John Alfred Prestwich 1874-1952

The Vintage Years

by

Jeff Clew

Foulis

ISBN 0 85429 458 9

A FOULIS Motorcycling Book

First published, 1985
© Jeff Clew 1985

Published by:
Haynes Publishing Group
Sparkford, Nr. Yeovil, Somerset
BA22 7JJ, England

Haynes Publications Inc.
861 Lawrence Drive, Newbury Park,
California 91320, USA

British Library Cataloguing in Publication Data
Clew, Jeff
J.A.P. — the vintage years.
1. J.A.P. Motor Company—History
I. Title
338.7'621'0941   HD9710.3.G74J3
ISBN 0-85429-458-9

Editor: Mansur Darlington
Page layout: Chris Hull
Printed in England by: J.H. Haynes & Co. Ltd.

Contents

Foreword

THIS IS the history of J.A. Prestwich and Co. Ltd which covers the lifetime of its founder John Prestwich. His initials were the origin of the trade mark of JAP which became universally known for motorcycle engines.

The story begins in a modest way in a suburban house in Tottenham, North London during 1874, the year of his birth. From early years there was an interest in mechanical things, as indicated by the making of a model steam engine while still at school. This model is still admired by model makers, who see it preserved in its glass case.

John grew up in a time when there were enormous strides in engineering in many different directions and this led him to express his mechanical bent by involvement in the cinema, aeroplanes, engines, motor cars and finally motorcycles leading eventually to industrial engines.

The close of the Second World War brought about the enormous economic changes which affected engineering in this country and especially the motorcycle trade, which has almost eclipsed our industry and extinguished so many of the names we all knew and respected.

Amalgamations and the development of larger concerns caused the smaller companies to close down and the change altered the policy of buying out components and making a much larger proportion of parts in their own works.

These changes were making themselves felt just at the time when John passed from the scene and sadly much of his work was lost in the absorptions of larger groups.

It is fitting these achievements are here recorded and many memories will be revived in the minds of those reading this book.

(Douglas Prestwich)

Preface

THERE WAS a time when I wondered why no one had written a complete history of Messrs J.A. Prestwich and Co. Ltd, manufacturers of the world famous JAP engines. The company itself had published a small booklet in 1951 to commemorate their Golden Jubilee, although strictly speaking it was then in its 56th year, the Prestwich Manufacturing Company having been formed in 1894. Other authors have covered specific areas of the story, often in great detail, but none the story as a whole. The reason soon became apparent — the sheer enormity of the task and the need for an almost unparalleled amount of research. Eric Corneliusen, a former JAP agent in Crosby, near Southport, said in an early letter to me, and with no small amount of truth, 'I doubt whether there is a man living who knows all the types of engine Prestwich made'. But someone had to make a start, here is the chronicle of JAP's vintage years which takes the story up to the end of 1925, when JAP closed their Racing Department and braced themselves for the coming recession. Its compilation represents almost four years of my leisure time, during which I have made innumerable visits to the National Motor Museum Library at Beaulieu, written a vast number of letters and conducted many interviews. On more than one occasion I seriously considered abandoning the whole project, simply because it had overwhelmed me and it looked as though I would never reach the end. But determination won through eventually, thanks to all the encouragement and assistance I received from those with whom I had made contact.

I lived in Tottenham during the mid-thirties, first at West Road and later at Coniston Road, neither address far from the JAP works. In those childhood days I had no interest in cars or motorcycles, so much to my regret I have no personal recollection of the factory or those associated with it, even though I must have walked along Tariff Road on so many occasions. It was not until I moved to Somerset towards the end of 1972 that I became fully aware of JAP's massive contribution to the world of motorcycling, an awareness that grew measurably when I met and got to know the late Cyril May — a true JAP enthusiast if there ever was one. Cyril and I had started to make tentative plans for a complete history of the company, which even Cyril considered an impossible task, but sadly he died before our discussions had progressed very far. So it then became a 'solo' venture, in the knowledge that others would be prepared to offer assistance along the way.

My greatest problem in writing this book has been the inability to interview many of those who made such a substantial contribution to the company's success. John Prestwich, affectionately known as 'the guv'nor', A.E. Bowyer-Lowe, Val Page, Bert

PREFACE

Le Vack, Stan Greening, George Tottey, E.C.E. Baragwanath and many others who made their mark are no longer with us, so that their contributions have had to be assessed by reference to the cold print in back issues of periodicals. It is often the human interest stories or personal anecdotes that make the most interesting reading, so my greatest fear has been that of producing a book that reads like a catalogue and does not have the life it should. But I have tried to make up for this whenever possible by setting the scene for motorcycling as a whole, whenever the opportunity presented itself. I trust that I have not missed any events of major interest or significance.

I realise that even now all I have managed to do is little more than scratch the surface, for the story is both deep and complex. Better this, however, than to have all that remains of the company's records contained within one cardboard box in the archives of Tottenham's Bruce Castle Museum, as I found on my first visit there.

Many queries will arise when it comes to engine capacities, as these have been misquoted on so many occasions, often in the motorcycle press and sometimes in the company's own announcements. I have made corrections whenever there has been factual evidence to support this need, but where areas of doubt have occurred, especially when recounting race results, I have used the figure quoted in print at the time of the release or report. The capacity discrepencies are small, but to the dedicated JAP enthusiast they will, nonetheless, be apparent.

If nothing else, I hope this book will help perpetuate the memory of a man who was a genius in two quite different fields — being one of the leading pioneers in cinematography for a decade before he transferred his affections to the then infant internal combustion engine, to become a leading manufacturer in his own right. Such an amazing achievement is indeed rare.

Jeff Clew
Sparkford
August 1984

Editor's note
Repeatedly, throughout the book, the word JAP has been used as a qualification after makers names to make it quite clear that a JAP engine was fitted to the particular machine referred to. In those rare instances where the word JAP was incorporated as part of the manufacture's official title a hyphen is used, as in Rex-JAP.

MJD

Acknowledgements

I HAVE many to thank for helping to make this book possible, so many that I am in danger of inadvertently overlooking someone. First and foremost must go my deep thanks to both Douglas and Edward Prestwich, who not only tried their best to answer my searching questions, but gave me every possible encouragement to see this story through to its conclusion. Ron Valentine, late of Weslake and Co. Ltd, was another anxious to see the JAP story in print. Wal Phillips entertained me in his home to talk about his uncle, Bert Le Vack, and about his own involvement with JAP. Lew Coffin and Nelson Harring provided much useful advice about JAP racing engines through their many years of preparing or riding machines fitted with these engines, as did the late Eric Corneliusen, who enjoyed similar experience as a JAP agent in the north of England. A letter to the now defunct *Tottenham Herald* brought forth useful correspondence from many who had at one time worked for 'the JAP', or who had in some way been involved with JAP engines. I would in particular like to acknowledge the help of Mrs E. Oldfield (neé Howard) who so kindly provided comprehensive information about the process of pencil making, the late Fred Butcher of the Wood Green and District MCC, L.J.V. Clements, R.E. Montague, E.H. Edwards, Mrs L.J. Sadler and W.E.N. Davies. My old friend, Ken Hodgson, supplied much useful technical information about JAP engines of the twenties, in his former role of Coventry Eagle Specialist in the Vintage Motor Cycle Club, and I am also indebted to Richard Chapman, who at one time worked for Francis Beart and Eric Fernihough.

John Barnes, of the Barnes Museum of Cinematography, St. Ives, kindly provided some interesting information about the early career of John Prestwich, as did the British Film Institute and the Science Museum, South Kensington. The Royal Aeronautical Society very kindly supplied an account of Willows' historic flight in a JAP-engined dirigible from Cardiff to London, and Roger Boyer-Lowe was able to fill in some gaps relating to his grandfather's part in the manufacture and development of JAP engines at Lansdowne Road. The late John Hempson corresponded with me about JAP aircraft engines, and very special thanks are due to the staff of the Reference Library at the National Motor Museum, Beaulieu, and especially to the Reference Librarian, Peter Brockes. I would also like to thank the staff of the Bruce Castle Museum, Tottenham, who so readily made their JAP archive material available to me, when I made them my first port of call.

It is important that any historical work should be well refereed, so again I am greatly indebted to Douglas and Edward Prestwich, who read through my manuscript

ACKNOWLEDGEMENTS

and offered various contributions. Dr Joseph Bayley, author and a recognised authority on Brooklands, World's records and record breaking, not only painstakingly checked speeds and record breaking figures quoted in the text, but also made many valuable observations about the racing scene that have been incorporated. Jack Bindley was another who checked data on the racing engines and provided some useful comment, through his specialised knowledge of racing during that era. John Clayton kindly provided information about the overhead camshaft engines that were, at one time, in his possession.

I must also acknowledge, yet again the welcome assistance of Ken Hodgson, whose critical appraisal of my manuscript did much to enhance its final presentation.

Photographs came from a variety of sources, but I would like to pay particular tribute to the staff of the Bruce Castle Museum, Tottenham, in which the JAP archive material is stored, for their sympathetic response to my requests and for printing off innumerable photographs from old and faded originals which I could identify only by brief, descriptive notes. I am also grateful to the Science Museum, South Kensington, who helped in a similar capacity. Other photographs came from the Prestwich family, Mrs Connie May, NUT historian Peter Sparkes, Morgan historian and author, Dr J. Alderson, Ken Hodgson, Richard Platt, and the Shuttleworth Collection. My good friend, Dr Helmut Krackowizer, took photographs of the rare dohc Le Vack engines that are now in Vienna, and of another 'mystery' engine. Ronald Clark very kindly gave permission for the reproduction of a number of his JAP engine drawings. To all I give my sincere thanks for letting me make use of their material.

I realise that there are many others whom I should have contacted, and indeed at one time meant to, but time was never on my side and after four years it seemed desirable to get something into print rather than delay matters even further. To them I can only offer my apologies and hope they will forgive this oversight.

Chapter One

A Pioneer in cinematography

THE EARLY pioneers in any new technology often make a quite significant contribution towards its advancement, to leave their mark in the annals of history in no uncertain manner. Most continue to remain closely associated with that particular activity for the remainder of their working career, but inevitably there are exceptions, albeit very few. One such person was John Alfred Prestwich who, in his early life, was one of Britain's leading pioneers in the field of cinematography. Yet within little more than a decade he became fascinated with the then infant internal combustion engine, which led to the complete diversification of his interests. Starting by designing and manufacturing his own engines, and progressing to the manufacture of complete motorcycles and forecars, he played a significant role in the creation of a giant industry, with which his name is the more closely associated. Soon, he became better known for the engines that bore his initials JAP, rather than for his substantial contributions to the cinema, and it is in this former context that his name has become immortalized.

John Alfred Prestwich was born in the Borough of Kensington on September 1st, 1874. His father, W. H. Prestwich, was a photographer by profession and a member of the Royal Photographical Society. Initially he had worked for the Singer Sewing Machine company, with whom he had undergone training in the USA. Later, he became interested in photography and perfected the method of working with gaslight paper, a process the details of which he sold to Eastman for £1,000. Edward, one of his grandsons, recalls visiting his grandfather and seeing photographic plates exposed to sunlight. Not unnaturally it was this background that most probably influenced his son's future ambitions. In due course the Prestwich family moved to Warmington House in Tottenham High Street, and it is this dwelling place that bears the number 744 which today serves as the headquarters of the Spurs Supporters Club, the Tottenham Hotspur football ground being close by. It was here that young John's mechanical abilities came to the fore when, at the age of 14, he constructed a working miniature stationary steam engine, having a nineteen tube boiler a foot high. Of quite exquisite workmanship, it belied the youth of its maker, and it won prizes wherever it was exhibited. Many years later, when J. A. Prestwich and Co. Ltd was well established in premises in Northumberland Park, Tottenham, it formed the centrepiece of the display of JAP engines and components in the reception area. It survives today, in the hands of Mr. E. S. Prestwich, the eldest survivor of John's five sons.

At school, John Prestwich showed a particular aptitude towards mechanics and excelled in mathematics and draughtmanship, Through the award of two scholarships he

The stationary steam engine with its 19 tube vertical boiler, built by John Prestwich at the age of 14. It is now in the safe keeping of Edward, his eldest surviving son. (Photo: Douglas Prestwich)

was educated at the City and Guilds School and the City of London School.

On his sixteenth birthday, he commenced work with S.Z. de Ferranti in Charterhouse Square, Aldersgate — the well-known electrical and scientific instrument manufacturers. Two years later he joined, as an apprentice, a heavy engineering company whose activites embraced a very wide area, ranging from the manufacture of compound locomotives to ice rink refrigeration equipment and wood carving machinery. The refrigeration equipment below the stage of the London Palladium was installed by John Prestwich, in connection with an ice rink that featured in a show at the time. Even now, he knew inwardly that he had not found his vocation in life, and he remained restless. Eventually, he resigned and at the age of 20 he decided to take the plunge and set up on his own by forming the Prestwich Manufacturing Company. It was his intention to make and sell electrical fittings and scientific instruments, using only hand tools and a treadle lathe, operating from modest premises in his father's garden at Warmington House — the greenhouse!

Quite by coincidence it was during February 1895, just after the time he had decided to set up on his own, that the motion picture industry achieved a considerable breakthrough. Although this industry was still in its infancy, it had become possible to project moving images onto a screen with reasonable clarity for the first time, and it was this that had a considerable appeal to the young Prestwich. In a comparatively short time he became deeply involved in the world of celluloid film, pausing only to marry a Miss Elinor Bramley of the Parish of Tottenham in 1896. They bought as their home a house in Lansdowne Road, a turning off Tottenham High Street that was relatively close to Warmington House. Their home was number 3 and by purchasing number 1 at the same time, John had the factory space he so urgently required. Conveniently, the outbuilding between the two houses became both the machine shop and the test shop, and later still the small complex was augmented by the acquisition of an old, disused chapel that adjoined number 1.

It was now that John's innovative capabilities became readily apparent and such were the magnitude of his contributions to cinematography that several of his inventions can be seen in the Science Museum, South Kensington, today. For a brief period he had an association with William Friese-Greene, to which John Barnes refers in his excellent book 'The Beginnings of the Cinema in England' (David and Charles). He makes reference to the Greene-Prestwich projector, which was invented and patented by them jointly in 1896. Using a special film 60mm wide, the apparatus is best

Left:
A photograph of the young John Prestwich taken at the time of his marriage in 1896. He always took great pride in his appearance and was a firm devotee of the winged collar. (Photo: Douglas Prestwich)

Right:
Elinor Prestwich photographed at the same time as her husband. She was always referred to by her family as Nellie. Photo: Douglas Prestwich)

Above:
The original premises in Lansdowne Road, Tottenham, photographed in 1895. The building exists to this day, as three seperate flats. (Haringey Public Libraries)

Below:
Inside the Lansdowne Road Works. The lady in the photograph is quite probably Elinor Prestwich, who often helped out in the office. Note the early typewriter and the cupboard full of scientific instruments. (Photo: Douglas Prestwich)

Opposite page, Top:
The old treadle-operated lathe on which John Prestwich made his stationary steam engine. Known as 'Grandfather', it was subsequently installed in this corner of the carpenters' shop at the Lansdowne Road Works. (Photo: Douglas Prestwich)

Opposite page, Bottom:
The machine shop of the Lansdowne Road Works at the turn of the century. Note the overhead shafts and pulleys, used to drive the lathes. (Photo: Haringey Public Libraries)

described as a 'double projector', the object being to eliminate film flicker and to permit projection speeds down to 16 pictures per minute without losing the motion effect. By using two projection lenses and two shutters, the screen was always illuminated by one or other of the two apertures, so that one picture 'dissolved' into the next, the film being advanced two frames at a time. Barnes claims that it was the outstanding engineering ability of Prestwich that made practical Friese-Green's somewhat woolly thinking and failure to appreciate the detail requirements.

Whilst it is not the intention to cover in detail in this book, the cinematographic achievements of John Prestwich, they none the less deserve mention because they occupied some ten years or so of his early career. The 1899 edition of Hopwood's 'Living Pictures', for example, devotes four pages to the machines made by Prestwich and makes reference to his intermittent claw mechanism for moving film, which he patented in 1898. This became the basis of his ciné cameras, which were subsequently used by many of the early British film pioneers. Scott's expedition to the Antarctic in 1910 was filmed on a Prestwich ciné camera, as was Queen Victoria's Golden Jubilee procession. There were even plans to film the Grand National one year and fourteen cameras were set up around the course. But on this occasion the attempt was in vain. A sudden snow storm coincided with the start of the race and everything was obliterated.

Amongst the many milestones in John Prestwich's cinematographic career were the making of the world's record length of film in 1897, a reel containing 2,500 feet, and being the only person with the ability to print from Lumiere to Edison perforations, and vice-versa. Reference to his 1905 catalogue gives some idea of the range of equipment he was able to offer, and the excellence of its quality, the catalogue cover mentioning the award of two Silver Medals. Basically, what he had to offer was as follows:

The Prestwich patent Kinamotograph camera model 4 at £35.00 with 2 magazines for 400-500 feet of film

The Prestwich tripod in best polished ash at £1.10s

Extra magazines in brass bound mahogany at £1.15s each

Extra lenses, leather bound carrying cases etc.

A note indicated that the Kinamatograph camera had the patented claw or pin movement and that the camera weighed 8½lb. Other equipment listed was:

The Prestwich patent Kinamatograph camera model 5 at £36.00 A self contained instrument for stage scenes or trick use

The Prestwich No. 7 projector at £25.00 complete with lantern and swing-out base. Suitable for film or slides

The Prestwich revolving camera tripod head at £6.10s For taking panoramic shots and following the centre of interest

The improved Prestwich printer at £25.00 (with patented claw movement)

The Prestwich film joiner at 10/6d

Prestwich perforating machines:
Rotary perforator at £30
Step perforator at £30

The Prestwich film measuring machine at £8.10s

An early Prestwich cinematograph projector with its reel of film. It is hand operated.
(Photo: Haringey Public Libraries)

In addition, he also sold some proprietary equipment marketed as Kamm's Oxygen Generator and Kamm's Carburetter, which was used by projectionists to produce the oxygen and hydrogen needed to boost the intensity of the arc lights used in their projectors. It was claimed the average projector used in a cinema or similar building required from 1000 to 2000 candle power for maximum effectiveness. The oxygen was generated by heating cakes of potassium chlorate and manganese oxide, which was then passed to the carburetter which contained an absorbent. Ether contained in the carburetter could be used as the hydrogen source, both gases then being led to the arc light by flexible tubing. One wonders what would have happened to the unfortunate projectionist if the ether escaped, since apart from its anaesthetic properties, it is also highly explosive!

Last, but certainly not least, an arc light could be supplied too, the proprietary Urban Arc Lamp model W, at £6.00. Strangely enough, the outside rear cover of the catalogue was devoted entirely to motorcycle engines of the type that had been manufactured at Landsdowne Road for the last couple of years or so, a strange combination of products that would appeal to widely differing interests. If nothing more, this was a pointer to the future. Already, the divergence of John Prestwich's interests had taken place, accentuated by the birth of the 'horseless carriage' around the turn of the century. Now the internal combustion engine was to attract his all-consuming   *17*

T. G. West using a Prestwich ciné camera in the making of a film entitled 'Our Navy'. It was subsequently screened at a polytechnic film show. (Photo: Haringey Public Libraries)

attention, so that his infatuation with the world of cinematography would begin to fade. One cannot help think, however, that his catalogue claim to have had 12 years experience of the design of internal combustion engines must have been made with tongue in cheek.

Chapter Two

The JAP engine makes its debut

JOHN PRESTWICH had been following with keen interest the development of the internal combustion engine, and even at the early age of 16 had filed some patents relating to engine design. By 1901 he had embarked on the design of his first complete engine, a single cylinder four-stroke to power a motorcycle, and by 1902 he was in a position to make the engine available on a production basis. Having bore and stroke dimensions of 70 x 76mm and a capacity of 293cc, it produced 2¼hp at 1600rpm, according to a description that appeared in *The Motor Cycle*. The crankcase was cast in two halves in the normal manner, separated in the vertical plane. The crankshaft followed what was to become accepted as the traditional design too, having two full circle flywheels joined by the crankpin, each having its own mainshaft. The cylinder head and barrel were cast in one, using the same material as that selected for the flywheels — cast iron. With regard to the valve gear, only the exhaust valve was mechanically operated. The inlet valve was of the atmospheric type that typified early engine design. Having only a light valve spring, it relied upon atmospheric pressure to force it off its seat, as the piston descended in the cylinder. Obviously it took some care to set up the valve spring pressure correctly, a technique that is today almost a lost art. The overall appearance of the engine was one of neatness, although the sparse finning of the cylinder gave it a long and spindly look. It resembled in many respects the Minerva engine of that period.

In many ways J.A. Prestwich's all-consuming interest in the internal combustion engine was well timed, for when Queen Victoria died on January 22nd, 1901, her passing marked the end of an era. Although at that time regarded as little more than a novelty, which many considered would pass unnoticed, the automobile was soon destined to become an established form of transportation, changing our daily lives and giving a degree of mobility hitherto unforseen. Only a few years later the 'flying machine' would become a practical proposition, too, when Orville and Wilbur Wright demonstrated the capability of their primitive biplane in a series of powered flights on December 17th, 1903. Although their first flight was of only 59 seconds duration, it represented a significant breakthrough in another field of technology. Many of the predictions of Jules Verne were beginning to come true.

One of the first advertisements about the new engine was published in the June 17th issue of *The Motor Cycle,* with a testimonial about its hill climbing capabilities. John A. Prestwich and Co. was the listed title of the manufacturer, the address being 1, Lansdowne Road, Tottenham. The advertisement also mentioned that the company

Above:
An original illustration of a 2½ hp JAP motorcycle fitted with the clip-on type of automatic inlet valve engine. It is dated 1902.

The 1902 2½ hp automatic inlet valve engine had bore and stroke dimensions of 70 x 76mm. This is a very early factory illustration of 1902. (Photo: Haringey Public Libraries)

could supply 'motors, motor sets and complete bicycles' and furthermore, that the engine had an automatic lubrication system.

Lubrication was, in fact, by means of the drip feed method that was widely adopted by engine manufacturers at that time. It was aided by the suction of the piston and worked on the total loss principle. Even so John Prestwich had appreciated the need for a crankcase breather and his engine incorporated a patented vacuum valve of his own design. This helped obviate the messy and often uncontrolled ejection of used or excess oil. The ignition system was powered by trembler coil, which worked in conjunction with a 'wipe' type of contact breaker, and the whole engine was designed to be fitted to a bicycle-type frame, in the form of a clip-on attachment, being suspended in front of the front down tube of the frame.

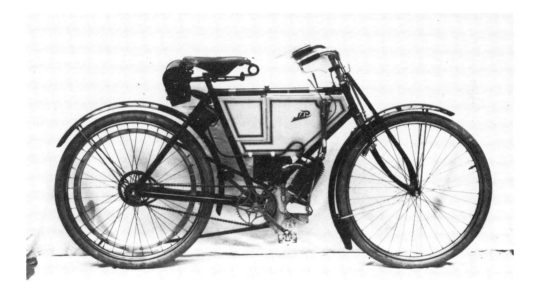

Probably taken during 1902 or 1903, this is the first photograph of a complete machine bearing the famous JAP motif. The specification of this model includes a surface carburetter and a trembler ignition coil. (Photo: Douglas Prestwich)

The first motorcycle manufacturer to use an engine of JAP manufacturer was the Triumph Cycle Co. Ltd of Coventry, who had marketed their first machine in 1902, using a Minerva engine of Belgian manufacture. It was claimed by the trade press of the time that Triumph's adoption of the 293 cc JAP engine in 1903 saved motorcycling from following the prediction of being no more than a passing craze, just like the roller skate. True or not, a few of the early motorcycle manufacturers had already faded from the scene or diversified into other engineering activities. Perhaps the JAP engine had shown that it was possible to make a sound, reliable engine of consistent quality on a production basis, and at the same time adhere to high manufacturing standards. John Prestwich was probably the first Englishman to use the production methods pioneered in the USA, where gauging and interchangeable manufacture had been in use from the 1860s. He had improved on the 'go' and 'no go' system of gauging, which allowed him to produce components that were commercially acceptable. Costs were kept to a minimum and the *21*

THE BEST BRITISH WORKMANSHIP BEATS THE WORLD.

This is in the

JAP

Cycle Motors, Motor Cycles & Motor Sets.

If you are buying Motors, call and see the **JAP** 2½ h.p. Can be seen running at any time. Owing to the high quality of materials, the excellence of the design and workmanship, the highest efficiency is combined with lightness. Its hill-climbing and speed capabilities are far in excess of any of the heavier and larger but less efficient motors. We are constantly receiving letters which affirm this, with repeat orders.

JAP Adjustable
Spark Gap. . .

Light, Neat, Strong Balanced, Glass Protection, Universal Clip.

Money returned if this is not the neatest and best finished Spark Gap on the market, or if not entirely satisfactory.

Price 2/6.   Liberal Trade Discounts.

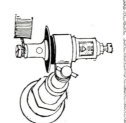

The technical expert on this Journal's staff writes:

We have recently had under inspection a 2½ h.p. motor made by J. A. Prestwich & Co., 1, Lansdowne Road, Tottenham, London, N. We have no hesitation in speaking of it as an excellent piece of workmanship in all its details, every part having that sharpness of finish so pleasing to the mechanical eye. The cylinder is 70 mm. bore and 76 mm. stroke (2½ by 3 inches), and has the combustion head cast in one piece with the cylinder. The contact breaker is very substantial, and operates in conjunction with an exhaust valve opener of clever design. Another specially good feature is a vacuum valve to keep a good vacuum in the crank case, and prevents the oil being blown out of the bearings. The top of the cylinder is provided with a handy screw tap for admitting paraffin at starting. See THE MOTOR, March 25th.

Sight Feed Automatic Lubricator, Special Vacuum Valve, Large Silencer of Polished Steel.

Ease, Elegance, and Comfort. No vibration, no short circuits. Clean, fast, & exceptional Hill-Climber.

The Motor for To-day and of the Future
Every part will stand the closest inspection.

MANUFACTURED BY

John A. Prestwich & Co.,

Telegrams: "Prestwich, Tottenham."
Telephone: 55 Tottenham.

1, Lansdowne Road, Tottenham, London, N.

An early advertisement for the JAP motorcycle fitted with the 2½ hp clip-on engine. It was published in the 29th April, 1903 issue of The Motor.

22

new gauging methods enabled him to identify the areas of the tolerance band so that the exact mating of parts was possible. This is, of course, the standard method used by all of today's automobile manufacturers. At this time an article in the weekly magazine *The Motor Cycle* claimed the JAP factory was the first to grind cylinder bores, a statement subsequently confirmed by Edward Prestwich.

A good example of the JAP-engined Triumph of 1903 is owned by NVT Motorcycles, and can today be seen on display in the motorcycle section of the National Motor Museum at Beaulieu. Strangely enough, the JAP advertisements seem not to have made capital of the use of their engine by Triumph, preferring instead to rely on slogans and what one would now classify as 'gimmicks. For example, in *The Motor Cycle* dated June 24th, the advertisement is headed 'Have motor bicycles come to stop? JAP motors have come to go'!, whilst in August the advertisement in the same weekly depicts a lion and has the heading 'JAP — The King of Motors'. But if proof of the engine's capabilities was needed, it came when John Prestwich submitted a factory-sponsored entry in the 1000 Mile Reliability Trial of 1903, organised by the Auto-Cycle Club, the forerunner of the Auto-Cycle Union. The entry was made in the name of a rider listed as Duffield and although no details of the actual machine are available, it is known that a 70 x 76mm 293cc engine was fitted and that the complete machine weighed 110lb.

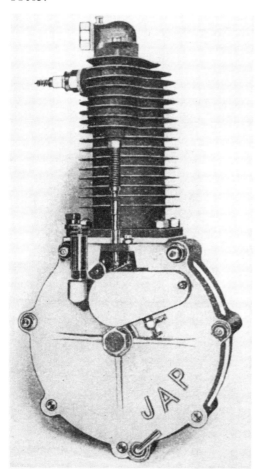

A vertically-mounted 2½hp engine followed in 1903, permitting a more conventional method of installation in a frame. It retained the automatic inlet valve arrangement. (Photo: Haringey Public Libraries)

The event took place on August 11th-21st inclusive, each run starting and finishing in the grounds of Crystal Palace, in South London. Nine days were spent travelling defined routes to a set time schedule, the tenth day taking the form of a speed test on the Crystal Palace track. Competitors had to cope with all the usual hazards, not excluding the weather, and some fell foul of the infamous police traps that characterised that era, when the motorist or motorcyclist was considered fair game by the local bench. Duffield made a disastrous start on the first day, when he came to grief just outside Maidstone. A victim of the 'dreaded side-slip,' he crashed heavily in the wet, damaging one of the cranks of his pedalling gear. Although uninjured, he was severely shaken by the incident and he returned to London, with his machine, by train. Fortunately he soon recovered and was able to present himself astride his machine at the Crystal Place, in time for the start of the second day's run. He successfully completed the remaining days' runs, and also the speed test at their conclusion, to qualify as one of the 28 finishers out of the total complement of 48 starters. In total, he lost only 20 marks throughout the entire event, and was awarded a 2nd Class Award. This accomplishment was subsequently mentioned in a JAP advertisement that appeared in *The Motor Cycle* dated September 16th. Although his christian name was never mentioned, it was the same Duffield who made the headlines again in a quite different context, when he was caught speeding *UP* Muswell Hill in North London. He was 'booked' at 20mph on October 17th, and summoned to appear before the Highgate Bench. The JAP advertisement at this time made capital of his offence as though it were some kind of a speed cum hillclimbing testimony, but whether the company paid his fine is not recorded!

The next big event, as far as the company was concerned, was the end of the year motorcycle exhibition, known as the Stanley Show, held in the Agricultural Hall, Islington. It was at this show that John Prestwich introduced his latest engine, which surprisingly was of the ohv type, with mechanically-operated valves. It would seem probable that Prestwich was the first to design and build a really practical production engine of this type in Britain, and perhaps the world. It was certainly a bold step to take because metallurgy was not too well advanced at that time and there was always the danger of a head breaking off a valve, which would then fall into the still revolving engine with disastrous consequences. Yet for all this, the engine seems to have proved reliable. The surviving example in the Science Museum, South Kensington, had seen active service right through to 1924, before it was finally pensioned off. It is interesting to note these engines were made to limit gauge and had interchangeable parts.

The new ohv engine was a much bigger unit than the original automatic inlet valve design, having bore and stroke measurements of 85 x 76mm, which gave a cubic capacity of 437cc. The distinguishing feature of this engine was the use of a single push rod operated from the timing chest, which either pulled or pushed the single overhead rocker arm. This action was achieved by having a cam formed on one side of the half speed pinion, with a hump in the correct position to lift the exhaust valve via a cam lever, and a corresponding depression into which a roller on the cam lever moved when a spring surrounding the push rod pulled it downwards to open the inlet valve. The valves were mounted vertically in a separate casting, comprising their seatings and the exhaust and inlet ports. This casting, which was detachable, could be likened to a miniature cylinder head and was retained in position by a bar that bridged the casting and was secured by a central stud. The overhead rocker was therefore a rocker in the true sense of the word, the bolt that secured the casting also acting as its pivot and allowing it to rock in either direction like the beam of an early steam engine. Also incorporated was an exhaust valve lifter, in the form of a pivoted lever. The remainder of the engine followed the general layout of the original 293cc engine and had the initials JAP cast in both crankcase halves. Advanced though it was for its time, an engine of this type obviously had its limitations, especially with regard to power output. Eventually, it was replaced by a modified ohv design that retained the vertically-positioned valves with detachable seatings, but which relied upon two separate push rods and modified timing gear for their operation. The detachable cylinder head was still a very long way off.

A photograph of the first JAP motorcycle to be built with the vertically-mounted 2½ hp engine. As yet there is no suggestion of using a spring front fork. (Photo: Haringey Public Libraries)

Apart from the new ohv engine, a complete machine was on display comprising an ohv engine fitted into a BSA frame that was complete with spring front forks, described ambiguously as the spring frame model. Stand 163 also displayed a sparking plug of JAP manufacture, having a recessed porcelain insulator that had been designed to eliminate short circuits and which utilised copper washers as the sealing medium. Other ignition system fittings were also shown, such as terminals and insulators. Advertising still continued to follow no set pattern and by the end of the year had taken on a Japanese theme. Using pseudo Japanese letters as a play on the initials JAP, the 'A' and the 'P' were said to relate to 'complete ALLIANCE to absolute PERFECTION'. One senses that John Prestwich himself originated the advertising copy and style; it is interesting to note that already he was using the JAP logo to form a source of corporate identity that much later was used on the timing covers of the competition engines. Mrs Prestwich

The 2½ hp vertical engine fitted into a Chater Lea frame and cycle parts. (Photo: Haringey Public Libraries)

Later in 1903 the surface carburetter was superseded by the more efficient spray type, as shown here. This machine is fitted with the overhead valve engine, using a single push-pull valve operating rod. It was the first overhead valve engine to go into quantity production. (Photo: Haringey Public Libraries)

suggested he should use as the accompanying slogan 'Just About Perfect', but it seems doubtful if this suggestion was ever taken up.

A consignment of 2½hp clip-on engines awaiting despatch from Lansdowne Road in 1903. (Photo: Haringey Public Libraries)

It would seem probable that the BSA-framed machine on display at the Stanley Show marked the first appearance of the JAP motorcycle as a complete entity, for in the December 9th issue of *The Motor Cycle* the JAP advertisement clearly stated that the complete machine was 'now available to order'. Not mentioned in *The Motor Cycle* report on the show, although covered in the contemporary report made in the pages of *Motor Cycling,* was that there was also a 2¼hp lightweight model on view at the same time. Described as being a remarkably strongly-built machine, despite its overall weight of only 84lb, it featured a spray carburetter, braced front forks and vee-belt drive, the frame being a Chater Lea manufacture. John Prestwich claimed it was the lightest machine made in relation to the power output available and that it would prove quite suitable for anyone up to 12 stone in weight.

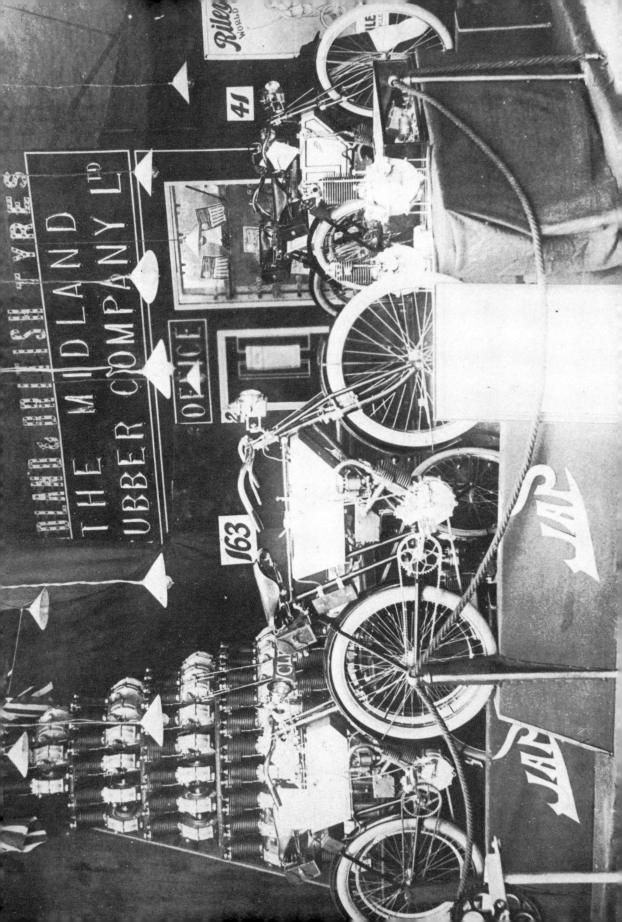

1904 marked a heightening of interest in the forecar, regarded by many as a convenient and civilised means of carrying a passenger without having to subject him or her to the indignity of being towed in a somewhat primitive trailer behind a solo motorcycle. Many embryo romances were terminated somewhat abruptly when the tow bar broke and deposited both trailer and occupant in a muddy ditch. Similarly the passenger often became the recipient of all the oil droppings and miscellaneous dust and filth thrown up by the rear wheel of the bike itself! The sidecar had yet to appear on the scene.

In some forecar designs, the passenger was seated comfortably in front of the driver and thereby had to contend with a completely different situation. Apart from suffering the almost total lack of weather protection and unwittingly providing a shield for the driver, the passenger also had an unparalleled view of any impending accident, to become the involuntary buffer between the obstacle hit and the driver! Fortunately, it was possible to effect a compromise and it was this line of approach that was adopted in the Prestwich design.

The forecar designed by John Prestwich had the driver and passenger seated side-by-side, in independently sprung upholstered seats. Between them, and projecting forwards, was a slim and graceful-looking petrol tank, to which was attached the main controls. A steering wheel turned the two front wheels, each of which was fitted with a stirrup brake operated by foot pedal. The rear wheel was driven by a propellor shaft and a patent worm roller drive, and had a powerful band brake operated by a hand lever in the centre of the chassis frame. The engine itself, a 4½hp single cylinder air-cooled side valve, was mounted in-line in front of an apron under the seats and like the petrol tank, was centrally disposed between the two front wheels. Mounting the engine with the crankshaft in-line proved convenient for the power take-off and also allowed a starting handle to be attached directly to the forward-facing mainshaft, via a dog coupling. Bore and stroke dimensions were 85 x 95mm, giving a cubic capacity of 539cc. The transmission contained a 24 leaf plate clutch, and critics claimed the weak point in the design lay in having the 4 foot long propellor shaft unsupported. The complete vehicle weighed 360lb and it was priced at 90 guineas. It formed a prominent feature of Stand 177, the location of the JAP display at the 1904 Stanley Show.

Preoccupation with the Dual Sociable, as it was first called, did not preclude attention to engine design or the continuing development of the motorcycle range. Once again, the factory made an official entry in the 1000 Mile Reliability Trial, organised by the Auto-Cycle Club. This year the event was held from August 15th-20th inclusive, with the start and finish in Avenue Road, close to Down Street where the machines were garaged whilst they were in London. There had been criticism about the way in which they had been stored overnight in a tent during the previous year's event, hence the reason for seeking more permanent, covered storage at the Club headquarters. This year, A E. Lowe was the JAP-nominated rider, having a machine fitted with an 82 x 76mm engine, rated at 3hp. The complete machine weighed 145lb and was regarded as a JAP motorcycle in its own right. Lowe, or Bowyer-Lowe to give his correct surname, had joined the factory in 1903, aged 17, as an Improver-Turner at 4½d an hour. This was not, in fact, his first appearance as a factory-sponsored rider. About a month earlier his name had come into prominence through the motorcycle press when he had taken part in a hill climb at Westerham, in Kent. The event had been organised by the

Facing page:
The JAP exhibition stand at the 1903 Stanley Show in London. Note the pyramid of overhead valve engines surmounted by Union Jacks. (Photo: Haringey Public Libraries)

Two views of a remarkably well preserved early JAP engine of the automatic inlet valve type, engine number 114. Note provision for taking the exhaust either forward or rearward from the cylinder. (Photo: G. Woodward)

The origin of this machine, fitted with an overhead valve engine, is unknown, as is the reason for the small diameter rim spoked into the front wheel. (Photo: Haringey Public Libraries)

The original Dual Sociable three-wheeler, fitted with a single cylinder 4½ hp engine mounted transversely between the front wheels. (Photo: Haringey Public Libraries)

CHAPTER TWO

Catford Cycling Club and Bowyer-Lowe had some strong words to say about a Club ruling that permitted pedal assistance. His JAP-engined machine compared favourably in terms of performance with that of a fellow competitor by the name of Chase, who was riding a machine of his own manufacture. Chase had been a professional cyclist and Bowyer-Lowe considered the Club ruling gave him an unfair advantage. In an attempt to mediate, the Club sanctioned a special Bowyer-Lowe v Chase Match Race at the conclusion of the event itself, and it was Chase who took first place in all four ascents of the hill, albeit by only a narrow margin. Although pedalling was not allowed during any of the four runs, Chase seemed to have a clear advantage because his machine started so easily as he pushed off. Bowyer-Lowe's comments are not recorded, but unfortunately the animosity between the two riders lingered on.

In the 1000 Mile Trial, Bowyer-Lowe acquitted himself well, despite the accepted hazards of inclement weather and police harassment. His only black mark was caused by belt slip, which set in during the observed ascent of Stepney Hill, near Scarborough. He lost valuable time in struggling to the top without seeking assistance, yet there was no inherent fault in the machine itself as it was the one he had used at Westerham and he was later able to record a good climb up London Hill, near Marlborough. He won a 2nd Class Certificate and a Silver Medal.

Surprisingly, it was at this time that Chase chose to discredit Bowyer-Lowe even further by writing a letter to *The Motor Cycle* in which he made reference to the Westerham Hill Match Race and the superiority of his own machine. Whatever his reason, this attempt to obtain cheap publicity at Bowyer-Lowe's expense backfired. Readers of the magazine soon voiced their disapproval of this ungentlemanly blow through the correspondence columns, including a few who had witnessed the respective performances of the two riders. Eventually, John Prestwich was drawn into the correspondence, stating that the whole comparison was based on a false premise. In the second of his two letters he went so far as to claim that whilst both machines were capable of 45mph, the machine ridden by Lowe could exceed 50mph. From thence onwards, the correspondence ceased.

Earlier in the year, it had been estimated that something like 22,000 motorcycles were registered in England, Scotland and Wales, registration having become a legal requirement with effect from January 1st, 1904. Under the Motor Car Act of 1903, all the machines had to carry registration plates, front and rear, having one or two letters that were indicative of the registration authority, and a following number of up to four digits. An extra letter to be added after the number was required for trade licences. From now on, it was possible to monitor the growth of the British motorcycle industry much more accurately, by deriving statistics from the licensing records.

Unlike many of the early pioneers, John Prestwich himself did not ride his motorcycles, although this conflicts with a report in *'The Motor Cycle'* that suggests he entered for a hill clmib organised by the Auto-Cycle Club in 1905. The event was held in the spacious grounds of Blackdown House, near Hazlemere, in Surrey, by kind permission of the owner, Sir Phillipston Stow. Riding a machine powered by an 82 x 76mm single cylinder engine of his own manufacture, it is alleged John Prestwich (more probably his entry) put up fastest time of the day in his class — Class 2, for machines having a capacity limit of 402cc. For this he became the recipient of a Silver Medal. There was one other competitor in the same event who also used a JAP engine. A.P. Tyler had entered on a JAP Traveller, powered by an 85 x 76mm engine, but he was much less fortunate. On his first run he took the first corner at such speed that he went straight on, through the line of spectators, fortunately without injury to himself or any of the onlookers. Sobered by this experience, he took the same corner on his second run with such caution that his machine stuttered to a stop some 80 yards along the incline

The three cylinder 70 x 82 mm 8 hp engine that was fitted to the later Tandem two seater three-wheeler. It was of very advanced design for that era. (Photo: Haringey Public Libraries)

that followed.

Bowyer-Lowe continued his run of successes for the JAP factory, winning outright the Auto-Cycle Club's 200 Mile Trial during May 1905, riding a 3½hp model. For this accomplishment he was awarded the Reeves Trophy. He was also successful in the later London-to-Edinburgh Run, winning a Gold Medal for the second year in succession, and in the Blackpool Motor Races where he put up fastest time of the day to win the Blackpool Corporation Cup. For reasons unknown, his luck deserted him in the Auto-Cycle Club's Six Days Trial of that year when he was forced to make an early retirement. Even so, he ended up the Auto-Cycle Club's Hill Climb Champion.

Racing was now beginning to take prominence in the motorcycle world, it having been recognised that racing successes made powerful advertising copy. In the early days, reliability had been the keynote in promoting sales, but as machines became more reliable as the result of continuing development and participation in competitions, it was racing that became the decisive factor in evaluating performance capabilities. Road races held on the Continent were beginning to attract British manufacturers and when France announced the running of the Coupe Internationale in 1904, around a 34 mile course near Dourdan, John Prestwich entered a rider by the name of W. Hodgkinson on a machine powered by one of his new ohv engines. Lagonda and Quadrant entered machines, too, yet sadly all three British machines failed to complete the race. Perhaps it was as well, for eventually the race was declared null and void. Certain 'irregularities' had come to light and there had been many squabbles amongst those who took part.

In an attempt to improve the quality of the British entry for the 1905 event, the

33

Open   Closed.

An illustration of the JAP variable-speed belt pulley, showing the arrangement of the toggles used to open or close it. (Photo: Haringey Public Libraries)

The JAP carburetter, a somewhat complicated device that relied upon multiple jets, each with its own independent air supply. (Photo: Haringey Public Libraries)

Auto-Cycle Club decided to hold selection trials in the Isle of Man. This was considered to be a suitable venue because a course had already been agreed over which the Gordon Bennett car race would be run during the month of May. It would be comparatively easy to extend the use of the course until May 31st for the Selection Trials to be run, for the Island had its own government and it was still possible to close the roads for speed events. Furthermore, there was no rigourously enforced 20mph speed limit, as there was on the mainland.

Amongst those invited to take part were seven riders of JAP-powered machines, six of them using 76 x 95mm 6hp engines and one an 8hp engine. On this occasion, Hodgkinson was sponsored by Charles Jarrott, the celebrated racing motorist, the others having entered under their own names, comprising C.B. Franklin, O.L. Bickford, H.A. Collier, C.R. Collier, J.S. Campbell and H. Rignold. The Collier brothers rode Matchless machines of their own design and manufacture, whilst J.S. Campbell had an Ariel. Rignold, a former Lagonda rider, rode the machine fitted with the 8hp engine, make unrecorded.

J.S. Campbell emerged as winner of the trials and was awarded *The Motor* cup. Selected to accompany him to France were H.A. Collier and C.B. Franklin, with H. Rignold as the reserve. In the International Cup event itself, the British entrants were again beset with troubles. Franklin's machine went out with a broken inlet valve, Campbell suffered ignition and other problems, whilst Collier had tyre troubles. None finished, and when the results were announced they again became the subject of controversy when the inevitable protests made them a complete nonsense. This apart, the future of the event seemed to be in the balance whilst the maximum weight limit of 110lb for all machines taking part continued to be upheld. Manufacturers were taking risks by reducing the weight of vital components, even to the very limits of safety. In consequence, 'freak' lightweight machines had begun to appear, which bore little or no resemblance to their standard production counterparts. One foreign rider had been observed setting about his machine with a giant hacksaw, cutting the ends off the footrests in order to scrape through the weight limit!

In *The Motor Cycle* report of the 1905 Stanley Show there is no mention of a JAP exhibit, although a new 6hp vee-twin engine was observed fitted to a BAT machine on Stand 93, a machine with spring front forks and a spring saddle pillar. Also on the same stand was a machine specially-made for one of BAT's customers, featuring a 3hp JAP ohv single. In point of fact, the vee-twin was not the first of its kind to leave the works at Tottenham. The first 70 x 95mm 6hp engine had been made in 1904, and like the water-cooled version that followed it, it had automatic inlet valves. An early photograph in the Tottenham Museum archives shows the air-cooled version fitted into a JAP motorcycle in 1905. There is also a photograph showing the use of an 'open' high tension magneto fitted in the forward mounting position, taken around the same time. A distinctive feature of this machine (CF 213) is the cylindrical petrol tank sporting the JAP logo, mentioned earlier. By now it was becoming more difficult to keep track of racing and other successes achieved by JAP engines because quite a few manufacturers were specifying them for use in their own machines. It had become necessary to know the make of engine as well as the name of the machine.

It would seem that the original JAP forecar design, known as the Dual Sociable, had achieved nothing like the success that had been anticipated. Without doubt there was fierce competition in this sector of the market, with many alternative makes and designs from which to choose. These included Riley and Lagonda, two manufacturers who were destined to make a much greater name for themselves in the world of four-wheelers at a later date. Undeterred by this setback, John Prestwich and Bowyer-Lowe evolved a variant, which was announced by the JAP works early in 1906.

The first vee-twin engine was made in 1904. This is a 1905 6hp engine fitted with automatic inlet valves and having bore and stroke dimensions of 70 x 95mm. (Photo: Haringey Public Libraries)

A complete vee-twin model of unknown capacity, but most probably manufactured at Tottenham during 1905. (Photo: Douglas Prestwich)

The JAP carburetter had been evolved in an attempt to provide an alternative to the widely used Longuemare carburetter of French manufacture. Although the spray carburetter had superseded the primitive surface carburetters used during the pioneer or experimental era, it too had its shortcomings, mainly in the need to manipulate the controls constantly in order to match the supply of the petrol/air mixture to engine requirements. John Prestwich was determined to have simplified control over mixture strength and with this in mind he set about the problem with his own individualistic approach.

The carburetter he designed was unsual in so far as it used multiple jets, each with its own air supply that could be opened or closed, depending on riding conditions. When all the jets were uncovered, and all the air orifices open, this was the equivalent to running on full throttle, with the air control fully open on the contemporary spray instrument. Conversely, when only one or two jets remained uncovered and a corresponding number of air outlets were open, this was the equivalent of closing the auxiliary inlet and having the throttle only partially open. By bringing in what amounted to more and more miniature carburetters, it will be appreciated that the JAP carburetter had been designed to give a smooth, progressive throttle opening.

Advertising copy claimed the JAP carburetter had the following attributes:

Simplicity, automatic action, no need for hand regulation
Easier starting. No jump or jerk
Slower, quieter and more flexible running
Greater speed and power with less fuel consumption
Simpler and easier control

In theory, it did have much to commend it, too. But in practice there was an annoying hesitance in throttle response that necessitated a major modification at a later date. Certainly only one control was needed to work the carburetter once it had been matched to the engine to which it was to be attached by means of pre-set adjustments. A milled screw on the outside of the insturment moved an adjustable shutter that controlled the orifice through which the fixed air supply entered, thus permitting the mixture strength to be varied and also temporarily enriched for easier starting from cold. In consequence, a limited range of adjustment was provided to match the carburetter with the operating conditions of the engine. A lever positioned at the base of the instrument could also be used to adjust the fixed air supply to suit the running requirements of the engine. Once set correctly, it was unnecessary to change its position under normal operating conditions.

Facing page, Top:
The high tension magneto eventually replaced the old trembler coil to provide a more efficient and reliable ignition system. This 1906 7hp vee-twin engine is fitted with a gear-driven Bosch magneto of the 'open' type. (Photo: Haringey Public Libraries)

Bottom:
For heavy duty use, the 9hp vee-twin engine could be obtained in either dir- or water-cooled form during 1906, with automatic inlet valves. (Photo: Haringey Public Libraries)

This unknown rider has an Ariel of about 1905/6 vintage, fitted with an automatic inlet valve vee-twin JAP engine. (Photo: Haringey Public Libraries)

It is also pertinent to comment on another JAP product, a sparking plug. The design had been originated in an attempt to improve on the products of decidedly poor or doubtful quality that were mostly being imported from the Continent. JAP sparking plugs were manufactured by a subsidiary company, the Prested Battery Company. They in turn liaised closely with another subsidiary company, the Prested Miners' Gas-

One of the 6 hp JAP-engined racing machines that were entered for the 1905 Isle of Man Selection Trials prior to competing in the later International Cup Race held in France. (Photo: Haringey Public Libraries)

Indicating Electric Light Company, who manufactured such items as accumulators, coils, lamps, terminals and insulators, as well as a compound for repairing damaged accumulator cases marketed under the trade name 'Celludine'. Some of these activities were short-lived, however, especially when the introduction of the high tension magneto obviated the need for trembler coils and the acid-filled batteries that formed the basis of *43*

C. B. Franklin with the racing model on which he represented England in the Austrian International Cup Race of 1906. The engine is a specially-prepared 8hp 90° vee-twin racing engine with bore and stroke dimensions of 85 x 85mm. (Photo: Haringey Public Libraries)

the ignition system of early motorcycles. Even the best of the trembler coils could prove temeremental on occasion, whilst the batteries soon disintegrated as a direct result of the terrible pounding they received from little or no springing and the surfaces of the unmade roads of that era. There were some things on which even John Prestwich himself found it difficult to improve.

Chapter Three

Entries in the record book

AS FAR AS the company's involvement with racing was concerned, 1907 proved to be a year of significance for it heralded the first of what would subsequently prove to be innumerable entries in motorcycling's record books. Many of the pioneers had been faced with a long and hard struggle to gain recognition during their formative years, and in a great many cases it was not until one of their machines had achieved a major competition success that the desired breakthrough came about. Once it had been proved that their machine was much better than many of its contemporaries, the orders began to flow in. Even the layman who had little experience of motorcycling could not fail to appreciate that a machine that had successfully withstood the rigours of harsh competition was likely, as a result, to be more reliable in everday use, and would embody many of the lessons learnt on the track.

Whilst the need to prove the qualities of a machine in such a dramatic manner may have been a matter of vital concern to many, it was not one of such immediate concern to John Prestwich. Already, his products had earned for themselves a good reputation through their advanced design and the care with which they were assembled after the essential working parts had been manufactured to limit gauge specification. It was his proud boast, which was repeated many times in advertisements, that all JAP engines were of identical design and workmanship and therefore there was no distinction from those used for records, races and competitions. Cylinders, pistons and piston rings, to name but three components, were all made to within 1/2000 of an inch.

Be that as it may, manufacturers who supported racing were coming to the conclusion that the easiest way in which to produce more power was to increase the capacity of the engine. This tendency seems to have originated in France, when Buchet, in 1904, produced a tricycle powered by what is almost certainly one of the largest capacity vertical twins ever made. Known as the 'Bete de Vitesse', the tricycle had an engine of no less than 4½ litres, which drove the rear wheels through a De Dion-type live rear axle. Although not exceptionally fast, it provides a good example of the way in which development was progressing at that time. Others followed suit and even Prestwich himself made a large capacity vee-twin, although it did not in any way approach the size of the Buchet engine. But by then he had another possible application for the engine at the back of his mind, as will become apparent shortly.

The big news of 1907 was the decision to replace the somewhat volatile International Cup Races previously held on the Continent by a race over closed roads in the Isle of Man, the Manx Government having agreed to act as hosts and at the same time to subsidise the event. And so the TT races were born, a prestigious series of races which, even today, some 70 or so years later, still draw the attention of the motorcycling world.

It is now history that Charlie Collier, riding one of his own Matchless machines powered by a JAP engine, won the Single Cylinder Class at an average speed of 38.22 mph. What is even more remarkable is that he averaged 94.5 mpg throughout the race, which put him well above the minimum 90 mpg that riders were compelled to meet if they were not to be disqualified from the results. As may be gathered from the foregoing, the early races were run on a speed and fuel consumption basis. Brother Harry, also riding a Matchless with a JAP engine in the same class, put up the fastest lap before he was forced to retire. To win a class in the first TT, and merit the first entry in the records of this historic annual event was no mean achievement for an engine manufacturer, even if the field was quite small (18 singles and 7 twins). The rough and dusty 15 mile course had to be covered 10 times before the welcoming finishing flag was put out and the minimum fuel consumption requirement met.

A check with the 1908 Buyer's Guide in *The Motor Cycle*, published during February that year, shows that more manufacturers were now fitting JAP engines to their motorcycles. The list detailed the following makes of motorcycle:

Anglian No.2	2½hp single
Ariel	5hp twin
BAT	3½hp single
	3½-4hp single
	5hp twin (two models)
	6hp twin
	9hp twin
	16hp twin
Clyde	4hp single
	6hp twin
Elleham	2¾hp single
Leader	2½hp single
	4½hp single
	6hp twin
	7hp twin
	9hp twin
Matchless	2½hp single
	3½hp single
	4½hp single
	6hp twin
	9hp twin

To this list should be added a 2½hp Matchless Ladies Model fitted with a single cylinder engine, and two forecars, the Zenette and the Zenith, both fitted with 6hp twins, the former having a water-cooled version. The forecar was now on its way out, the sidecar having taken its place as a more convenient means of carrying a passenger in comfort and safety.

On April 13th, 1908, a racing motorcyclist by the name of Harry Martin decided to attempt some record breaking at the Canning Town track and in order to do so, he borrowed Harry Collier's 1907 TT 3½hp Matchless JAP single. He was successful too, breaking all the World's records for 101-120 miles and 160-244 miles. The 200 mile record was broken by no less than 22 minutes, whilst the 6 hour record was exceeded by 16 miles. His achievements were soon capitalized upon in a JAP advertisement, which for some strange reason also reproduced testimonials from satisfied users of the JAP carburetter.

An event of great historical significance took place on Easter Monday, April 20th, when the first official motorcycle race was held at the newly-opened Brooklands track. The building of the track had been implemented by H. J. Locke-King, a wealthy hotelier who owned a large estate at Weybridge, in Surrey. Aware of the lack of a suitable test-cum-race track in Britain to aid the development of cars and motorcycles, he took it upon himself to finance this ambitious venture, with the whole-hearted support of the local council and many leading motorists of the day. As a result, a 2¾ mile banked track was laid down at a cost alleged to be in the order of £150,000 — a not inconsiderable amount of money in those days. The building of the track is a story in itself for it was quite a remarkable civil engineering achievement. Very little was known at that time about the laying of reinforced concrete in large slabs. Locke-King's foresight and generosity had far-reaching consequences and until the outbreak of World War 2, Brooklands was in constant use for both racing and testing from June 17th, 1907, when the official opening ceremony took place.

Although the first car race had been held on July 6th, 1907, the very first motorcycle 'race' had been staged quite unofficially, for at that time the track had not been seriously considered for motorcycle use. Two Oxford undergraduates staged a match race there on February 25th, 1908, and in doing so attracted the attention of the Clerk of the Course, Mr. E. de Rodakowski. Seeing the possibilities that existed for motorcyclists too, he set about the organisation of the Easter Monday meeting, a scratch event.

The winner was W. E. Cook, riding a machine of his own design that had a vee-twin Peugeot engine. Not unexpectedly, JAP-engined machines were also in evidence, foremost amongst them being the machines ridden by the Collier brothers. Riding the machine he had used in the last International Cup Race, a Matchless fitted with a vee-twin JAP engine of 861cc capacity, Charlie Collier was placed third. Harry was out of the running, despite the fact that he was riding his own 3½hp TT single, the machine he had lent to Harry Martin a few days earlier for his record-breaking spree.

Not everyone was interested in track events, however, or for that matter in record breaking, for this was now the era of the long-distance trial. This type of event attracted riders of standard road machines, and two of the major events in the calendar were the London-to-Edinburgh Run and the End-to-End, the latter a road trial that started at Land's End and ended at John O'Groats. Three JAP-engined machines took part in the 1908 End-to-End, which necessitated completing a course of 893 miles. All three acquitted themselves well, each rider being awarded a Gold Medal in recognition of his performance. Both J. Tassell and A. M. Tatham rode 3½hp Matchless JAPs, whilst the third man, A. F. Wilding, placed his faith in a 6hp BAT JAP twin.

Still the racing successes piled up. The JAP advertisement in *The Motor Cycle* dated August 12th, lists 2 firsts, 2 seconds and 2 third places in the Cambridge Sports Motor Races, a first, a second and a third each in Classes 1 and 2 of the Dublin Centre Hill Climb, organised by the Motor Cycle Union of Ireland, and 3 firsts in a Crystal Palace meeting — in the 5 miles Handicap (1st from scratch), the 1 Mile Handicap (1st from scratch) and in the 5 Miles Scratch Race. Presumably all were amateur riders, for their names were not mentioned. If nothing else, this suggests there was a great deal of truth in the statement put out by the factory about the capabilities of the standard, over-the-counter engine.

News about the 1908 TT entries abounded, and special attention was drawn to the fact that Harry Bashall would be entered by the factory on a machine fitted with a 20hp vee-twin engine, specially designed for the purpose. Of the 90° type and having bore

A 1908 overhead valve engine made specially for New Hudson. (Photo: Haringey Public
Libraries)

and stroke dimensions of 120 x 120mm (which gave a capacity of 2714cc), the engine filled the frame. The extra wide angle between the cylinders (most JAP vee twin engines were 80° at that time) permitted a nicely radiused inlet pipe from the big, updraught carburetter of the spray type. Although the cylinder heads were not detachable, the valve guides and the inlet and exhaust manifolds were bolted to them, following standard JAP practice with ohv engines of this type. By dismantling the valve gear and removing the bolt-on parts, the flat top of each cylinder head could be observed and the condition of the ports and valve seats examined.

Before the TT, Charlie Collier made an attempt on the World's Hour Record for machines of 76 x 76mm capacity, riding a single cylinder Matchless JAP. He was successful too, covering 52 miles, 1560 yards in the allotted time. Yet for some inexplicable reason, his ride achieved little by way of publicity.

In the 1908 TT there were seven JAP-engined entries, three in the Single Cylinder Class and four in the Twin Cylinder category. In the former, Charlie and Harry Collier each rode a 4hp Matchless single, fitted with the 85 x 76mm vertical-valve ohv engine. The third rider, C.B. Franklin, had a 3½hp Chater Lea. Bert Colver headed the twin cylinder class with a 7hp Matchless, R.M. White and W.H. Bashall having 6-7hp BATs. The fourth rider in this class, Noel Drury, had a machine of JAP manufacture, fitted with a 5hp 85 x 60mm engine that had been specially built for the race. It will thus be realised that Harry Bashall was not riding the monster 2714cc 90° vee-twin as had originally been intended. Extremely powerful, he had found it too much of a handful long before he got to the Isle of Man, as had Charlie Collier who had ridden a Matchless fitted with an identical engine. In consequence, the engines were set aside, and used ultimately for another, quite different application. Perhaps it was as well in some respects, as a minimum fuel consumption of 80mpg had been specified for the Twin Cylinder Class this year (100mpg for the singles!).

In the Single Cylinder race, Charlie Collier brought his Matchless JAP into 2nd place, after having to stop and change a plug when a misfire set in. Harry Collier ran out of petrol and Franklin struggled in to finish 6th. The JAP-engined runners in the Twin Cylinder Class fared almost as well. Harry Bashall took second place, a puncture having caused him to stop and effect a repair at the time when he was in the lead. Drury finished 6th and Bert Colver 9th, the latter having suffered the same fate as Harry Bashall when he was on his 7th lap. Only White failed to finish; the magneto drive bevel pinion had shed its teeth towards the end of the race, and put him out of the running.

On October 8th at Brooklands, using the 7hp Matchless JAP ridden by Bert Colver in the TT, Charlie Collier decided to make an attempt at the World's Hour Record, which had been established during 1905 by J. Giuppone, riding a Peugeot. The attempt proved highly successful and at its conclusion the 85 x 85mm vee-twin ohv engine had carried rider and machine a total distance of 70 miles, 105 yards. The fastest lap was timed at 72.89mph.

At the annual Motor Cycle Show there was again no separate JAP exhibit, although a display of the Company's engines could be found on Stands 97 and 128, in the names of BAT and Collier and Sons, respectively. Three new JAP engines had been announced, an 8hp 85 x 95mm side valve vee-twin, a 4hp 85 x 85mm side valve single, and a redesigned 2½hp lightweight engine of 70 x 76mm, which retained an atmospheric inlet valve. This last engine was a totally redesigned version of the original lightweight design, having enclosed timing gear and mainshafts fitted to the flywheels by taper, key and nut, unlike the boss and screw method used previously. The new engine was on show, fitted into a Chater Lea frame. Significantly, there was no mention of the JAP carburetter in the Show reports, although it was later advertised at the reduced price of 36/-.

The 1908 version of the 90° vee twin racing engine used in the International Cup Race of 1906. The sparseness of the cylinder finning is a most outstanding feature in this 85 x 85mm bore and stroke engine. (Photo: Haringey Public Libraries)

Mention should be made of two other JAP developments that occurred during this period; a patented variable pulley that was toggle-operated to provide continuous changes in gear ratio, and a patented automatic lubrication system. The advantages of the former were claimed to be a complete lack of parts that would be subject to wear, the ability to run as a solid pulley at top speed, no end thrust on the engine mainshaft, and a convenient means of being able to alter the gear ratio.

The lubrication system used a conventional sight feed, but relied upon the partial vacuum created in the crankcase to draw oil from a reservoir, via a vacuum valve. This rendered the traditional hand pump unnecessary.

Before the year came to a close, John Prestwich had made an application to the Local Council in the form of a request for permission to erect a temporary shed 35 feet square on the Lea Marshes for 'experimental purposes in connection with a flying machine'. His request was duly referred to the Parks and Open Spaces committee on October 6th, but on November 3rd the committee gave notice that they were not willing

An even bigger, 16hp, overhead valve racing engine was available in 1908, with bore and stroke dimensions of 120 x 120mm, giving a cubic capacity of 2714cc. The exhaust valve push rods appear to conflict with the exhaust port outlets. (Photo: Haringey Public Libraries)

to agree to this request. Subsequent events seem to suggest that they must have relented as the result of further pressure, possibly after Bleriot made his historic crossing of the English Channel on July 25th, 1909, thereby demonstrating in a most convincing manner the practicability of the aeroplane as a future mode of transport.

Not unexpectedly, John Prestwich had been following with keen interest the progress of the early aviators, ever since the Wright brothers made the first powered flight at Kitty Hawk, in the USA. He could forsee this was another area in which the internal combustion engine would play a vital role, the engine being designed for this purpose rather than being adapted from a design intended for propelling road vehicles. When the big 2714cc 90° vee-twin had been made for Harry Bashall to use in the 1908 TT, it had been suggested that an engine of this type would have the ability to run with a minimum of vibration, and it cannot have escaped Prestwich's attention that it could also prove very suitable for use in an aircraft, where it would run at a fixed speed. Indeed, there is evidence to suggest that one of the three engines of this type made may have been fitted into the ill-fated Matchless monoplane, of which mention is made later.

The end of the year saw the production of the last complete JAP motorcycle. With and ever-increasing demand for engines of all kinds, it made good sense to concentrate on their manufacture alone. Many manufacturers had at least one JAP-engined model in their range, so that the prospective purchaser had a wide choice of individual designs to choose from, even when he had specified the make of engine was to be a JAP.   *51*

F. A. McNab is the rider on the extreme left of this trio of competition riders. His mount is a Trump JAP of his own manufacture. The wooden box strapped to the front fork contains the trembler coil used to power the ignition system. (Photo: Haringey Public Libraries)

Early in 1909, a JAP advertisement drew attention to a revised design of the JAP carburetter, which now had an extra air plate sandwiched mid-way in the main body of the instrument. It had been found necessary to incorporate this in order to overcome the annoying hesitance in throttle response of the original design, which meant introducing artificial drag into the petrol/air mixture flow. This was accomplished by adding an extra plate in the form of a disc with additional air passages covered by brass balls, one extra inlet being provided for each jet after the first one had been uncovered. In practice, the balls did not vibrate on their seats but either remained seated or lifted off completely. The modification worked, but it had been applied too late to save the instrument from extinction. It was expensive to manufacture and eventually it became apparent that it would be much cheaper to buy-in one of the proprietary products which were being made in very large numbers.

The 1909 Buyer's Guide published in a February issue of *The Motor Cycle* listed additional manufacturers who were now fitting a JAP engine into at least one of their models. The newcomers were Corah, Max, NLG and Norton, the last-named also having a 2½hp ladies model. Corah could offer 2½hp and 3½hp singles, as well as 6hp and 8hp twins.

With Brooklands in constant use, a useful extension was the opening of the Test Hill early in the year, and this had not been in use for long before attempts were made to climb it against the clock, from a standing start. One of the earliest record attempts was made by Freddie Barnes, who took a 3½hp Zenith JAP up the hill in 18.633 seconds on March 29th. Just under a couple of months later, Harry Collier took over the track itself to attempt the 24 Hour Record, using a 76 x 95mm JAP engine in his Matchless. It was on May 5th that he covered 775 miles, 1340 yards with this single cylinder machine, and another JAP record went into the Records Book.

Only a fortnight later, during a One Hour Scratch Race that formed part of the Second BMCRC Members Meeting, F.A. McNab set the first officially recorded 500cc Hour Record at 48.22mph, riding a Trump JAP of his own design and manufacture. The date was May 19th and he succeeded in retaining the record until H.H. Bowen raised it to 59.27mph almost three months later, riding a BAT JAP. It went again towards the close of the year, but by only 0.49mph, when O.C. Godfrey took the honours for Rex. Record breaking was about to become a regular occurrence at Brooklands and lead to an unwritten code of ethics whereby the successful record breaker would be allowed by other riders to retain his record long enough to qualify for the bonus payments he could expect from the machine manufacturer and those whose accessories were used. The record would then be broken again, but only by sufficient margin to have it recognised officially. After the following 'agreed' delay, the original record breaker was then free to try his luck again, alonside other likely contestants.

One of the big events of the year was the Auto-Cycle Union's Six Days Trial, held from July 5th-10th inclusive. Amongst the many entrants were six who had JAP-engined machines, namely T.H. Tessier, W.H. Bashall and H.H. Bowen, all on 7hp BAT JAPs, A.D. Draper riding a 3½hp Matchless JAP, and A. Weatherilt and F. Barnes, both riding 3½hp Zenith Gradua JAPs. All put up an outstanding performance to win a Gold Medal each, Tessier in addition being awarded a Silver Cup. The success of his BAT JAP machines is best summed up by quoting the remarks made by *The Motor Cycle* reporter who covered the event: 'The behaviour of the BAT JAP machines on all the hills throughout the Trial has been remarkable'.

As far as the 1909 TT was concerned, it was Harry Collier who emerged victorious on this occasion, when he brought his 738cc Matchless JAP twin home in first place. A change in the regulations for the event had dispensed with the separate single and twin cylinder classes, permitting both types of machine to compete against each other in the same race. There was, however, a 500cc maximum capacity limit for the singles and one of 750cc for the twins, it being considered the multis were much less reliable than the singles. Fortunately, the fuel consumption requirement had been dropped at the same time. Harry was using the new 85 x 65mm ohv twin cylinder JAP engine, identical in design to the 85 x 85mm engine, but having shorter cylinders. In the following JAP advertisement, great play was again made of the fact that the TT had been won on a standard production engine, in accordance with the company's earlier claims.

An interesting feature of the 1909 TT machines ridden by the Collier brothers was the adoption of a Bosch magneto for the ignition system, in place of the usual battery and coil. It is claimed that this was the first appearance of the new vee-twin Bosch magneto in Britain, which may have given the riders an added advantage. Neither machine had spring forks or a spring frame, so that if a battery and coil system had been fitted, these components would have taken quite a hammering.

It was Charlie Collier who encountered misfortune on this occasion. Alleged to have the faster of the two machines, it was the belt drive that let him down. On the opening lap the belt fastner broke and in so doing caught in his rear brake, putting it permanently out of action and forcing his early retirement from the race. Many would have liked to see how he matched up to the challenge provided by Lee Evans, who was riding a 5hp Indian twin with a two-speed gear and all-chain drive. As it was, brother Harry had his work cut out to take the lead from Evans and win at an average speed of exactly 49mph.

Continuing on a racing theme, it should be recorded that the Matchless riders pulled off a surprising win during the October Handicap Meeting held at Brooklands, when Harry Collier, brother Charlie and Bert Colver finished in 1-2-3 order. Harry, who rode a 946cc Matchless JAP, won at an average speed of 70mph, setting a new three-lap record in the process. Bert Colver rode a similar mount, starting 20 seconds ahead of Harry, who was scratch man. Charlie used a 738cc machine, and he started 10 seconds ahead of his brother.

Again there was no JAP exhibit at the 1909 Stanley Show, although one of the models on the BAT Stand featured the new 5-6hp twin cylinder engine, a side valve vee-twin of 76 x 85mm bore and stroke dimensions. It was significant that the production Matchless JAP models now featured magneto ignition and that furthermore they could be obtained with a choice of Amac, Brown and Barlow or JAP carburetter. The days of the JAP carburetter were numbered, on grounds of economics alone.

During November, W.E. Cook discarded the Peugeot engine previously fitted into his NLG and in its place used one of the big 20hp JAP vee-twin engines. His objective was to attempt some record breaking at Brooklands, but he was out of luck when the timing system at the track failed. A week later, Harry Martin tried his luck with an 85 x 85mm BAT JAP, but he too experienced problems. After a struggle he managed to break the 3 Hour Record at an average speed of 55.17mph before he had to call it a day.

Facing page, Top:
An early racing NUT JAP stripped of all but the barest essentials. Note the unsprung front fork and the wooden box containing the trembler coil for the ignition system, the advance and retard lever being mounted on the cylinder barrel. (Photo: Peter Sparkes)

Bottom:
Noel Drury rode this 5hp overhead valve vee-twin JAP in a speed event held at Enniskerry on St. Patrick's Day, 1909. He achieved a maximum speed of 72mph.

Almost unnoticed amongst the motorcycle competitors at Brooklands this year was a young rider by the name of Malcolm Campbell, riding a machine fitted with a 4hp JAP engine. During the final meeting of the year he managed to take second place in one of the two lap handicap races run during the afternoon. Soon, he would become part of the Brooklands scene, but on four wheels not two.

F. A. McNab's success in taking the first officially recorded Hour Record with a 500cc machine clearly encouraged him to capitalize on this by adding a Trump JAP TT model to the somewhat limited production of machines that originated from Liphook Motor Engineering. This latest model, announced in *The Motor Cycle* dated January 10th, 1910, was a single cylinder machine fitted with an 85 x 85mm JAP engine. Ignition was by coil and battery, and a JAP carburetter was specified.

The 1910 Buyer's Guide, published in the same magazine, listed just two more manufacturers who were now using a JAP engine — New Comet and Waverley. The former had a 4hp single and 2½hp ladies model, the latter a 3½hp single. Those who had previously offered machines with a JAP engine still retained their allegiance to the Tottenham factory.

During the month of April, when motorcycling emerged from the usual spell of inactivity brought about by the winter months, Harry Martin decided to have another attempt at record breaking. On this occasion he used an ASL JAP twin, but once again his luck was out when engine troubles set in. Harry was dogged by misfortune during most of his early record breaking attempts, yet at many of the Brooklands race meetings he invariably showed excellent form. If nothing else, he appeared to be learning from his experiences, for one may presume he chose the ASL for this latest attempt because it was quite unique in having pneumatic front and rear suspension. The track was notoriously bumpy and a good suspension system would certainly prove advantageous.

Even though the record breaking attempt failed, Harry must have been satisfied with the way in which the machine handled. When he next appeared at the track, his 344cc Martin JAP had ASL front forks fitted. Later that year, everything came right when, on August 17th, he broke the 500cc flying start kilometre and mile records during the BMCRC Six Monthly Race Meeting, at speeds of 68.28mph and 65.97mph respectively. These results were achieved when riding his 344cc Martin JAP, a quite remarkable performance for a 350cc machine at that time.

Amongst the regular performers at Brooklands was J.T. Bashall, one of Harry Bashall's brothers. For general speed work, he was using an MAB JAP, a single cylinder machine fitted with an 85 x 60mm JAP engine. Nicknamed 'Bizzy', he made his mark, too, later in the year, when he set up a new 750cc One Hour Record during the Brooklands 60 lap TT Race, held on June 22nd. On this occasion, however, he was riding a 666cc BAT JAP twin. Also to be seen amongst the competitors this year was a rider as yet unknown, E.B. Ware, who during 1910 rode a somewhat obscure 8hp twin known as a King's Own. This machine had a 946cc JAP vee-twin engine and featured all-chain drive via a two-speed P and M gear. Later, Ware made quite a name for himself racing Morgan three-wheelers and became closely associated with the JAP factory.

Early news about the 1910 TT suggested that Charlie Collier would be riding a Matchless fitted with an 85 x 58.5mm vee-twin JAP engine that had Bosch magneto ignition. But before much attention could be given to happenings amongst the contestants in this event, the JAP name had come to the fore in quite a different world — that of aviation.

Chapter Four

JAP takes to the air

IT WAS on April 10th, 1910, that a JAP-built aeroplane, powered by a 40hp eight cylinder, air-cooled side valve engine of JAP design and manufacture took to the air from the Lea Marshes. Known as the JAP-Harding monoplane, it was based on the successful Bleriot designs and had been built for the pilot, H. J. Harding, under the direction of John Prestwich himself. As mentioned in the previous Chapter, permission to erect a temporary building on the marshes for the express purpose of building this, and perhaps other aircraft, had been turned down by the local Council. Ultimately they must have relented, but sadly they quickly withdrew their permission soon after the flights began. A local farmer complained that the aircraft made his horses restless, and this effectively brought the JAP aviation project to an abrupt halt.

The flight from the Lea Marshes was by no means the first occasion on which a JAP engine had been used in an aircraft. As far back as 1906, one of this country's pioneers of aviation. A. V. Roe, had used a 6hp vee-twin JAP engine of the atmospheric inlet valve type to power an early biplane of his own design and construction. Initially, he had been working in a shed at Brooklands, the scene of the birth of many of the early aircraft made in this country. But when Brooklands began to get heavily involved with both car and motorcycle racing, Roe considered aviation looked like taking a back seat and he became sufficiently disenchanted to transfer his activities to premises under a railway arch in Hackney. Being in close proximity to Tottenham, it was inevitable that Roe and Prestwich should be drawn together, with the result that a JAP engine was supplied as the power unit, driving the hand-made propellor of the biplane by belt. Flights, or to be more correct, attempts to get airborne, were made from the Hackney Marshes, which necessitated transporting the aircraft there by horse and cart. Unfortunately these 'flights' were soon terminated, after complaints from local residents. These complaints were probably well justified, too, as most 'flights' would have had to be made at early dawn, when there was little or no wind. Undaunted, Roe moved premises yet again, this time to Wembley Park, making personal visits to the Tottenham factory a little more difficult. But his change of work place did not take place until late in 1909, after he had built and flown a more ambitious triplane, powered by a 9hp vee-twin JAP.

Characteristic of the method of construction used in those days, Roe's triplane comprised a wire-braced spruce wood fuselage, the undercarriage of which was made by using standard bicycle wheels and front forks. The wings were built from a combination of spuce spars and pine ribs, with the interplane struts in ash, braced by piano wire.

Covered initially with fabric-reinforced brown paper, the flying surfaces were ultimately replaced by proofed cotton fabric. This machine, alleged to be the first British-made aircraft to take to the air, first took off from the Hackney Marshes on 23rd July, 1909, to cover a distance of some 900 feet before touching down. It marked the early beginning of one of Britain's best-known aircraft manufacturers, for during the year that followed, Roe set up his own business under the name of Avro.

The A. V. Roe Triplane of 1909 outside the railway arch at Hackney, which served as Roe's workshop. (Photo: Crown Copyright)

By now, John Prestwich had come to the conclusion that aircraft needed an engine specially-designed for the purpose in mind and that it was no good merely to adapt a motorcycle engine thus obtaining some form of compromise. When the big 90° vee-twin had shown it was not at all well-suited in its dual-purpose role, he set about the design of a series of four and eight cylinder engines, and by 1910 he could offer the following, all specially-designed for aviation:

A vee-four 85 x 110mm side valve engine

A vee-eight 85 x 95mm ohc engine, developing 35hp

A magneto ignition vee-twin JAP engine was used to power Roe's Triplane. Note the vee-belt drive to the large diameter pulley, which is attached to the propellor by means of a long shaft. (Photo: Science Museum)

A vee-eight 90 x 110mm ohv engine, developing 50hp
A vee-eight 85 x 110mm side valve engine, developing 40hp

With the exception of the 50hp ohv engine, all were air-cooled. The 50hp engine was water-cooled and weighed about 190lb, some 10lb heavier than its air-cooled counterpart. All had short exhaust pipes, pointing upward, and another distinctive feature was the use of ported cylinder barrels, a practice that was at one time very popular in the design of racing engines. It was believed that this formed a convenient way of disposing of the residual exhaust gases and spent oil, albeit at the risk of having an 59

engine that was messy on its exterior. Keeping the engines light in weight was always a problem, particularly those that were water-cooled. To ease the problem in this latter case, John Prestwich made the water jacket in copper, using the 'lost wax' process, which involved coating the cylinder barrels with wax and then applying an exterior layer by electro-depositing copper. Advice about this method was later given to Rolls-Royce, when they showed an interest in it.

It has been alleged that John Prestwich hoped to have one of his own aircraft make the first Channel crossing, but he was pre-empted by Bleriot in this respect. On several occasions he had visited France, and Le Mans in particular, to watch some of the early flying machines being put through their paces, whilst during October 1909 he attended an air display at Blackpool. Later, he arranged for H.J. Harding, a local aeroplane enthusiast, to take his monoplane to France, so that he could obtain his flying licence, due to the embargo that was placed on the use of the Lea Marshes. Also worthy of note are the facts that a JAP engine of unknown type was used in a Martin biplane made by Martin and Handisyde, that a JAP engine powered the first aircraft to fly mail in Australia, and that Malcolm Campbell made an aircraft that had a JAP engine as its power source.

More or less coincident with the assembly of the JAP-Harding aircraft was the construction of the Matchless monoplane, a project that commenced during 1909. A friend of Harry Collier's owned a timber yard in Woolwich and was able to provide not only all the basic materials of construction but also the space for the erection of the aircraft. In March 1910 the frail machine was completed and after a four-cylinder JAP engine had been installed, it was taken to the near-by Plumstead Marshes for its inaugural flight. With Harry at the controls it became airborne and stayed aloft for about a half mile before it touched down. Later, it was taken to Brooklands, where eventually it was more or less written off as the result of a bad landing. From contemporary accounts, several different engines were installed during the aircraft's short life, including one of the big 2714cc 90° JAP vee-twins that had been used by either Harry Collier or Harry Bashall in a racing motorcycle.

It was not aeroplanes alone that used JAP engines either. The Willows dirigible, a light airship made in Bristol, was powered by one of the air-cooled vee-eight engines, in this instance the 85 x 95mm ohv engine of 4,400cc capacity. It is this engine that can be found in the Shuttleworth museum and it is interesting to note that the crankshaft runs on five sets of white metal bearings, the big-end bearings being of the roller type. A JAP multi-jet carburetter fed the mixture to the cylinders through long, polished copper pipes, one pipe to each pair of cylinders via a branched manifold. This engine is said to have developed 47hp at 1,600rpm.

Having made a successful flight from Cheltenham to Cardiff, Willows was keen to show the capabilities of an airship, and more particularly one of his own design. A follow-up flight from Cardiff to London was somewhat hastily planned and it was during the evening of Saturday, 6th August that he set off for the Metropolis, preferring to travel by night so that he could follow the lights in towns. Wearing a leather-lined coat, and with a cork lifebelt around his midriff, he became the first man to cross the Bristol Channel in a powered aircraft. Despite having two tugs standing by in the channel to cope with any emergencies, he reached Clevedon within thirty minutes and managed to pick out the lights of his father's car, which was to have acted as a guide but had broken

Facing page:
Preparing for a flight from Lea Marshes. The pilot, A. V. Roe, seemed to be somewhat precariously seated in this frail aircraft. (Photo: Crown Copyright)

Above:
What was described as 'a busy corner in the JAP Aeroplane Works' on Lea Marshes.
(Photo: Haringey Public Libraries)

Facing page, Top:
This impressive 47hp vee-eight ohv aircraft engine was made by J. A. Prestwich and Co. Ltd in 1908. Bore and stroke dimensions are 85 x 95mm, giving a cubic capacity of 4400cc. Two of these engines, one air-cooled and the other water-cooled, were the only British engines at the first Aero Salon in Paris, held on 24th December 1908.
(Photo: Science Museum)

Bottom:
Another view of the vee-eight ohv engine; showing the gear-driven magneto and the ported cylinder barrels. The long induction pipes from the single JAP carburetter contributed, almost certainly, to icing problems. (Photo: Science Museum)

down. To make matters worse, the battery that powered a powerful light he carried on board failed, so that he had to rely solely on a pocket torch to read his maps.

By 9.30pm he had reached Bristol, where he had the misfortune to throw out his refreshments along with some ballast. Undaunted, he passed over Chippenham, Calne, Marlborough, Hungerford and Reading, following his prescribed route. It was over Reading he reached his greatest altitude, 2,800 feet. But many times he had need to drop close to ground level, so that he could shout through a megaphone to startled passers-by for directions. A compass was useless in such close proximity to all the metalwork.

Sleep was out of the question, but before he had time to get drowsy, the engine ran out of petrol, presenting yet another problem. Plans to refuel en route had gone awry when his father's car broke down, so Willows decided to land, being over Sydenham at the time — quite close to the Crystal Palace where he had intended landing. But his efforts were in vain when his grapnel caught in a tree and broke. Passing over his alloted landing spot about an hour earlier than expected, he drifted on to Lee, near Mottingham, where he persuaded some astonished railway workers to grab his trailing rope and haul down his airship after he had released some gas. Despite all his problems, he had managed to make the longest cross-country flight in Britain, covering the 140 miles in just under ten hours.

He made his way to the Crystal Palace, his proposed destination, on the day following. This gave him time to refuel, effect temporary repairs to the damaged gas bag before topping up with gas, and even show his dirigible to onlookers at 6d per head! It took him just 18 minutes to complete the final 5 miles. The engine had performed faultlessly throughout the flight, running out of petrol being the only problem. Now a JAP engine held an aviation record too!

H. J. Harding at the controls of the JAP Monoplane in 1910. It bore a resemblance to the Bleriot design which made the first successful crossing of the English Channel. (Photo: Crown Copyright)

Monsieur Gilmour with the JAP Monoplane in France during 1909. (Photo: Haringey Public Libraries)

The overhead valve engine used to power the Willows dirigible during its record-breaking flight from Cardiff to the Crystal Palace on August 6th, 1910. It can be seen in the museum of the Shuttleworth Collection, where it is on loan from the City of Birmingham's Department of Science and Industry. (Photo: City of Birmingham Museum of Science and Industry)

65

CHAPTER FOUR

It seems probable that Prestwich's interest in aviation would have continued longer than it did but for two factors that influenced a change of direction. The first of these was that the demand for JAP motorcycle engines was still on the increase as more and more manufacturers decided it was preferable to buy in a reputable, proprietary engine rather than to design, develop and manufacture one of their own. Alternatively, such was the popularity of the JAP engine that those who had a range of machines of their own design and manufacture decided to add at least one JAP-powered model to the range, to provide a little variety. The second, and perhaps the more important factor, was that the rapidly growing aircraft industry, although still in its infancy, was beginning to demand more powerful engines, which in turn was leading to greater complexity in their design. Already, some engine manufacturers such as Anzani, were specialising in aircraft applications alone, so that they could concentrate all their development work into this single area rather than seek compromise with road applications, the requirements of which were beginning to diverge. There was only one reasonable decision that John Prestwich could make, and this he did, thereby bringing to a premature end his brief excursion into early aviation. It was a decision he made not without some regrets, although he had the consolation that he had already made his mark. Testimony to this exists in the form of the JAP monoplane, that has survived intact and can be seen today in the Science Museum, South Kensington, where it takes pride of place amongst the early aviation exhibits. At least four of the multi-cylinder engines have survived too. One fell into the hands of the Villiers Engineering Company, of Wolverhampton, when they acquired JAP in the fifties, and another is in the museum of the Shuttleworth Collection, at Old Warden, Bedfordshire, as mentioned previously.

The JAP Monoplane has survived and now forms part of the Aeronautical Collection of the Science Museum in South Kensington, London. (Photo: Science Museum)

Reverting to the company's continuing motorcycle activities, it was the 1910 TT that again drew the attention of the capabilities of the JAP engine, for it was Charlie Collier who brought his Matchless JAP into first place at an average speed of 50.63mph. The field comprised no less than 83 riders, 12 of whom rode a machine fitted with a JAP engine, either a single or a twin. The expected challenge of the all-chain drive Indian failed to materialise and after the usual early incidents, Charlie found himself in the lead at the half-way stage, with brother Harry close behind. These positions remained unchanged by the time the race ended, although it was by no means a walk-over victory. Amongst the many famous names who had offered a challenge were Harry Martin, Noel Drury, H.H. Bowen, F.A. McNab and Harry Reed. The third member of the Matchless team, Bert Colver, finished tenth.

Soon after the TT it was the BMCRC 5th 1910 meeting at Brooklands that focussed attention on some of the JAP-powered entrants. During the Record Time Trial event, Charlie Collier set up a new Class E record for sidecars, taking the flying start mile at 80.18mph and the flying kilometre at 78.45mph. Bert Colver took the flying kilometre in Class D (up to 750cc solo) with a 666cc Matchless JAP at 70.61mph, whilst S.A.M. Witham took the flying mile in the same class at 71.72mph, riding a BAT JAP of similar capacity. Later, F.A. McNab won the up to 500cc July Junior Handicap on a 498cc Trump JAP, and Bert Colver the up to 1000cc July Senior Handicap on his 666cc Matchless JAP. It was McNab's second major success in less than a month, for at the end of June he had won the up-to-500cc Singles Class of the Brooklands 60-Lap TT Race, on the same machine. H.H. Bowen had finished second in the Multi-Cylinder Class on a 666cc BAT JAP twin, beaten only by Arthur Moorhouse on an Indian.

During July, a photograph in *The Motor Cycle* showed a JAP engine being used to drive an electrical generator to power what was termed a 'wireless operating box' used by the Royal Engineers, Aldershot, who were encamped at Rowlands Castle, Havant. This is one of the earliest photographs of a JAP stationary engine, yet another application that was to prove of increasing importance in later years.

During the same month, the End-to-End Trial came into the news again, but this time for a quite different reason. One of the contestants who should have done well was T.H. Tessier, manufacturer and rider of the BAT JAP motorcycle. His machine went well for the first couple of days, but on the third day the big-end expired prematurely and put him out of the running for the remainder of the Trial. The occurance was so unusual that a post-mortem was conducted back at his works, whereupon to the amazement of everyone concerned, two test tubes-full of silver sand were scraped from the inner surfaces of the flywheels. This quite unexpected act of sabotage incensed John Prestwich and a photograph of the evidence was published, coupled with the offer of a £20 reward from J.A. Prestwich and Co., for information that would lead to the conviction of the saboteur. History does not record whether the reward was ever paid, or the culprit traced.

In August, another of the lesser-known makes came to the attention of readers of *The Motor Cycle* when mention was made of the Priest JAP 3½hp single. Manufactured by Priest and Co., of 66, Bishop Street, Birmingham, one of these machines had competed successfully in the A-CU's Quarterly Trials, held on July 23rd. Shortly afterwards, there was mention of a new Chater Lea JAP, fitted with a 5hp ohv twin engine.

In one of the November issues of the same magazine, the annual Buyer's Guide showed and even more imposing list of manufacturers who now had a JAP engine fitted into at least one model in their 1910 range. The list comprised the following entries:

Single cylinder motorcycles		Twin cylinder models	
ASL	3½hp	BAT	5hp, 7hp
BAT	3½hp	Chater Lea	6hp*
Chater Lea	2½hp, 4hp	Clyde	6hp
Clyde	4hp (2 models)	DOT	6hp, 8hp
DOT	3½hp	Hazel	5hp, 6hp, 7hp
Frays	2½hp, 3½hp	Matchless	6hp, 8hp
Grandex	2½hp	Moveo	4hp, 8hp
Hazel	2½hp, 3hp, 4½hp	Pilot	6hp, 8hp
Martin		Trump	6hp
Racer	2¾hp	Waverley	6hp, 8hp
Martin		Zenith	
Tourer	4hp	Gradua	6hp
Matchless	2½hp, 3½hp		
Moveo	2½hp, 3½hp	**Ladies models**	
New Hudson	2½hp, 3½hp	Norton	2½hp
Oakleigh	4½hp		
Pilot	4hp	**Passenger models**	
Trump JAP	3½hp	Oakleigh	4½hp
Trump TT	3½hp	Oakleigh	
Waverley	3½hp	Sociable	8hp
Wilton	2½hp		
Zenith			
Gradua	3½hp		

* no mention of the 5hp model, listed in an earlier issue

It is also worth mentioning the 8hp Morgan Runabout, which was listed in the Guide for the first time. This three-wheeler, which was soon to eclipse the old and fading forecar, and similar designs listed as passenger models, was fitted with a side valve vee-twin engine of JAP manufacture.

The year ended on a high note, when S. A. M. Witham broke some kilometre and mile records at Brooklands at the end of November. Riding a 5hp Zenith Gradua JAP twin, he set new records as follows:

Kilometre, standing start 50.1mph
Kilometre, flying start 64.08mph
Mile, standing start 63.57mph
Mile, flying start 65.86mph

From the way in which the story of the company has progressed so far, it will be evident that Messrs J. A. Prestwich and Co. Ltd had an almost exclusive market in the supply of proprietrary engine units. There could be little doubt about the quality of their products or the way in which they could be expected to perform under a wide variety of operating conditions. Furthermore, there was a large number of capacities and designs from which to choose, so that those who wished to buy-in rather than design and make their own engines (often a question of basic economics) could fulfil their requirements with comparative ease. Yet there was no room for complacency. During June 1910, F.E.

Baker had commenced the manufacture of motorcycle engines from premises in

Birmingham, using the trade name Precision, in an area that formed the very centre of the motorcycle industry. In a very short period of time, this rival, proprietary engine, began to offer a serious challenge to the Tottenham factory and for a brief spell there were more motorcycle manufacturers using Precision engines than those who put their faith in the tried and proven JAP designs. The challenge was met aggressively and JAP soon regained the upper hand. By the mid-twenties, the Precision engine was in danger of becoming little more than a memory.

Early in 1911, the company found it necessary to move to new premises, as further expansion had become impossible at the now very cramped site in Lansdowne Road. Fortunately, an alternative site was acquired in Northumberland Park, which was still within the Borough of Tottenham and only about ¾ mile away. The Northumberland Park address remained the home of J. A. Prestwich and Co. Ltd, until the works closed down completely during 1963. By now the Prestwich family had moved to Westcliff-on Sea, in Essex, as Arthur, one of John's sons, suffered from asthma. At this time his family comprised four sons, Vivian, Arthur, Edward and Roland, in order of seniority. A fifth son, Douglas, was born whilst they lived in Westcliff. But by 1914 they had moved back to the London area again, this time to settle in Muswell Hill.

There is an unusual story relating to the new factory because when it was half built there was a builders' strike. Unwilling to accept this unexpected delay in completion, John Prestwich employed the builders himself and had the job finished on target. It is also interesting to learn he was responsible for naming the road. It got its name — Tariff Road — due to the fact that the Government had introduced a discriminatory tax on motorcycles from abroad, notably the American Indian, to discourage their importation.

Spurred on by his successes at Brooklands, F. A. McNab announced a new Trump JAP during February 1911, a 4hp single with dropped handlebars and an engine having a ported cylinder barrel, the drillings being similar to those seen on the aircraft engines. Officially referred to as 'auxiliary exhaust ports', McNab had a surrounding cover placed about them, to act as a guard and deflect ejected oil from the drive belt and engine pulley.

During the month of March, the Northumberland Park factory announced plans for the engines that were to be used in the 1911 TT. Three different designs were to be made available, including a lightweight 60 x 60mm 340cc side valve vee-twin which was, in effect, a miniaturised version of the existing 8hp twin. The two other designs mentioned were a 76 x 65.5mm single, and an 85 x 85.5mm single. All three types of engine were to have ball bearing crankshafts and big-ends, and would also have what was described as 'more durable exhaust valves'. Announced at the same time was a simple but ingenious design of valve cotter extractor, which took the form of a forked steel plate. By placing the forked end around the valve stem, immediately under the valve spring cup, the spring could be compressed quite easily so that the valve stem cotter could be withdrawn.

As far as the TT was concerned, 1911 proved to be the first occasion on which the famous Mountain circuit was used, which meant a lap of 37½ miles against the previously used 15 mile triangular course from St. Johns to Peel, and back again to St. Johns. Furthermore, for the first time separate Senior and Junior races were to be held, each with their own clearly defined capacity limits. In the Junior race, Harry Collier brought his single cylinder 297cc ohv Matchless JAP into second place, at an average speed of 40.09mph. Still retaining his allegiance to belt drive, his machine had the advantage of an Armstrong three-speed hub gear in the rear wheel. In the Senior race, Harry was joined by brother Charlie, both of them riding 580cc ohv Matchless twins. The machines ridden by the Collier brothers were fitted with the new Matchless six-speed variable gear, which relied for its operation upon two long levers mounted on the right-hand side of the machine. The levers worked together in a double rack on the right-hand side of the tank, and were made of spring steel, one arranged to spring inwards and the other outwards, so that they would lock themselves in one of the eight pairs of inward-facing notches in the rack. One lever opened and closed the engine pulley whilst the other moved the rear wheel backwards or forwards in a sub-frame attached to the rear stays of the main frame. One lever was topped by a ball and the other by a cup, so that when gripped with the right hand the ball was forced into the cup, thus releasing both levers from their respective notches in the rack. When released, they would spring inwards and outwards respectively, to lock themselves in the selected position. The system worked quite satisfactorily, although there was no means of compensating for belt stretch.

It was the Senior race that attracted the greatest attention, for amongst those on the starting line was a famous American board track racer — Jake de Rosier — with his all-chain drive vee-twin Indian. He was one of four Indian riders, similarly mounted, and it was expected that the race would develop into a battle for supremecy between the rival Matchless and Indian camps. But as so often happens, a twist of fate took away all the excitement. Harry, then Charlie, ran out of petrol quite unexpectedly, whilst later in the race Jake stepped off his machine, sustaining some machine damage and injuring himself in the process. But he carried on after straightening things out, only to be disqualified for taking on fuel other than at his pit. After finishing second, Charlie Collier was disqualified too, for the same reason, with the result that the remaining Indian riders took the first three places. This result had some significance, the more so because a Scott two-stroke had put up the fastest lap. It had not passed unnoticed that the successful machines all had chain drive.

With the Indian v Matchless challenge unresolved, Jake de Rosier stayed on after the TT to take part in a special match race against Charlie Collier at Brooklands, on Saturday, July 15th. For the occasion, Charlie used one of the new but now legendary '90 bore' JAP engines, a 90 x 78.4mm vee-twin with overhead valves. Clearly he had taken much care in machine preparation, for the Matchless was red enamelled and it could be seen that he had dispensed with the customary 'auxiliary exhaust ports', preferring to use relatively short downward pointing exhaust pipes. The results of that classic match race are now history, Jake winning two of the three races and thereby taking the series on aggregate. But even then the results were hardly conclusive as each rider had experienced his share of unforseen troubles. Perhaps it was a little premature to use the new JAP engine, for less than a month later, the Matchless recorded 91.31mph at the same track, regaining the Class E flying start 5 miles and kilometre records for Britain, and the later in the day, the flying start mile. The respective speeds 83.72mph, 89.48mph and 91.31mph, the Flying Start Kilometre attempt representing a new world record and the Flying Start Mile the first occasion on which a British rider had exceeded 90mph. It seemed as though Charlie Collier had been correct when he claimed the 90 bore engine had needed more time to bed down than he had anticipated when he had started preparing his machine for the earlier Match Races.

When Charlie entered the same machine for the final BMCRC meeting of the season at Brooklands on September 23rd, it could be seen that he had converted it to all-chain drive, using a countershaft and what was termed a 'slipping clutch' in lieu of a shock absorber. As yet, no firm decision had been made about the form of drive to be preferred, for like many other riders, Charlie and his brother Harry continued to use belt drive machines right up to the time of the Great War. It had one desirable attribute, that of providing a relatively 'soft' drive that obviated the need for a shock absorber. But it had its drawbacks too, especially the tendency to slip badly in the wet and also to stretch or alternatively to pull out the fastner, when highly stressed.

During the second half of the year, more manufacturers were fitting a JAP engine to at least one of their model range, some of the more famous names included. Royal Enfield, for example, had a new 6hp two-speed Enfield JAP, which, with sidecar attached, had been ridden in a Midland Inter-Club Reliability Trial by Bert Colver. Another make, the long-forgotten Roulette JAP, was using a 2½hp single. Made by the Roulette Cycle Company of Gosford Street, Coventry, this latter machine weighed only 122lb, and had a twin top tube frame and a cantilever saddle pillar. Yet another machine seen around at the same time was what was presumably an experimental vee-twin New Hudson, fitted with a 425cc 60 x 76mm JAP engine. It too had been entered in one or two of the 1911 competition events.

As the year drew to a close, it could be seen that several spring-frame machines were included amongst the list of JAP-engined models offered by quite a large number of manufacturers. These comprised the 3½hp PV JAP (60 x 76mm side valve vee-twin), the ASL JAP (3½hp and 5hp side valve vee-twins), the Edmund JAP and, as previously listed, the BAT JAP. Strictly speaking, the last two did not have a spring frame in the generally-accepted sense. On the former, the saddle and footrests were spring-mounted in unison with each other, whilst the latter had a spring saddle pillar which later was interconnected with the footboards in a similar manner to that of the Edmund.

Reference to the end of the year's Buyers Guide in *The Motor Cycle* showed that some manufacturers were now offering the option of either a JAP or a Precision engine, whilst the overall count revealed that more models were available fitted with a Precision engine than a JAP, the ratio being 38 to 34. Amongst the newcomers in the list, the following manufacturers were now specifying a JAP engine, or in some cases, the option of a JAP or a Precision:

Campion
Edmund
Ixion TT
New Hudson
NLG
NYE
Portland
PV
Rex-JAP
Swan
VS

Undoubtedly there were many more not listed who manufactured machines in relatively small numbers, of which the Roulette JAP mentioned earlier is but one example.

The end of the year marked the appearance of the cyclecar, in the form of what was to become one of the better-known makes, the Bedelia. The cyclecar represented a bold attempt to construct a lightweight and somewhat primitive car, powered by a motorcycle engine. Many of the designs featured belt drive to the rear wheels and tandem seating of the driver and passenger, often with the passenger in front of the driver. It was a cult that grew very rapidly in the years prior to the Great War and created sufficient interest for a new weekly magazine, *The Cyclecar,* to be launched on November 25th, 1912. But the craze expired almost as quickly when, after the war, the light car and the three wheel runabout presented decidedly better prospects. Even so, the cyclecar era formed another important outlet for proprietary engines, such as the JAP, especially the vee-twin. It was significant that the Bedelia used a JAP vee-twin for its motive power, having the engine in line with the chassis.

Serious thought was now being given to the use of variable gears on motorcycles and particularly whether they should be of the epicyclic type fitted into the hub of the rear wheel, or whether a countershaft with a simple form of dog clutch arrangement would not offer a better solution. Opinions remained divided, although it had not passed unnoticed that one or two makes of machine, such as the Indian and the Douglas, had a two-speed gearbox that was proving highly successful. When machines so equipped started to win major competition events, other manufacturers began to sit up and take notice. When Harry Bashall won the 1912 Junior TT riding a Douglas fitted with a two-speed gearbox, he claimed it was the gearbox that had proved his greatest asset. He knew he had made the right choice when he passed the previous year's winner, P.J. Evans, early in the race. Evans was struggling hard to maintain forward progress with his hub gear Humber in rain that had turned the course into little more than a muddy track. From now on, the fate of the three-speed hub gear was sealed. Already, Harry had started to show his true potential, when he took an 8hp Matchless JAP twin to a hill climb at Gometz-le-Chatel, in France, during December 1911. It was a highly successful trip from his viewpoint, for he recorded fastest time of the day.

With so much going on, it could be inferred that John Prestwich was more than fully occupied. Yet surprisingly he managed to find time to rough out some arangement drawings for what is described as a light coupé car and had requested the Drawing Office to originate a set of blueprints from them as a 'background job' whenever they had time to spare. The car was intended for his own personal use and quite probably was of the cyclecar type, having an engine rated at 11.9hp. Eventually a prototype was built and handed over to him for testing, and it is alleged that this led to the construction of a second, 'improved' version, embodying a number of modifications that he considered necessary as the result of the many miles he had covered. Unfortunately, very little is known about either car, although it would seem certain that the outbreak of war in 1914 precluded the possibility of the JAP car going into production, even in quite small numbers. John Prestwich continued to use the second, 'improved' car, right through the war years, often on work of national importance. When eventually the car was broken up, it had covered in excess of 150,000 miles.

Although John Prestwich himself had been involved with most of the design work since his company started manufacturing engines, it is obvious that he alone could not retain this sole responsibility unassisted as the business began to expand. One of his early assistants had been A.E. Bowyer-Lowe, mentioned earlier, who had joined the Lansdowne Road works in 1903 as a young lad of 17 and had been taken on in the capacity of improver-turner. It is alleged that he had aided Prestwich in the design and development of the original 473cc capacity ohv engine, learning from his master as he went along. Later, he helped with the preparation of the engines used by some of the British competitors in the International Cup Races.

Now that Brooklands had become well-established, the advertising potential to be gained from race results had diminished, so that manufacturers were always looking for new avenues to explore. Early in 1912 a sudden interest in ascending steep gradients came to the fore, with the seeking out of 'freak' hills that had so far proved unclimbable, or alternatively, those that could be climbed, but only with great difficulty. A typical example of one of these publicity 'stunts' was reported in the January 18th issue of *The Motor Cycle* when Harry Reed climbed Stoney Brow, considered to be Manchester's 'worst' hill (1:7), from a standing start with an 8hp DOT JAP sidecar outfit. Whilst this in itself may not seem too remarkable today, it should be explained that the sidecar carried three well-built male passengers throughout the test.

Harry Reed of DOT Motors, the driving force behind this old-established manufacturer, based in Manchester. He scored numerous competition successes with a variety of JAP-engined machines of his own manufacture. (Photo: Haringey Public Libraries)

CHAPTER FOUR

Another unusual happening was the successful opening of a provincial Motor Cycle Show in the City of Leicester by one of the local clubs. Although comparatively few machines were on display, they included three that had a JAP engine fitted — Clyde, Rex JAP and Campion, representing makers based in Leicester itself, Birmingham and Nottingham respectively. Sufficient local interest was aroused to call for a repeat on a much larger scale the following year.

The opening of the 1912 racing season at Brooklands marked the appearance of Harry Martin at the wheel of a Morgan Runabout. Differing in many respects from the cyclecar type of design, the Morgan had an air-cooled vee-twin ohv JAP engine mounted across the front of the car, completely exposed to the elements. Like the car's inventor, H. F. S. Morgan, Harry would soon bring the Morgan name to the fore, when it began to take part in cyclecar racing events. It is also of interest to note that another name, also to be more closely associated with the Morgan name and the JAP engine in a few year's time, was appearing regularly at Brooklands on a Zenith JAP, both solo and sidecar. The person in question was E. B. Ware who, in 1912, made his first entry in the Isle of Man Senior TT Race, mounted on a 498cc Zenith JAP. Sadly, his efforts were in vain, for he was forced to retire without completing the race — as indeed proved to be the case the following year.

In Europe, the political situation was far from happy, and already the clouds of war were beginning to form in an ominous fashion. The Army had started to give serious thought to the role a motorcycle could fulfil should hostilities commence, and during May a so-called Mobilisation Day was held in Daventry to see what response would be forthcoming from those who had volunteered for motorcycle service in a reserve capacity. 99 out of a total of 173 who had pledged their support turned up on the day in question, many of them having travelled a considerable distance. Military observers often appeared at competition events, and it was Harry Bashall's belief that the presence of observers during the 1912 TT led to the order for Douglas motorcycles when war was declared on Germany only a couple of years later. Other motorcycle manufacturers were awarded government contracts too and the sidecar outfit took on a new role — that of a mobile platform on which a machine gun was mounted. Some War Department trials were held at Brooklands towards the end of January 1912, with the prospect of a government contract for the manufacturers whose machines seemed to match up to the requirements of the officials present. These tests were conducted on both the track itself and on the Test Hill, the latter apparently to show a machine's hill climbing abilities.

Records were broken early in the season when Freddie Barnes won the first 100 Mile Race of the season at a record speed of 48.50mph with his Zenith Gradua sidecar outfit, powered by a vee-twin JAP engine. In so doing, he also took the 50 Mile Record at 49.74mph, the Hour Record at 49.73mph and the Two Hour Record at 48.64mph, all in the sidecar Class E category (750 - 1,000cc). It was in the first cyclecar race to be held at the track, run in conjunction with the same meeting, that Harry Martin took first place with the Morgan mentioned earlier. His race speed was 57.31mph, over 13mph faster than the second man, who was driving a Sabella JAP.

The 1912 Isle of Man TT proved something of an anticlimax for the Collier brothers who had entered for the Senior Race only. Fitted with the same six-speed variable gear as used during the 1911 Senior TT, only one long gear lever operating in a single rack was used on this occasion. The lever that opened and closed the engine pulley had been reduced to half its original length and now worked in a small rack that was attached to, and moved with, the long lever. Apart from having only the one lever to move, it was now possible to compensate for belt stretch by moving the second short lever a notch or two either way, as appropriate, quite independently. Both machines were no match for the flying Scott of Frank Applebee. The best Harry could manage was third place, with Charlie following closely behind in fourth berth. From now on, their interest in the TT seemed to wane, and 1914 marked the last occasion on which they took part in this historic event. Ironically, it was the 496cc Matchless JAP twin of 1912 on which both had entered that provided them with the last opportunity to have their names recorded in the list of results. Both were forced to retire in the 1913 and 1914 Senior Races, without being able to complete the course. The JAP engine used in 1912 was a 70 x 64.5mm ohv vee-twin. Harry averaged 46.5mph throughout the race, and Charlie 45.43mph.

With more and more different makes of cyclecar appearing on the market, there was need for a specially-designed engine with heavy flywheels rather than having to use an existing engine that had been designed especially for motorcycle use. Towards the end of September, the JAP factory released details of their new cyclecar engine, which took the form of a 90° inlet-over-exhaust vee-twin, with an extra-large crankcase. Rated at 10hp, the engine had the rocker arms for the overhead inlet valves pivot on a standard cast *in-situ* with the inlet domes. Other proprietary makes of cyclecar engine also came into being around this period, including the water-cooled Blumfield.

Prior to the 1912 Motor Cycle Show, advance details became available about the Matchless range for the 1913 season. The machines to be fitted with a JAP engine comprised an 8hp side valve vee-twin, with all-chain drive and a countershaft of simple design, a 3½hp ohv vee-twin, and a cyclecar fitted with the 90° 9hp I0E vee-twin engine (85 x 85mm) already mentioned. From all accounts this can be regarded as the 'Chain Drive Show', this form of transmission having proved its superiority and its compatibility with the countershaft type of gearboxes that were now being developed. The belt was at last on its way out.

When *Motor Cycling* described the 1913 Matchless range in their issue dated 19th November, 1912, it became apparent that the alleged cyclecar fitted with a 90° 10E vee-twin engine was not a cyclecar at all, but a three-wheeler, with bevel drive to the rear wheel via a two-speed gearbox. It would seem probable that only the prototype exhibited at the Olympia Show and one or two more were made, because little was heard about them afterwards, apart from the fact that they were expected to sell at 110 guineas. Yet the major part of one has survived, having spent at least 25 years immersed in a stream where it had served as a temporary dam! Skilled hands succeeded in taking it apart without breaking any vital components and plans are afoot to rebuild it with a replica body.

Although there was no direct JAP representation at the Show, JAP engines were much in evidence and could be seen fitted to the following makes: Trump, New Imperial (2½hp single and 6hp twin), Rex-JAP, BAT (8hp 85 x 85mm twin) and Matchless (9hp I0E twin), in addition to those who had shown JAP-engined models on previous occasions. Although in many instances a Precision engine was offered as an optional alternative to a JAP engine, reference to the end of the year's Buyers Guide confirmed that the Tottenham factory had regained their premier position as the largest single supplier of proprietary engines to the British motorcycle industry, being associated with each of the following makes:

Single cylinder models

Campion	4hp	Hobart TT	2½hp ohv
Clyde	4hp ohv	Hobart	3½hp ohv
Corah	3½hp	Kynoch	4hp
Edmund	3½hp	Martin	4hp
Hazlewood	2¾hp	New Imperial	2½hp
Hobart	2½hp	New Imperial	3½hp

75

New Imperial	4¼hp		Royal Ruby	3½
New Imperial	4hp		Royal Ruby	3½hp ohv
Pilot	4hp		Sun	3½hp
Portland	4hp		Swan	3½hp
Rex-JAP	3½hp ohv		Trump JAP	3½hp ohv (2 models)
Rex-JAP	4¼hp ohv		Zenith	3½hp
Royal Ruby	2½hp			

Twin cylinder models

BAT TT	5-6hp (2 models)		NLG	6hp ohv
BAT TT	7-8hp		NUT	2¾hp (2 models)
Campion	6hp		NUT	3¼hp
Campion	8hp		OK	6hp
Clyde	6hp		Pilot	6hp ohv
Corah	3hp		Pilot	8hp ohv
Corah	6hp		PV	3¼hp ohv
DOT	6hp		PV	5hp ohv
DOT	8hp		PV	6hp ohv
Edmund	3hp ohv		Rex-JAP	3½hp
Edmund	6hp		Rex-JAP	6hp
Hazlewood	3½hp		Rex-JAP	7hp ohv
Hazlewood	5hp		Rex-JAP	8hp
Ixion	3¼hp sv or ohv		Royal Ruby	3¼hp
Kynoch	6hp		Royal Ruby	6hp
Lea Francis	3¼hp		Royal Ruby	8hp
Martin	6hp		Sparkbrook	6hp
Martin	8hp		Trump JAP	3¼hp
Matchless	3½hp ohv		Trump JAP	6hp
Matchless	6hp		Trump JAP	8hp
Matchless	8hp		Wulfruna	6hp
New Comet	8hp ohv		Zenith	6hp (2 models)
New Imperial	6hp ohv			

Three wheelers

Autotrix	8hp		Lambert	8hp
Enfield s/c	6hp		Morgan	8hp
Ixion s/c	6hp (2 models)			

Cyclecars

ALC	JBS
Arden	Kendall
Autocrat	Leo
Crescent	LM
Duocar	Rolo Tandem
Flycar	Sabella
Gilyard	Tiny Car
Gordon	Walcycar
Invicta	Whippet

In addition, both Hobart and Swan marketed a ladies motorcycle, both makes using a single cylinder 3½hp JAP engine. The ratio of JAP to Precision engines was now 25 (38) in the single cylinder range, 49 (4) in the twin cylinder range, three-wheelers JAP only and cyclecars 18 (2), the comparable Precision figures being in brackets. Already, the JAP factory was starting to concentrate on twin cylinder engines, this representing the area in which there seemed to be the greatest growth potential.

At the end of the year, it was interesting to take a close look at the Records Book, if only to see how many had been achieved by a motorcycle or a three-wheeler powered by a JAP engine. The situation up to December 31st 1912 was as follows:

Class A *(Solo up to 275cc)*

H. Martin	Martin JAP	Flying kilo	66.42mph
		Flying mile	64.75mph
		Flying 5 miles	50.79mph
		50 miles	59.76mph
		1 hour	54.17mph

Class D *(Solo up to 750cc)*

H. Hunter	Corah JAP	Flying kilo	77.80mph
		Flying mile	76.04mph

Class E *(Solo up to 1000cc)*

C.R. Collier	Matchless JAP	Flying kilo	91.23mph
		Flying mile	91.37mph
H.A. Collier	Matchless JAP	400 miles	43.92mph
		500 miles	39.06mph
		600 miles	35.30mph
		700 miles	32.66mph
		9 hours	44.00mph
		10 hours	41.10mph
		11 hours	40.53mph
		12 hours	39.29mph
		24 hours	37.32mph

Class E *(Sidecars)*

G.F. Hunter	Zenith	Flying kilo	72.72mph
		Flying mile	67.03mph
F.W. Barnes	Zenith	50 miles	52.14mph
		100 miles	49.15mph
		1 hour	52.17mph
		2 hours	48.45mph

Cyclecars

H.F.S. Morgan	Morgan	Flying kilo	58.94mph
		Flying mile	58.86mph
		50 miles	59.43mph

Awaiting confirmation were S.T. Tessier's attempts on the flying kilo and flying mile with a BAT JAP at 48.45mph and 48.42mph respectively, and A.W. Lambert's kilo and mile attempts with a Morgan three-wheeler at 58.94mph and 58.86mph, respectively.

CHAPTER FOUR

In many respects, the end of the year marked the beginning of an era of change, which would set the broad pattern of motocycle development for the next decade or so, taking into account the disruptive effects of the now imminent war with Germany. Already the evolution of the countershaft gearbox as we know it today had commenced, and belt drive had begun to give way to the all-chain drive that had been pioneered by Indian, Scott and others. Perhaps even more significant was the appearance of the cyclecar and its companion, the three-wheel runabout. Offering an alternative to the sidecar outfit, each had its own particular attributes and would ultimately lead to the development of the light car which would offer serious challenge to the motorcycle industry in the mid-to-late twenties.

Chapter Five

Progress and reward

ALTHOUGH a couple of years had passed since the company moved into its new premises in Northumberland Park, John Prestwich was proud of the progress that had been made, and more particularly, in the way in which he had been able to expand and modernise his production facilities. It seemed an appropriate time to organise a visit from one of the professional institutions associated with the car and motorcycle industry, so during January 1913 the Institution of Automobile Engineers included a visit to Tottenham in their winter programme. They were shown around by John Prestwich himself and according to a report on the visit in *The Motor Cycle* of January 18th, members found much to interest them. One of the highlights was a demonstration of how a flywheel could be fully machined in 12 minutes, this including the setting-up time, machining of both sides of the flywheel, and the drilling out the centre for the fitting of the mainshaft. The boring of cylinder barrels drew the attention of the visitors, too. Four cutters were used to take the bore to within 0.003 inch of its intended size, this remaining fraction being removed by a separate grinding operation. The visit proved a great success, bringing home the high standards that were maintained throughout the entire production cycle.

One news item that is so easily overlooked because it was of little significance at the time was the employment on 1st January, 1913, of Stanley M. Greening. In the capacity of Technical Advisor, he made his own unique contribution to the success of the company during the fifty years he remained at Tottenham, as will become apparent as the story progresses.

With the chain-or-belt and hub-or-countershaft gears arguments still going on, it was interesting to see that early in February a two-speed countershaft gear of the dog-clutch type had been announced by the Collier brothers. Of the bottom bracket type, the gearbox represented a radical departure from what had appeared previously on the standard production models. Necessitating all-chain drive, the gearbox also had provision for a kickstarter and a foot-operated clutch that relied upon steel and phosphor bronze 'friction' surfaces. The gearbox had already undergone rigorous testing in the hands of Charlie Collier, who had used it fitted to the Matchless he rode in a North Middlesex MCC open trial.

The Leicester Show, mentioned earlier, was continued again in 1913, with more entries on this occasion. Amongst the newcomers was the Morrison, a 6hp vee-twin fitted with a JAP engine, which came from Dover Street in the City itself. Previously associated with the manufacture of a spring wheel sidecar, A.E. Morrison and Co. had decided it was time to make their own motorcycle, too.

With so many speed events taking place all over the country, the tuning specialist was coming into his own and much was being learnt about valve timing, reducing the weight of reciprocating parts, and the advantages of valve overlap. As if a prelude to the Isle of Man TT, *Motor Cycling* published an article on tuning a 4hp JAP engine in their April 1st issue, which gave some sound advice, based on the practices of the day. The article centred around the famous 90 bore engine, as this was considered to be the best of all the JAP engines for serious competition work. Surprisingly, the author recommended retaining the JAP carburettor, although he did admit that he preferred the special racing type when he rode at Brooklands.

One of the forgotten makes of the pre-Great War era, this ohv Blenheim-JAP has been built with racing in mind, judging from its stripped condition. The year of manufacture is probably 1913/14. (Photo: Haringey Public Libraries)

As far as the 1913 TT was concerned, three new engines were announced by the JAP works early in May. The first of these was a 70 x 64.5mm ohv vee-twin, having new timing gear that necessitated the use of three timing pinions only, the second engine was a 76 x 58mm twin, having oil scoops fitted to the perimeter of the flywheels, and the third the one that represented the greatest breakaway from established practice, thereby necessitating a much more detailed description. Of 64 x 77mm dimensions, this last engine had the camshaft mounted between the cylinders, so that the valve gear was

Above:
This Chater Lea, carrying a Scottish registration number, is fitted with a large capacity ohv water-cooled JAP vee-twin engine, and features all chain drive. Note the massive radiator fitted between the machine itself and the sidecar chassis. (Photo: Haringey Public Libraries)

Left:
This photograph of an unknown make of JAP-engined sidecar outfit accompanied a testimonial written by the owner, a Mr. A. W. Tarry of 93, Lea Road, Northampton. He claimed to have covered 3,000 miles with this outfit in 12 months, carrying his family, and without need to fit replacements. His wife looks somewhat apprehensive! (Photo: Haringey Public Libraries)

located at the front of the front cylinder, and at the rear in the case of the rear cylinder. Both cylinder barrels had detachable heads and another unusual feature was the provision of a flexible drive for the magneto so that it could be mounted behind the engine by means of a special coupling. All three engines were of the belt drive type, being supplied with a pulley. The 64 x 77mm engine was specified for use in conjunction with an Armstrong MkV hub gear.

A few weeks later, a special feature article in *Motor Cycling* showed that no less than 15 different types of engine were currently in production, ranging from the 2½hp single to the 8hp twin. Reference was made to the 85 x 85mm IOE single as used by the Collier brothers, the inlet pipe having a cast-in guide for the inlet push rod which had an adjustable tappet. The side exhaust valve was not adjustable in a similar manner, but followed what had been the standard practice in the past — adjustment being effected by placing shims of appropriate thickness on top of the fixed tappet, which were then held in position by a dust cover. This obviated the need for grinding off the end of the valve stem as and when the clearance decreased below the recommended limit.

The lubrication system, always very thorough in any JAP engine, demanded special attention. Oil was fed to the crankcase in the traditional manner, the revolving flywheels picking it up and using the splash method to lubricate the pistons and cylinder walls. Oil draining back found its way to a sump that was integral with the crankcase and was forced up a vertical pipe via a non-return valve, by pressure from the descending pistons. It flowed around the revolving timing side mainshaft, to be caught within a recess formed within the boss of the timing side flywheel, when a hole in the crankcase wall aligned with a hole in the flywheel recess. The oil then passed to the crankpin and big end bearings, via internal passageways. The TT engines had the added refinement of a lip on the back edge of the front cylinder piston. The revolving flywheels flung oil on to this lip, the extra oil being carried by the piston for lubricating the cylinder walls. The front baffle plates were removed from the crankcase mouth too, to ensure thorough lubrication of the front cylinder and piston. Contrary to popular belief, the rear cylinder usually runs the coolest, as under normal running conditions it has the advantage of better oil distribution.

The 1913 TT differed from the earlier races in this historic series in so far as both the Senior and the Junior Races were run in two stages, on two separate days, with a rest day in between. In consequence, competitiors had to cover three (Senior) and two (Junior) laps on the first day, and then four laps each on the second day. A new requirement was the need for all riders to wear a helmet, and because the Senior and Junior Races were to be run concurrently on the second day, the Senior riders had to wear a red waistcoat, and the Juniors one coloured blue.

As mentioned earlier, both the Collier brothers were out of luck in the Senior Race, neither of them managing to complete the course on the first day. Ironically, this proved to be the first occasion on which they had pinned their hopes on the Swiss-made MAG (Motosacoche) engine in preference to the JAP designs they had used in the past. Three prototypes had been prepared prior to the event, all having the new 64 x 77mm MAG engine. One had the Matchless six-speed variable gear as used in the 1912 Senior TT, another had a 2-speed countershaft gearbox, and the third an Armstrong 3-speed hub gear. It was the last of these three designs that was used in the race, but it is interesting to note that the 2-speed model with all-chain drive still exists, at one time being owned by Ivor Mutton who rode it on several occasions in the Vintage MCC's annual Banbury Run. It was not the engine, but a couple of punctures that put Charlie out of the running during the second lap, whilst Harry had gone out earlier with a broken exhaust valve cap and unspecified gear trouble, so their demise could hardly be attributed to the change of engine. No one could keep pace with the flying Scott of Tim

Wood, although A.R. Abbott and Alfie Alexander tried hard, being Rudge and Indian-mounted, respectively.

In the Junior Race it was a totally different picture. It was Hugh Mason, riding a JAP-powered NUT twin who took the honours, fighting off a strong challenge from Billy Newsome, on a Douglas. The story behind Mason's win is worth relating, for he was anything but fit and had been in hospital the day before the race started, returning there on the rest day, and again at the conclusion of the race on the second day. To have completed the course under these circumstances would have been a minor miracle, but to have won with such a severe handicap gave testimony to his sheer grit and determination.

A 1913 vee-twin NUT fitted with an ohv JAP engine, most probably photographed on Redcar Sands. One wonders what the onlooker proposes to do with the hammer he is carrying! (Photo: Peter Sparkes)

The trouble started as the result of an accident whilst practicing on the Monday that preceded the first day of the Junior Race. Caught in early morning mist around Snaefell, he failed to take the corner just before the Bungalow and fell heavily, cutting his face and biting his tongue. He rendered himself unconscious too, because he remembered nothing more until almost twelve hours later, when he was found by the Collier brothers. A doctor was summoned and he was taken to the Bungalow for a brief examination before being returned to his lodgings. When he regained consciousness, he requested his mechanics to salvage his machine from the scene of the accident and transfer the engine to a spare frame. He was then taken to the Fort Ann Hotel, whereupon he again became unconscious. When he awoke later, he found himself in hospital, being attended to by a doctor. He pleaded to be allowed to return to his lodgings, but the doctor persuaded him to stay.

The next day he had rallied sufficiently well to be taken by car to the Drill Hall, where the machines were being scrutineered. An A-CU official told him that his machine had been handled by his mechanic in his absence and he could return to bed, which he did, to be awakened on the Wednesday morning for the start of the race. His machine was ready for him, so he sat down and waited patiently for his turn to start.

Even now he was far from well and he claimed that it was not until he fell off at Quarter Bridge that he started to liven up. Before he reached the Mountain, he passed eleven riders who had started before him. The excitement of the race kept him going, but soon his head started throbbing and he vomited several times whilst on the bike. The worse he felt, the slower he went, yet he managed to complete those vital two laps and, unbelievably, take first place.

He returned to hospital and slept throughout the Thursday, being fit enough to get to his machine on the Friday for the final four laps. He stopped at Braddan to refuel and take on oil, being passed by one of the Junior riders whilst he did so. But he had overtaken the new race leader by the time Glen Helen came into sight. On the second lap he stopped at Ramsey to query his position and was told that if he kept going as he was, he would win the race. Thereafter he stopped on each lap to oil his gears. Once more he was taken ill with a thumping headache and bouts of vomiting, so that he dare not ride fast. On reaching Ramsey on the third lap he was told he was 36 seconds behind the leading Junior, which caused him to remonstrate as to why he had not been given this news on the previous lap. But he was told that he had not been given this information in his own interests, as it was considered unsafe for him to go any faster. The incentive had been provided and somehow he did manage to go faster, so that by the time he reached the finish he knew he had made up all the lost time.

Having finished, he had an overwhelming urge to go to sleep, but by a superhuman effort he helped the A-CU official by taking his engine down for the customary post-race examination and verification of capacity. Only then did he go to sleep, to wake up again in hospital late on the Saturday.

Asked about his machine, Mason claimed he had found out quite by accident that he was getting quite extraordinary results from one of his engines. He made careful note of all the settings and found that the timing differed on one cylinder as compared with the other. He set his next engine up in similar manner, to get identical results, and it was on this basis that he had prepared his TT-winning engine, starting as early as January. He had taken his Brooklands engine to the Isle of Man as a reserve, this engine having a lower compression ratio, but being identical in other respects. It was interesting to note that it was his practice to use cut-down valves from the 8-10hp JAP engines and that he had 'cleaned' the valves when he stopped at Braddan to take on fuel and oil.

Irrespective of Mason's gallant ride, fierce controversy raged after the 1913 TT, largely as the result of high speeds and the allegedly lurid cornering style of some of the

Left:
Hugh Mason and an unknown Ivy rider at Brooklands. (Photo: Peter Sparkes)

Right:
Hugh Mason is assisted away from the finish, after winning the 1913 Junior TT on his NUT JAP. A very sick man, he had not fully recovered from the crash he experienced during practice. (Photo: Peter Sparkes) 5/6

Hugh Mason astride a vee-twin model similar to the one on which he won the 1913 Junior TT for NUT. (Photo: Peter Sparkes)

faster riders. Quite a few competitors had been injured during both practice and racing, whilst one unfortunate, F. E. Bateman, had been killed during the Senior Race when his Rudge got into a rut at Keppel Gate. All the usual suggestions were made, such as reducing the maximum engine capacity and reducing the length of the race itself, but in the end the controversy died down and the races continued, much as before. Only the two-day system was abandoned and the number of laps reduced.

It is interesting to speculate on the underlying reasons that caused the Collier brothers to change allegiance from JAP to the Swiss-designed MAG engine. Jack Bindley, who had proved so very helpful in providing information on the early days, believes the JAP engine designers may have tended to rest on their laurels a shade too long, and that this had become apparent to very forward-looking Collier brothers who had been so pro-JAP in the past. He may well be correct, as the cylinder head and valve gear, for example, had not changed in design since 1908 — surely a limiting factor? Certainly there is reason to suspect that JAP soon got the message because there are rumours that an ohv JAP engine had made a brief re-appearance at Brooklands prior to the 1914-18 war. So far it has not been possible to substantiate this, although there is ample evidence of such an engine after the war at the time when Bert Le Vack joined the factory.

Designed in 1912 and built in the MAG factory in Scrubbs Lane, Willesden, the new 496cc MAG vee-twin represented a considerable advance in technology, having inclined overhead valves in a hemispherical cylinder head. There was also the 1912 TT Alcyon to be taken into consideration, which had a two port hemispherical cylinder head, with four overhead valves, radially disposed. Although these engines may have had their structural weaknesses, they represented a considerable improvement on the then current JAP designs. It was the weakness inherent in the crankpin of the MAG engine that most likely persuaded the Collier brothers to opt for belt drive rather than risk the harshness of transmission by chain.

More or less coincident with the TT came the news that yet another of the better-known motorcycle manufacturers had added a sidecar machine to the range, powered, of course, by a JAP vee-twin. The manufacturer was Sunbeam, famous already for building machines of high quality and finish. A 6hp 76 x 85mm engine was specified, of the side valve type, it being hinted that the JAP engine would be used only until John Marston Ltd had time to perfect a vee-twin engine of their own design. A striking feature of the engine unit was the very long magneto drive chaincase, the magneto being mounted behind the rear cylinder but quite high up.

During August there was news that a patent had been granted in the name of John Prestwich, to safeguard the type of timing gear arrangement currently in use. British Patent 22135 of 1912 related to the use of forked rockers in conjunction with two camwheels, each of which had two cam contours. This obviated the need for four camwheels in the timing chest of a twin cylinder engine, thereby reducing the size of the timing chest and simplifying the timing gear drive. No doubt the reduction in mechanical noise proved to be an added bonus.

The three-speed countershaft gearbox was now becoming much more popular, as evidenced during the 1913 Scottish Six Days Trial. Even the Collier brothers had gone over to this arrangement, Charlie using a sidecar outfit so equipped as one of the Matchless team. There was, however, one other development taking place, which was of not direct interest to the Tottenham factory. This was the advent of the motorcyclette, a small capacity lightweight runabout that could be regarded as the forerunner of today's moped. Many such models began to appear on the market at this time, most of them powered by a two-stroke engine and having a simple, two-speed gear. As there was nothing suitable in the lower capacity range, none had a JAP engine.

The Precision engine was now being made in several different forms and the sheer number of engines being produced made it necessary for F.E. Baker to have a new factory built in Kings Norton. Furthermore, the Swiss-built MAG engine, amongst others, had taken over some of the market previously held by JAP. From this, it may be inferred that something of a crisis was presenting itself at the JAP works, yet there was certainly no evidence to substantiate this. Indeed, it seemed doubtful whether John Prestwich was even worried to any extent. Although manufacturers such as Matchless were experimenting with other makes of engine, they were still specifying JAP engines for their standard production models — in common with many others. If anything, the list of manufacturers who had at least one JAP-engined model in their range was growing, whilst as tensions mounted within Europe, a substantial amount of government contract work was being awarded to JAP. In consequence, the output of JAP engines continued to accelerate and many years later the company claimed they had retained a constant one eighth of Britain's entire trade in motorcycle engines at the time when competition was at its fiercest.

Building on his earlier Junior TT win and other racing successes, Hugh Mason used his 2¾hp NUT to good effect to win the Junior Class of the Scottish Speed Championship, held during September. The Heavyweight Class was won by another JAP-engined machine, an 8hp Martin JAP ridden by R.J. Braid.

For the coming 1914 season, the speciality in the Matchless range was to be a 3½hp twin, with chain primary drive from the JAP engine to a simple countershaft. Final drive was by belt, to a 3-speed Armstrong hub gear in the rear wheel. Also added to the range was a new 7hp sidecar outfit, having an 82 x 94mm ohv engine of JAP manufacture, with fully enclosed valve gear and tappet rods. This particular model had a three-speed dog clutch countershaft and all chain drive. Matchless, like so many others, were now forsaking the belt in favour of all-chain transmission, even though they appeared to have a foot in either camp.

A couple of weeks later, when JAP announced their own plans for the 1914 season, they stated quite clearly that they would henceforth tend to specialize in twin cylinder engines. Four new twins were planned, 5hp (70 x 85mm), 6hp (76 x 85mm), 8hp (85 x 85mm) and 10hp (85 x 95mm). The last mentioned had been developed for use in cyclecars and had large diameter flywheels. All twin cylinder engines now incorporated the modified timing gears, which used the forked rocker arrangement that had been the subject of the 1912 patent application. In addition, there was a change in the mode of operation of the exhaust valve lifter, the revised design operating on the rack and pinion principle.

The lubrication system also received attention, mainly in the form of a refinement of the scheme already in use. As in the past, a separate chamber was cast into the offside crankcase, which acted as an oil receptacle, the oil being collected when the descending pistons forced it through a non-return valve from the crankcase itself. In this manner the chamber filled until about the half way mark. The vertical pipe within the chamber (another JAP feature) had now been extended at its uppermost end until it was virtually flush with the revolving mainshaft of the timing side flywheel. When the pistons commenced ascending, oil was drawn up the pipe by the vacuum created and the pressure of the air above the collected oil. A flat on the mainshaft uncovered the end of the pipe, permitting oil to flow to the crankpin and the big end assemblies. In consequence, the flat in the mainshaft acted in the same manner as a rotary valve, having the advantage of a fixed timing sequence that could not be upset.

The 1913 Buyer's Guide presented in *The Motor Cycle* showed the following manufacturers had at least one JAP-engined model in their range:

Single Cylinder Models

Clyde	NLG
Hazlewood	Oakleigh
Hobart	Royal Ruby
Juno	Trump
New Imperial	

Twin Cylinder Models

Campion	New Imperial
Clyde	NUT
Hazlewood	Rex-JAP
Ivy	Royal Ruby
Lea Francis	Sun
Martin JAP	Sunbeam
Matchless	Trump
New Comet	Zenith

Sidecars

Clyde	Rex-JAP
Hobart	Royal Ruby
Matchless	Sparkbrook
Morgan*	Sunbeam

Cyclecars

Carden	LM
Cumbria	Marshall-Arter
Gordon	Paragon
JBS	

three-wheeler

For comparative purposes, Precision engines were now used by the follwing manufacturers, a few still providing the option of either a JAP or a Precision engine:

Single Cylinder Models

ASL	Juno
Brown	Mead
Campion	Monopole
Dene	Pilot
Grandex	Sun
Ivy	Victoria
Ixion	Win

Twin Cylinder Models

ASL	Mead
Calthorpe	Pilot
Dene	Sun
Grandex	Victoria
Precision	

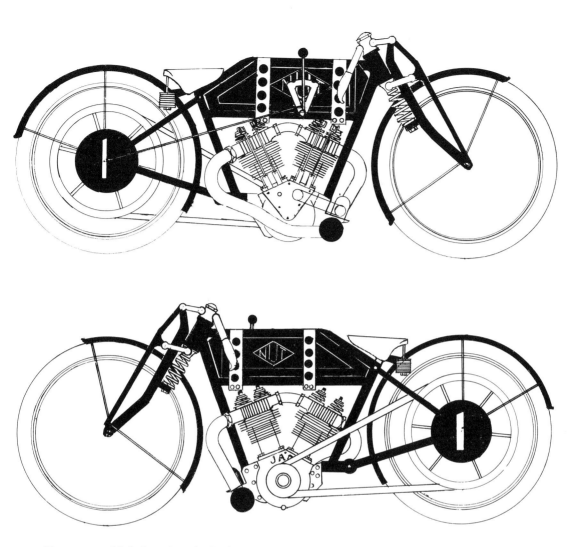

Two pen and ink drawings by Robin Bownass, of the 1914 Senior TT machine on which he was forced to retire. (Drawings: Peter Sparkes)

Sidecars

Calthorpe	Pilot
Ixion	Wall Tricarriage

Cyclecars

Armstrong	Ranger
DEW	Tiny Car
PDA	Warne

From these listings it will be evident that JAP were particularly strong in the twin cylinder market, in which they held the major share of proprietary engine manufacture. It will also be seen how the cyclecar market was changing, with several new names appearing and some of the originals no longer included in the list. An intensely

A water-cooled side valve vee-twin engine on dynamometer test at Northumberland Park. Note the correlation of bhp output and the rpm readings, painted on to the cooling duct above the engine. (Photo: Haringey Public Libraries)

competitive market, there was scarcely a week that went by without the announcement of at least one new manufacturer in either of the two motorcycle weeklies, or later, in the magazine that catered especially for this market, *The Cyclecar*. Such had been the success of this new publication that it was reputed no less than 100,000 copies had been sold of the initial launch issue.

Morgan three-wheelers continued to assert themselves in speed and reliability trial events throughout the 1913 season, in most cases using a JAP vee-twin engine unit, either air-or water-cooled. In the first sidecar and cyclecar race of the season, held at Brooklands on April 3rd, A.W. Lambert brought his 880cc (85 x 77.5mm) Morgan into third place at 54.96mph, to be awarded *The Motor Cycle* cup. Soon, E.B. Ware appeared at the helm of a 744cc (76 x 82mm) version of the three-wheeler, to lap at 48.92mph and mark the start of an association with the JAP factory that ultimately led to his full-time appointment to the Northumberland Park staff. Even abroad the Morgan was showing its paces, W.G. McMinnies having submitted an entry for the Cyclecar Grand Prix at Amiens in conjunction with those of H.F.S. Morgan, Rex Munday and a driver named Holder. A member of *The Cyclecar* editorial team at this time, McMinnies was one of the two motorcyclists who had staged an impromptu and entirely unofficial motorcycle 'match race' at Brooklands during 1908, before the track began to run official events for the two wheel fraternity. All of the Morgan entrants struck trouble of one kind or another during the race, but after coping successfully with a puncture, and then a fractured truss rod, McMinnies emerged the winner. Like Morgan, he had put his faith in a 90 x 77.5mm water-cooled vee-twin JAP engine, but with typical gallic evasiveness the race officials duly declared his Morgan to be a sidecar outfit and not a bona fide cyclecar. In consequence, the driver of a Bedelia cyclecar was awarded the spoils of the victor. At this time, several different makes of engine were being evaluated for installation in the production versions of the Morgan, the other two cars in the Grand Prix being fitted with a water-cooled vee-twin Blumfield and a Precision engine,

E. B. Ware with a Zenith JAP sidecar outfit in the Paddock at Brooklands during 1913. (Photo: Dr. J. D. Alderson)

respectively. Whether or not the final decision was influenced by the results of the Grand Prix is not known, but it was the JAP engine that was eventually selected.

E.B. Ware made news when he won the Cyclecar Handicap Race during the second BMCRC monthly meeting of the season at Brooklands. The Morgan he drove on this occasion featured a special wedge-shaped body of distinctive styling, claimed to have a wind-cutting effect. Later in the year it was announced that a new 1082cc (90 x 85mm) water-cooled vee-twin JAP engine had been specially designed for use in a Morgan, the valve porting having been given attention by Ware himself. Other improvements were also incorporated in the design, which owed much of its development to Ware's racing successes.

E. B. Ware with the 740cc Morgan in which he won the Three Lap Cyclecar Handicap Race at Brooklands on April 18th, 1914. The engine is a 740cc side valve vee-twin JAP fitted with a bevel-driven Bosch magneto. (Photo: Dr. J. D. Alderson)

The need for TT riders to wear helmets was further reinforced for the 1914 races when it was decreed that the wearing of a specially-designed safety helmet would be compulsory. It was a welcome move, designed to offer better protection than the leather flying helmet worn by many of the riders in the 1913 races. Clearly, anything that represented a positive move in the interests of safety would be seen as a step in the right direction at the time when the future of the races hung in the balance. Amongst the entries was a racing DOT JAP powered by a 70 x 64.5 ohv vee-twin, a Wolf JAP, and a 70 x 64.5mm Zenith JAP fitted with a Gradua gear and having front cylinder oiling, to be ridden by A.J. Moffat. Other entries featuring a JAP power unit included F.W. Carryer's 70 x 64.5mm Royal Ruby, which had a Jardine two-speed gearbox, and a 60 x 61.5 Martin JAP with heavy flywheels and a three-speed Armstrong hub gear. Sadly, none of the JAP-engined entrants finished either race holding a leader board position.

With the outbreak of war seeming inevitable, military motorcycling events were being reported upon in the two motorcycle weeklies, together with news items about new models being developed for use by the armed forces. The appearance of the first British-made magneto appeared about this time, a necessity because, until now, most manufacturers had relied upon the Bosch magneto, imported in significant numbers from Germany. The interest in the lightweight class of machine continued almost unabaited, no less than 55 lightweight models, the majority powered by a two-stroke engine, being listed during the month of July. In the four-stroke world, the MAG engine was now beginning to have an impact in the proprietary engine market. The vee-twin engine was already being used by Matchless and Morgan, amongst others, the racing version having four valve cylinder heads. But when Britain eventually declared war on Germany on 4th August, it was obvious that motorcycle development would soon have to come to a halt whilst manufacturers turned their attention to work of national importance. Even so, it was not until 3rd November, 1916, that a directive from the Ministry of Munitions terminated the production of all motorcycles for use by civilians 'for the duration'.

Pride of place in the 1915 JAP production programme was given to the 1082cc water-cooled ohv engine referred to earlier, which was intended for use in a Morgan. A distinctive feature of this engine was the large diameter crankcase necessary to contain the heavy flywheels, which obviated the need for a separate heavy flywheel clutch. Apart from this engine, the range included 2½hp and 4hp singles, and 4, 5 and 6hp twins.

One further change in the lubrication system was announced at the same time. Henceforth, provision would be made for a powerful jet of oil to be forced through the customary non-return valve in the crankcase to the timing side main bearing. Part of this oil feed would pass through a hole in the bearing, and part behind the bearing bush itself. This latter flow would issue from a nick between the aluminium housing and the bronze of the bush itself, to be carried round the crankpin and thence to the big ends. More oil would be passed to the front cylinder through a pipe, and there would be a further separate feed to the plain bearing on the drive side of the crankcase.

The battle for a sizeable proportion of the proprietary engine market continued, with Precision still the major competitor, although the Blackburne engine was now beginning to come on to the scene. The 1914 Buyer's Guide published in a late issue of *The Motor Cycle* showed the listings much as before, with JAP still retaining the upper hand, though now mainly in the twin cylinder class. Those who preferred a JAP engine, or in some cases still presented the option of JAP or Precision, comprised the following makes:

Single Cylinder Models

Campion	Mead
DOT	Royal Ruby
Hazlewood	Trump
Lea Francis	Zenith
Martin JAP	

Twin Cylinder Models

BAT	Lea Francis
Campion	New Comet
Clyde	NUT
DOT	Rex-JAP
Excelsior	Royal Enfield
Hazlewood	Sparkbrook
Hobart	Sun
Ivy	Torpedo
Juno	Trump
Kumfurt	Zenith

From this list it will be seen that many of the manufacturers still retained their long-standing association with the JAP engine, which obviously had given exemplary service, although for reasons not apparent the New Imperial name was a significant omission from this list. As far as those who preferred the Precision engine were concerned, the current listing was as follows:

Single Cylinder Models

Campion	LMC
Dene	Martin Junior
Dunkley	Mead
Endrick	Pilot
Grandex	Sun
Juno	Westovian
Kumfurt	

Twin Cylinder Models

Dene	Pilot
Dunkley	Regal
Elswick	Victoria
Grandex	Westovian

Cyclecars were no longer listed, as this sector of the market was now being catered for in *The Cyclecar*. It is interesting to note that the Precision engine had now much more of a foothold in the single cylinder market, although it should be appreciated that the JAP emphasis was now more on twins and that furthermore, some of the makes listed were of the 'motorcyclette' category for which no small capacity JAP engine equivalent was available.

Towards the end of the year another make, Wulfruna, joined the ranks of those using a JAP engine by announcing three models, a 2½hp single (70 x 76mm), a 4hp single (85.5 x 85mm) and a 5hp twin (70 x 85mm). But even this announcement was overshadowed by details of the 6hp Royal Enfield JAP sidecar outfit fitted with a 770cc side valve engine, which was to be fitted with a machine gun for military use and used in considerable numbers by the armed forces. Zenith was another manufacturer that offered an outfit to somewhat similar specification; the days of the continued production of civilian motorcycles were beginning to dwindle.

One event that seems almost to have escaped notice during the year was the appointment of Valentine Page as a draughtsman. He had built his own motorcycle from

A New Hotspur JAP single cylinder side valve model of 1913/14 manufacture, made by Messrs. Strutter and Abrey of Tottenham. (Photo: Haringey Public Libraries)

A catalogue illustration of the 1914 Model 2 DOT, fitted with a 70 x 84.5mm side valve vee-twin JAP engine and two-speed gear.

a combination of Fafnir and Chater Lea parts in 1908, whilst he was apprenticed to a firm of motor agents. Later, he bought a Calthorpe JAP, which originally was fitted with a 250cc side valve engine. But this was soon changed for one of the 350cc vee twin engines from the same factory, which enabled him to attach a sidecar. It seemed appropriate that he should join the Tottenham factory, with whom he stayed until he took position with the Air Ministry during the war.

As the year drew to a close, a look at the Records Book showed that few, if any, of the old records remained intact, the situation with regard to JAP engine users being as follows:

Class A *(Solo up to 275cc)*

H. Martin	Martin JAP	Flying kilo	50.16mph
		Flying mile	50.42mph
		Flying 5 miles	47.82mph
		Standing 10 miles	46.66mph

Class E *(Sidecars up to 1,000cc)*

A.V. Sumner	Zenith JAP	Flying 5 miles	53.25mph

Cyclecars

E.B. Ware	Morgan JAP	50 miles	47.52mph
		1 Hour	47.26mph
		Flying kilo	65.10mph
		Flying mile	63.09mph
		Flying 5 miles	61.22mph
		Standing 10 miles	59.50mph

All of the above records had been established during the 1914 season, record breaking forming a significant part of the activities that took place on the Brooklands track. As explained earlier, the contestants adhered to a strict, but unofficial, code of practice, so that all stood a reasonable chance of being rewarded for their efforts in the form of bonus payments from the machine and accessory manufacturers.

A 1913 catalogue illustration of the 2¾hp NUT TT model. It sold for £50, with an extra 10 guineas if a three-speed hub gear was specified as an optional extra. (Photo: Peter Sparkes)

Chapter Six

Times of war

WHEN BRITAIN went to war with Germany on 4th August 1914, the effect on motorcycling in general was not felt for some considerable time. The production of machines for the civilian market continued for more than two years and events of various kinds were run much as before, although with gradually diminishing entry lists as motorcyclists either volunteered or were conscripted for military service.

1915 had scarcely come into being when an announcement was made about the production of the Seal double-seated sidecar outfit, which was made by Haynes and Bradshaw, of Stretford Road, Manchester, and powered by an 8hp vee-twin JAP engine. It demanded attention on account of its unusual construction and the method adopted for seating both the driver and the passenger. Although it looked very much like a conventional sidecar outfit at first glance, there was no provision for seating the driver on the machine itself. Instead, he sat in the sidecar, next to the machine and alongside his passenger. The outfit was steered by a car-type steering wheel in front of him, which was linked to the front forks of the machine itself. In consequence, the driver, as well as the passenger, had full weather protection. Like most unconventional designs, few were sold at 80 guineas, even though the idea seemed appealing. The Seal soon lapsed into obscurity, but not before one or two others had produced their own variations.

The new Martin JAP lighweight was introduced too, having a 2¾hp JAP side valve engine and an Enfield 2-speed gear. Fitted with chain-cum-belt transmission, it was of a pattern that many other lightweight machine manufacturers followed.

The usefulness of the motorcycle in war had not been overlooked, and JAP engines were used in vee-twin form to power some of the larger sidecar outfits that had been modified for use as machine gun carriers. The trend had been set by both Scott and Royal Enfield, the latter using a JAP four-stroke engine, and soon both Clyno and Zenith had similar outfits to offer to the armed forces, the latter also having a vee-twin JAP engine. A Vickers machine gun was mounted on the sidecar chassis, which was devoid of body. Mounted on a specially-made tripod, the machine gun could also be used to fend off aircraft attacks, the aeroplane now coming into its own as an instrument of war.

Other new models announced early in 1915 were the 6hp Sun, designed mainly for sidecar use, with a JAP vee-twin engine and a 3-speed Sturmey Archer counter-shaft gearbox, the 6hp chain-cum-belt Royal Ruby sidecar outfit that had the option of the larger 8hp JAP vee-twin engine, and the 3hp vee-twin Lea Francis. A road test published during this period commended the 6hp Hobart JAP which, like the Sun, used

Air Raid Wardens used Royal Enfield sidecar outfits such as this to give advance warning of air attacks or to announce the all clear at their conclusion. Powered by a vee-twin JAP engine, this particular outfit is being used by members of the Metropolitan Special Constabulary. (Photo: Haringey Public Libraries)

JAP-engined Royal Enfield sidecar outfits were also used to form mobile machine gun units such as the example shown here. The gunner looks particularly ferocious in this photograph. (Photo: Haringey Public Libraries)

Royal Enfield machine gun outfits lined up outside the Northumberland Park works during the Great War. The gun mountings are already in position. (Photo: Haringey Public Libraries)

a similar 3-speed Sturmey Archer gearbox. The three-speed hub gear was at last on its way out.

When the Tottenham factory announced their improvements for 1915, these could be categorised as follows. First, there was a new 2½hp side valve engine having bore and stroke dimensions of 70 x 76mm. Secondly, all engines henceforth were to have cooling fins of larger area, larger diameter valves and valve ports, and screwed, adjustable tappets fitted with dust covers. Larger bearing surfaces were used to cope with the additional increase in power and the induction system was made more airtight in an attempt to improve the slow-running characteristics of the vee-twin engines. As a further aid, the clearance between the inlet valve and its guide was reduced to 0.002 inch by making the guide of cast iron and having internal grooves cut so that the oil trapped in these grooves would serve as both an effective lubricant and a gas seal. It worked too, yet another example of how a simple approach to a problem is often the most effective.

The annual listing of machine specifications showed that in the single cylinder class, JAP engines were used by Calthorpe, Campion, Clyde, DOT, Hazlewood, Martin JAP, Mead, NLG, Royal Ruby, Trump, Wolf and Zenith. In the twin cylinder range, the list of manufacturers comprised BAT, Campion, DOT, Hazlewood, Hobart, Ivy, Juno, Kumfurt, Lea-Francis, New Comet, NUT, Rex-JAP, Royal Ruby, Sparkbrook, Trump JAP and Zenith. Although production continued at a steady pace amongst those who were not directly involved in contract work, one major problem was beginning to make itself felt. Until hostilities had started, many British motorcycle manufacturers fitted a German-made Bosch magneto, a very fine instrument that rarely gave trouble and gave an outstandingly good spark. There were no British-made equivalents on the market at that time, with the result that when war was declared, the

Bosch supply was cut off virtually overnight. Machines without magnetos were stockpiled whilst other sources of supply were sought. Initially, Dixie and Splitdorf magnetos were obtained from the USA, but this was only a short term resort until British-made magnetos came from indigenous manufacturers such as BTH and EIC.

Other JAP improvements that followed on from the earlier announcement included a new type of exhaust valve lifter that operated externally in conjunction with the new screwed tappets, and what was termed an Apex oil union. This latter device was designed to feed oil to the front cylinder and thence to the crankcase by means of a right-angled union, the union having a tiny ball valve inside to act as a one-way valve and prevent blowback.

The 1915 Royal Ruby twin, announced earlier, seems to have had a very short life, for only a matter of three months later it appeared in redesigned form having all chain transmission with either 6 or 8hp engine. The intended all grey finish seems to have been abandoned at the same time, even though it had been described as making the machine look very attractive. The war had brought with it a feeling of drabness and a grey finish would hardly help to detract from this!

Whilst most of the traditional motorcycling competition events continued to be run, appeals began to appear in the two motorcycling weeklies for volunteers to enlist as drivers and gunners in the machine gun service. These appeals appeared more and more frequently, the magazines ultimately publishing the names of those who had responded

E. B. Ware with a 4-speed Grand Prix Morgan fitted with a water-cooled '90 bore' ohv vee-twin JAP engine. This photograph was taken during May 1915, when the vehicle was being used for magneto testing. (Photo: Dr. J. D. Alderson)

as in a Roll of Honour. Yet there was still no real shortage of competitors in civilian-type events, despite the fact that so many of the younger fraternity were becoming involved in an event of a far more serious nature on the Western Front.

In May, the 6hp 770cc chain-cum-belt Ivy sidecar outfit joined the ranks of those fitted with a 3-speed Sturmey Archer gearbox, as did shortly afterwards the Dunkley Runabout, an air-cooled three-wheeler with the option of a 4hp JAP single or a 5 or 6hp vee-twin. With the engine and the two wheels at the front, transmission to the 4-speed constant mesh gearbox was by a very long chain, the gearbox being mounted mid-way on the chassis. Final drive to the rear wheel was by belt. Made by Dunkleys Ltd, the three-wheeler came from Jamaica Row, Birmingham.

BAT sprung a surprise only a month later when their JAP-powered sidecar outfit appeared with dynamo lighting and a sprung sidecar wheel. Of Lucas manufacture, the dynamo was mounted to the rear of the rear cylinder, in line with the frame. It was driven by a separate chain from the gearshaft and relied upon bevel gears to turn the drive through 90°. A few weeks later, New Imperial announced their 2½hp model, which was fitted with a 70 x 76mm JAP single having an EIC magneto and chain-cum-belt drive. The belt was having its final fling as it provided a very smooth drive without having to use a shock absorber in the transmission system.

It was now becoming apparent that servicemen were being denied the opportunity to ride regularly in events and that there was no single event that catered specially for them. Matters were brought to a head when F.C.M. Houghton of the 25th Division Cycle Company proposed to the British Motor Cycle Racing Club that a special 'All Khaki' meeting be held at Brooklands, a proposal that was accepted even though the circuit was in a poor state of repair due to the pounding it had received from solid-tyred RFC lorries. The meeting was held during August after some temporary track repairs had been carried out, but by then it had become a combined services meeting as the Royal Naval Air Service had provided entries from their armoured car section, as had the Royal Navy. The meeting provided some light relief, too, for some of those convalescing from war wounds, for conspicuous amongst the spectators were the light blue uniforms of those who had been able to make their way from St. George's Hill Hospital, Weybridge. About 170 competitors made up the entry and the event must have proved a success, as it was followed by a second, similar meeting, in September.

The 1916 models were now beginning to be announced, one of the first being the Regal JAP, another machine with a four-speed gearbox and chain-cum-belt transmission, intended primarily for sidecar use. The Calthorpe JAP sidecar outfit followed, which was fitted with a 4hp twin cylinder engine of 496cc capacity (70 x 64.5mm). This machine was particularly attractive on account of its Zeppelin-shaped petrol tank which was lined in gold leaf. The general specification included an Ericson magneto and Enfield two-speed gear. The 4-5hp Ivy JAP that followed used a 3-speed countershaft gearbox and chain-cum-belt transmission. It is worthy of mention because the vee-twin engine featured another JAP improvement, as yet unannounced by the factory. A new type of exhaust valve lifter was fitted, which was controlled externally by a rod and cable. The transition between rod and cable was made at the point where a cable adjuster was fitted, this being threaded into a lug that had been cast into the induction pipe that joined the two cylinders.

Some of the new 1916 models, such as the New Imperial JAP, featured only minor improvements, and those mainly to the ladies model. Royal Ruby announced their intention to market a spring frame model, whilst Vindec (made by Brown Bros, of Newman Street, London.) had decided to market a sidecar outfit powered by a 6hp vee-twin JAP engine. NUTs were another make that continued virtually unchanged, apart from substituting a Sturmey Archer gearbox with chain-cum-belt drive for the hub gear they had used in the past. Zenith relied upon their countershaft clutch and Gradua gear, leaving Campion to make the most news. Their 8hp sidecar outfit, which had a 4-speed gearbox, was claimed to be fitted with a new JAP vee-twin engine that had improved balance, and was fitted with a Splitdorf magneto. They also listed a 70 x 76mm lightweight of 2½hp fitted with footboards and Jardine 2-speed gearbox. With a black-painted petrol tank and chain-cum-belt transmission, an unusual feature was interconnected hand and foot clutch control. It was not until November 18th that the JAP factory finally disclosed their programme for the 1916 season, engines for which were already in production.

It had been decided to concentrate production on the long stroke engines, with the result that the 90 x 77.5mm short stroke engine would henceforth be discontinued. In consequence, the engines available for the 1916 range were as follows:

2½hp single 70 x 76mm 293cc
3½hp twin 70 x 64.5mm 496cc
5hp twin 70 x 85mm 654cc
6hp twin 76 x 85mm 770cc

In addition, an 8hp Morgan engine would be available with a special magneto fixing that permitted bevel drive. Air-cooled, this engine had bore and stroke measurements of 85 x 85mm. In addition, a cyclecar engine with a heavy crankcase would also be available. Of 85 x 95mm bore and stroke dimensions, this engine had a capacity of 1,078cc. Both engines were, of course, vee-twins.

Dealing firstly with the single cylinder engine, this now featured a new design of piston with increased bearing surface and a series of annular grooves cut in the skirt to trap oil and improve lubrication. The cylinder had fins of increased surface area to improve cooling, and larger and more streamlined valve ports.

In the twin cylinder engines, it had been JAP policy to use a forked and centre connecting rod layout because it was considered this eliminated the binding strain that would otherwise have been due to the rods being out of centre with the pistons. Even so, problems arose in being able to get sufficient bearing area for the big ends, and to keep them adequately lubricated, when inertia stresses applied heavy loads at high speeds. Previously, a phosphor bronze bush inside the forked rod had been used as a bearing surface, and to improve on this the bush was made of steel, lined with phosphor bronze. In turn, this necessitated fitting the centre rod with a phosphor bronze bush which would bear on the outside of the steel bush carried inside the forked rod.

The 8hp heavy twin engine had shown a tendency to overheat under certain conditions, and to ease this problem extra cooling fins had been added. In addition, both exhaust valve caps were provided with star-shaped fins as an extra aid to improved cooling.

A further week passed before more details were released about the latest improvements. These related in the main to yet another design of exhaust valve lifter, which was contained within the timing chest and therefore fully enclosed. On twin cylinder engines a cable-operated actuating arm was attached to twin cams, which could be rotated to bear on heels attached to the exhaust valve rockers and so cause the rockers to lift. But perhaps of more significance the revised method of engine lubrication which was described in detail and accompanied by the line drawing reproduced here, to make the explanation easier to follow.

In the so-called pressure system successfully employed by JAP, the pressure is provided by the descending piston. This forces oil through hole at the base of the crank chamber into a passage and through a non-return valve into a reservoir cast onto the exterior of the timing side crankcase. The reservoir is so designed that it will contain a sufficient head of oil to provide a continuous flow. The only means of oil escape is

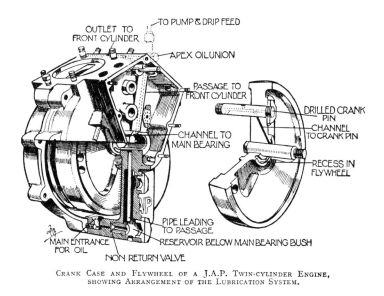

CRANK CASE AND FLYWHEEL OF A J.A.P. TWIN-CYLINDER ENGINE,
SHOWING ARRANGEMENT OF THE LUBRICATION SYSTEM.

Fig. 6.1 The JAP 'pressure' oiling system.

through a pipe which leads to a recess under the timing side main bearing bush, the oil being transferred to a recess semi-circular in shape which is cut into the outside of the timing side flywheel boss. This boss presses tightly against the side of the crankcase and it is when the two recesses align that oil under pressure is fed to the centre of the crankpin through an internal passageway in the flywheel itself. This lubricates the big-end assembly in an adequate manner before it descends to the drive-side main bearing. Another passageway takes oil from the main bearing to a hollow bolt running through the top of the crankcase assembly, where there is an outlet to the front cylinder. This bolt communicates with an apex oil union to which oil flows from the auxiliary pump or drip feed into the crank chamber via the front cylinder. It is provided with a ball valve to prevent any blowback through the oil feed pipe. The non-return valve which controls the supply of oil from the crankcase to the oiling system takes the form of a flat steel disc 'flap valve' offering simplicity with absolute reliability and the addition of only one extra moving part as compared to the possible complexity of a mechanical pump. Leakage from the main bearings is obviated by cutting threads on the inside of the bushes, to force back any excess of oil.

As the year drew to a close, it was becoming apparent that much was being learnt from aircraft engines under conditions of active service, reliability being a major factor. Much of the expertise gained would prove of benefit to engines of all kinds, including those used in motorcycles. As part of their war work, the JAP factory was already undertaking the overhaul and repair of aircraft engines under government contract, especially Clerget rotary engines. Contemporary reports claim the noise of aircraft engines under test was almost continuous and that the engine of the aircraft that shot down a Zeppelin at Stag Hill had been on the JAP workbenches that same morning — this latter accomplishment at the time when the Zeppelins were raiding the London area during 1916.

As mentioned earlier, the Precision engine had made an unsuccessful bid to dominate the proprietary engine market. Now it was the turn of the vee-twin MAG engine, to which the Collier brothers had changed allegiance. MAG were equally unsuccessful, the war in this instance being the limiting factor.

Right at the end of the year, W.J. Green of Coventry, manufacturers of Omega motorcycles, decided to add a 2½hp single, powered by a 293cc (70 x 76mm) single cylinder JAP engine, to their range. Similar in many respects to the lightweight machine of that era, it was fitted with an EIC magneto and had 2-speed chain-cum-belt transmission. The intention was to offer an alternative to the Omega two-stroke that was already in production, as some like Coventry-Eagle, admitted to problems or were expressing doubts about the capabilities of the early two-stroke single with their generally low power output. What better than to double-bank against the possibility of losing out in the bottom end of the market. Whether by chance or intention, competition soon came in the form of a Diamond JAP lightweight to almost similar specification that was announced only a matter of a week or two later.

Royal Ruby sprung a surprise quite literally by unveiling a spring frame model in which the rear end had a form of swinging arm suspension controlled by a leaf spring. It was an odd-looking machine, the rear suspension having a very disjointed appearance. In the event this design was short lived, for when full Royal Ruby programme for 1916 was announced a couple of months later, all the machines had rigid frames. 4-speed transmission was the order of the day, using a Jardine gearbox and chain-cum-belt transmission. Four models were available, all fitted with JAP engines — a 3½hp single and twins in the 3, 4 and 5hp categories. About this time, Dunkley Ltd, who made the three-wheeler mentioned earlier, added a 5hp sidecar outfit fitted with a JAP vee-twin engine. This too had 4-speed transmission, using the familiar chain-cum-belt arrangement.

As may be expected, the civilian motorcycling scene was beginning to change quite dramatically, with so many young riders now in uniform and fighting for their country in France and Belgium. Comparatively few competition events were being run and of those that were, the proceeds were being directed towards the Red Cross or some similar deserving need. Club members took the war wounded on runs or outings, despite the increasing price of petrol which had reached 2/6d per gallon by early 1916! Discussions about the taxation of motorcycles were under way and one sensed there was a general resentment that motorcycling as such had been allowed to continue almost unimpeded, apart from a ban on the import of foreign-made machines. Yet in some quarters it was acknowledged that the manufacture of motorcycles for purposes other than war needed to continue, as their exportation brought in a substantial revenue at the time when Britain needed all the money it could raise. Furthermore, motorcycling provided a convenient means of relaxation for those who worked long hours in munitions factories or on war work of various kinds. Even the events organised for those who served in the armed forces had now been opened up to include factory workers, such as the Service and Munition Workers Trial held during April 1916. Yet despite all these considerations, the pressure for a complete clamp-down on motorcycling activities and the cessation of manufacture of machines for the civilian market was beginning to mount. *The Times* newspaper added weight to this by their crusade against private motoring, which came into prominence during the middle of the year. Now it became a public issue, that is, until government intervention took a hand. With the shortage of petrol becoming more acute as time progressed, rationing was introduced with effect from August 1st. Under the new petrol allowance scheme, motorcyclists were allowed 6 gallons for 3 months, irrespective of the capacity of their machine, whether or not it had a sidecar attached, and whatever distance had to be covered during that period. Controversy raged over the fairness or otherwise of the scheme and if nothing else, it encouraged motorcyclists to look at ways of extending their meagre ration. Some used

A cutaway view of the 6 hp JAP engine fitted to the vee-twin Sunbeam, showing the layout of the valve operating mechanism.

white oils or paraffin as an additive, whilst paraffin vaporisers became the vogue. The engine was started on petrol and once it became warm, the fuel was switched over to paraffin — necessitating a two-tank arrangement — the change-over being reasonably acceptable by the low compression, relatively 'soft' engines of the day. But one important factor had been overlooked, as soon became obvious. The change of fuel, or the reduction of the actual petrol content, brought about lubrication problems by reducing the viscosity of the engine oil.

Somehow, motorcycling managed to survive, even if riding for pleasure was taboo. Spot checks led to the need to carry what was known as an 'exemption card', which would certify that the rider was engaged on government work or work of national importance. Quite a few who had dodged conscription into the armed forces were caught in this way.

As casualties at the front mounted in alarming numbers, *The Motor Cycle* continued its recruiting campaign, along with its rival, *Motor Cycling*. The campaign was provided mainly for the benefit of the Motor Machine Gun Service, which by now was accepting 18 year olds as the minimum age qualification. The basic requirements were age between 18 and 40, physical fitness and agreement to 'sign on' for the duration of the war. Those accepted were paid 1/2½d a day (all found, as the advertisement said!) plus a dependant's or separation allowance if this applied. The 'reward' for signing on through either of the two magazines was to see one's name in very small print in a register of applicants that was published at regular intervals. Small compensation indeed for the horrors of the Somme that soon were to become only too evident, with not too good a chance of surviving unscathed. It is strange to reflect how popular motorcyclists become in times like these.

By the end of the year, quite a few manufacturers were announcing new models and it is interesting to find that there was a marked tendency towards the use of a flat-twin engine. Apart from Douglas, who had set the trend in 1907 and was later followed by ABC, Bradbury, Brough, Humber and Matchless, Montgomery now showed similar intentions, with at least one flat twin design in their range. Two exceptions were New Imperial, who intended to continue much as before, and Zenith, who had a leaf spring version of their Gradua model. But all these announcements were made in vain. Early in 1917 it was announced that the production of motorcycles was to cease with effect from February 15th, except in cases where the manufacturer was engaged upon war work. In these latter cases, the Ministry of Munitions would issue a permit for production to continue.

Apart from the machines already in use by the armed forces, Excelsior were one of the first to announce a new twin for overseas and military use. Using a 4hp 70 x 64.5mm vee-twin JAP engine of 496cc capacity, this new model was fitted with a Sturmey Archer three-speed countershaft gearbox and chain-cum-belt transmission — still a favourite with overseas users. Sunbeam followed suit, with an 8hp vee-twin outfit that was intended for use as a stretcher carrier for the British and French Red Cross. Using a JAP engine, the outfit was supplied with a minimum 6 inch ground clearance, brought about by the use of 28 x 3in. wheels, all fully interchangeable and fitted with Parsons non-skid chains on the rear wheel. Obviously designed for heavy duty, the clutch had double the number of bronze and steel clutch plates, drilled to help obviate the build-up of debris that would tend to promote slip.

With the petrol shortage getting worse the use of vehicles by private individuals on other than government work had to come to an end. With effect from the end of March, no more petrol would be available — a bitter blow to those who had already taxed their vehicles for the year. Now even the substitute fuels were out, with just one exception —coal gas. As subsequent events will show, there were some who looked even

The 1915 Campion single cylinder model, fitted with a 494cc side valve JAP engine and three-speed hub gear.

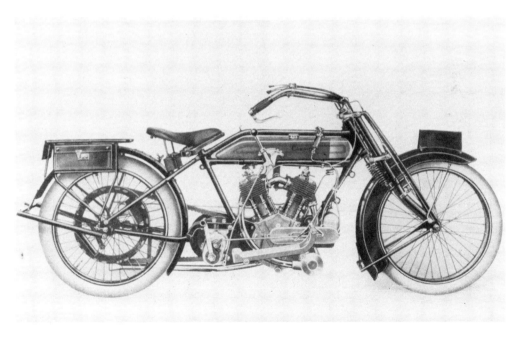

The JAP-engined vee-twin model from the same manufacturer, which could be supplied with the option of either a 770cc or 988cc side valve engine.

The 293cc side valve New Imperial JAP was always a popular model. This is the 1915 version.

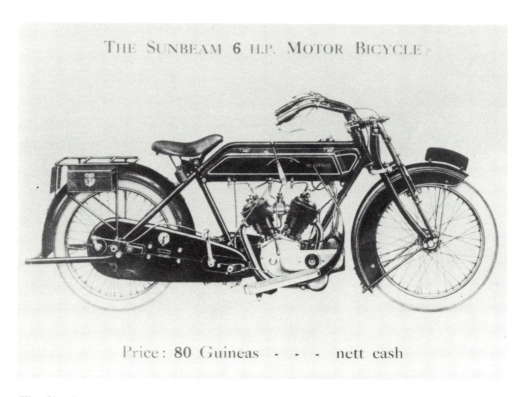

The 6hp Sunbeam had a reputation all its own, and used a 798cc side valve vee-twin JAP engine. Finished in true John Marston tradition, the rear chain is fully enclosed in an oil bath.

in this direction, refusing to accept defeat.

Russia was now beginning to show an interest in motorcycles for war use, particularly in terms of the big sidecar outfit. During April 1917, New Imperial announced the manufacture of an 8hp outfit against a contract from Russia, using the 85.5 x 85mm JAP vee-twin of 976cc capacity that was being supplied to Sunbeam for similar use. The Excelsior twin boasted 6¾ inch ground clearance and had all-chain drive. At the same time, the Sunbeam contract was extended by Russia to include a 3½hp and a 5hp solo, the latter having a 654cc vee-twin engine.

During June, Matchless followed suit with their own 976cc vee-twin, which was built to Russian specification that included the use of the big vee-twin JAP engine. Designated their 8B2/M model, it had instructions in Russian painted on the tank top. But sadly, it would seem that some of these orders were highly optimistic, to say the least. By September that year it had become apparent that not all of the orders were to be taken up. Excelsior in particular lost out in this respect, and it was suggested the completed outfits would be made available to private purchasers, as soon as conditions permitted. How the contract problem was solved, and whether Excelsior ever received any compensation, is not known. Possibly there is no answer as the impending Russian revolution soon changed everything.

As mentioned earlier, motorcyclists had begun to experiment with the use of coal gas as a fuel in lieu of petrol. The basic problem was the need to accommodate the huge, flexible container that was needed to carry the gas, which resembled a miniature barrage balloon. One charge, usually of about 40-50 cubic feet, was sufficient only for about 10 miles, the container taking up the space normally occupied by a large sidecar. Several variations of storage arrangement were tried, including a cradle mounted above the machine, rather like the upper deck of a bus. But the problems were always there — physical size in relation to distance to be travelled, the effect of high winds, rubbing of the bag wherever it was attached to its cradle, and the difficulties of recharging — the mains gas pressure being insufficient. Cox Gas Trailers of West Norwood were foremost amongst the early experimenters, but it seemed obvious that the only way in which the use of coal gas would be really feasible would be to store it under high pressure in special reinforced containers. Wood Milne was one company that came up with a practical solution in this respect. By storing gas under a pressure of 1,800psi, their container would provide the equivalent of running on 2 gallons of petrol. It had the advantage of being small enough to be carried on a solo machine. But inevitably, the use of coal gas had its snags too. Although it could be fed directly into the engine, without need for a carburetter, the running costs were approximately doubled in the cost of fuel alone. To this needed to be added the cost of the container in which the gas was stored, and the cost of recharging it, from time to time, under pressure. In consequence, the practice was not widely adopted.

The Tottenham factory had its own facilities for running engines on coal gas, mainly to conserve petrol when engines were under test. A special engine testing bench was arranged for this purpose, with full read-out facilities. Much data had been gathered by running a 4hp single in this manner.

The petrol shortage continued to get worse and by the beginning of 1918 there was a coal shortage too. This led to restrictions on the use of coal gas as a source of motive power for vehicles. Basically, its use for pleasure purposes was out altogether, but dispensations were made when a vehicle needed to be used for other than governmental or war work, such as for normal household affairs, performance of public duties, Red Cross work etc. By now, event the more patriotic types of motorcycling event had faded into obscurity and there were no more so-called Ordnance Workers or Special Constables hill climbs. With little to report, the two motorcycling weeklies fell back to reminiscences of the past from famous riders, discourses on various aspects of design and even aviation — *The Motor Cycle* running a series of articles on stunt flying. An article published by this latter magazine during the month of October makes particularly interesting reading today because it related to the throttle-controlled lubrication of engines. S. A. Lamplugh Ltd, of Tyseley, Birmingham, had taken a particular interest in this and had published an article during January 1917. Although the Japanese are today credited with this innovation, all this took place a half century before their own application started to make the headlines.

As far as the Prestwich family was concerned, 1918 was a year to be remembered on at least two counts. First, John Prestwich had the honour of being awarded a Silver Medal and Certificate by the Franklin Institute of America, for what was termed, 'work of distinction in promoting the mechanical arts'. The award was made for the Prestwich Fluid Gauge, a gauge that he had invented primarily for use in his JAP works at Tottenham. Having no moving parts, the instrument comprised a chamber filled with coloured spirit, a very fine graduated glass capillary, and a flexible diaphragm. Depression of the diaphragm caused the spirit to rise in the tube, the movement being so rapid that one hundred readings per minute could be taken by an unskilled person to an accuracy of 0.0002 inch. In consequence, John Prestwich was quite possibly the first Englishman to use production methods pioneered in the USA where gauging and interchangeable manufacture had been in use since the 1860s. He had improved on the 'go' and 'no go' system of gauging by the design of his fluid gauge, which allowed him to produce components that were commercially acceptable. Costs were thus kept to a minimum and the new gauging method enabled him to identify the areas of the tolerance band so that the exact mating of parts was possible — the standard method used by automobile manufacturers today. The Prestwich Fluid Gauge was used extensively in America, hence the prestigious award.

Secondly, it was during early 1918 that John's eldest son, Vivian, joined the Royal Naval Air Service, not long before it was amalgamated with the Royal Flying Corps to become what we know today as the Royal Air Force. Barely reaching the qualifying age for acceptance, it seems fitting that Vivian should have wished to learn to fly after his father's earlier all-consuming interest in aviation, quite apart from possessing the desire to follow a career in mechanical engineering. But as it so happened, he did not see much active service. The war had taken a turn for the better as far as Britain and her allies were concerned, so much so that by November it was all over and life could start to resume its more normal pattern. Before the year was out, several manufacturers had announced new models for 1919, mostly with flat twin engines. Just two vital questions remained to be answered: when would the new models be available, and at what price?

The end of 1918 marked the end of an era in the continuing story of JAP. During the year the company was registered with limited liability, the name being changed to J. A. Prestwich and Company Limited in order to reflect this. The days of the old Prestwich Manufacturing Company had at last come to an end, and with them the original association with cameras and cinematographic equipment. Involved with the administrative work in effecting this change was J. Watkins Richards, who became the secretary of the new company. His first involvement with the Tottenham factory had occurred when he turned up during the first year of the war, clad in the ill-fitting uniform of the Volunteers. It was his job to audit JAP war production for part of each week.

Before closing this chapter about the war years it is worth noting the wide-ranging contribution made towards the war effort by the JAP factory. Quite apart from the manufacture of engines for machines used by the armed forces of Britain and her allies, and the repair and overhaul of aircraft engines, millions of casings and fuses for small

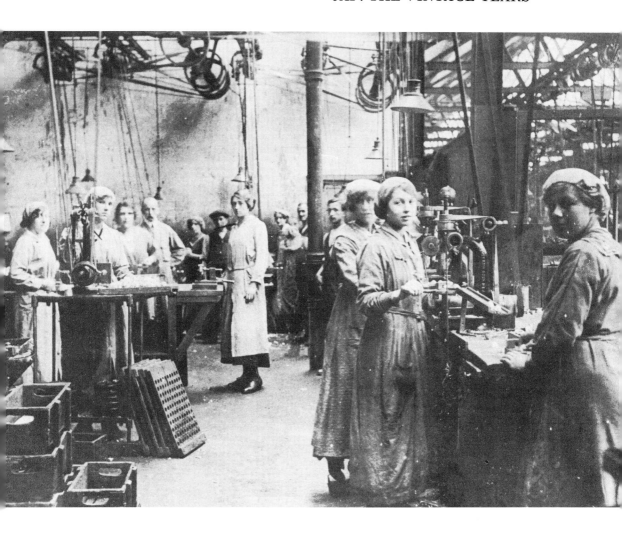

During the Great War, girls were recruited for working on munitions in the Northumber-land Park Works. Note the protective overalls and headgear. (Photo: Haringey Public Libraries)

calibre shells and Mills bombs were made. Also some aircraft components, mainly airscrews, wings, and ailerons. As may be expected, the workforce was expanded considerably to cope with these activities, and new machinery installed. Many of the extra staff were women, who adapted themselves to war work particularly well. They even found time to train as first-aid workers and stretcher bearers, should these useful attributes be needed in the event of an air raid or some major disaster. By the time the war had ended, the total JAP workforce numbered approximately 1200. Their record in these times of war was indeed one of which they were justifiably proud.

Chapter Seven

Prosperity – and pencil making

WITH THE prospects of a new year ahead of them, British motorcycle manufacturers were anxious to get their 1919 models into production at the earliest possible opportunity, by which time the regulations forbidding sales to the civilian market and to overseas customers should have been lifted. Some had already announced their new model range, whilst others were known to have been perfecting new designs as patent applications towards the end of the war had shown. Quite a few had been experimenting with spring frames of one kind or another, but in the end most were content to save time spent on development work by getting into production with what amounted to little more than an updated version of what they were selling in 1915 or 1916. It was anticipated that prices of the new models would be about 25% up on those in force during 1914, but as subsequent events would reveal, this was a very conservative estimate indeed.

The general scene in 1919 was very much that of a seller's market, with an outstanding demand for new machines. Quite a large number of machines had been impressed by the army when war was declared, whilst more than a few had either been disposed of, or had suffered badly from storage whilst their owners were fighting on the Western Front, many never to return. For those unable to find sufficient money for the purchase of a new model when it became available, the prospects of an ex-WD machine looked attractive, especially if the latter had been reconditioned prior to its sale. But with no knowledge when the first of the new machines were likely to arrive in dealers showrooms, or when the army would start to dispose of all its surplus models, there was no way in which the demand was likely to be met for some considerable time. The effect on the market was dramatic. Machines such as a new, good quality 500 were listed in the region of £140, whilst a good quality reconditioned mount, such as a Model H Triumph, fetched around £90. To add insult to injury, some of the more unscrupulous dealers requested a premium over and above the list price of a new machine, to guarantee early delivery. A payment varying from 10-12½% would ensure that the person willing to acquiesce to this blackmail would have his name high on the list of impending deliveries. Fortunately, it was not a situation that could prevail for too long. As supply began to meet demand, then overake it, the market stabilised and eventually (although not until towards the end of 1921) became one to the buyer's advantage.

Royal Ruby were one of the first to announce a new model in 1919, when details of their 8hp sidecar outfit, using a vee-twin JAP engine, were announced early in January. The specification included a Sturmey Archer 3-speed countershaft gearbox and all-chain drive, a form of specification that was now becoming more common. The three-speed hub gear and pedal starting had gone out of fashion during the war, as had belt drive to some extent.

The advantages of all-chain drive and a separate countershaft gearbox with kickstarter were becoming only too apparent.

To help readers keep pace with new models, the motorcycling weeklies published a list of delivery dates obtained from the various manufacturers. By the end of January the first very small batch of ex-WD machines had been sold and just a couple of weeks or so later, unrationed benzole became available as a fuel. The wartime restrictions were lifted during the early part of March, and motorcycling started to get back onto a peacetime footing. Many of the new models were described as 'peace' models at the time of their launch, so that it was evident they embodied improvements, however small, over their counterparts made until production during the war years came to a close. Towards the end of the month, a further batch of ex-WD machines as sold, this time about 400. It was a welcome move and all were eagerly snapped up.

With high prices appertaining to both new and second-hand machines in the larger capacity range, there was an incentive to produce quite a number of small capacity models, mostly powered by proprietary engines of the two-stroke type. Scooters came onto the market too, some with no provision for seating as it was considered the rider would prefer to stand up for the short distance to be covered. Contrary to popular belief, the scooter craze started in Britain, as early as 1907, when the Triumph-powered Max made its debut. The post-war interest in scooters was short lived, it was not until after the Second World War that the scooter came back into favour. By then it had been extensively restyled by the Italians and bore little resemblance to its forebears.

The first JAP-engined 'peace' model to become available to the general public was the 2¾hp Wolf lightweight, a two-speeder with chain-cum-belt transmission. For those who required something with more power, a 4hp model, also JAP powered, was available with a Sturmey Archer gearbox and all-chain drive. Omega had a somewhat similar 2¾hp lightweight, whilst Chater Lea brought out an experimental spring frame model which used leaf springs, fitted with a vee-twin JAP engine.

By July 1919 competition events had restarted, although some time would pass before Brooklands could re-open due to damage caused to the track surface by solid-tyred military vehicles stationed there. The first major competition event of any consequence was the Scottish Six Days Trial, held two months later than usual. It was won by J.W. Wills riding a 5-6hp Rover JAP. That JAP engines would retain their supremacy was shown when they figured prominently in the awards list of the Essex Speed Trials held that same month.

Other sidecar outfits powered by vee-twin JAP engines were soon on the market, including the Model H Matchless that had a unique spring frame and special provision for direct oiling of the clutch bearing from its 8hp engine unit. British Excelsior had a somewhat similar outfit using the 85.5 x 85mm vee-twin engine, but without the rear springing. Using a Sturmey Archer gearbox and all-chain drive, a particular and distinctive feature was the use of disc wheels, a trend that developed during the early post-war years. At this time the make had the word 'British' appended so that it could not be confused with its American namesake.

E.B. Ware, who was now working in the capacity of development engineer for the JAP factory, brought out an experimental four-seater Morgan three-wheeler, using an 8hp water-cooled JAP engine. Of conventional vee-twin design it had a die-cast crankcase and provision for heating the induction passages from the water jacket. He used the vehicle as a means of transportation for himself and his family, a convenient mobile test bench.

Later in the year, BAT and DOT announced new models, the former offering 6

A close-up of the experimental 8hp water-cooled JAP engine fitted to the four seater 'family' Morgan three-wheeler, developed by E. B. Ware in 1919. The engine features a large capacity oil sump, a die-cast crankcase and has a water-cooled induction system. (Photo: Dr. J. D. Alderson)

and 8hp JAP-powered vee-twins having countershaft gearboxes but retaining their original type of rear suspension. The DOT range comprised a 2¾hp single and an 8hp twin, the latter much to the same formula but without the rear springing. Some engines were again being exported overseas. The French-made GL sidecar outfit, marketed in the UK by Vivian, Hardie and Lane off Bond Street, was fitted with the standard 8hp vee-twin engine.

It was during the year that a man named Hepplethwaite, soon to become better known as 'Old Man Hep', opened up a JAP spares business in Wilcox Street, South Lambeth, living over the shop with his wife and youngest, unmarried, daughter. In his late forties, he was soon regarded as quite a character amongst motorcyclists, his business proving so popular that in due course during the mid-twenties, he needed to move to more spacious premises at Northcote Road, Clapham Junction. It was his practice to preface his advertisements in the motorcycling magazines by a simple, four line rhyme, of which the following are typical examples:

Old Man Hep, you all know. Lots of gas, not much dough.

Old Man Hep, lobster sup. Millionaire, then woke up.

Old Man Hep, Put and Take. Send some dough, for goodness sake.

In later years he became acquainted with some of the leading JAP personalities, such as Bert Le Vack and E. C. E. Baragwanath, and was able to supply any type of racing JAP engine if the customer was prepared to pay the price. Most of his customers bought cheap parts for the standard production engines.

Quite a number of other firms kept a comprehensive stock of spares for all types of JAP engines and, in some cases, sold complete engines, too. These included Firfield Motors of Leamington Spa, The BAT Motor Company of Penge, South London (manufacturers of the BAT motorcycle mentioned in earlier chapters), and Hemmings, of Hale, Liverpool. Some, such as Hemmings, sold very cheap spares, which were factory rejects. Although considered sub-standard by the Tottenham factory, these parts could often be used with slight modification or a little ingenuity on the behalf of the purchaser, and kept many a machine running that would otherwise have been off the road whilst the rider saved up for the much-needed yet more expensive genuine replacement parts. Hemmings also specialised, during later years, in conversion kits to transform a side valve JAP engine into one of the overhead valve type, giving an allowance against the old side valve cylinder. Scott enthusiasts will know of Hemmings too, for they made and supplied special parts for these water-cooled two-stroke twins.

Towards the end of the year, the annual passenger machine review printed in *The Motor Cycle* listed 13 sidecar outfit and light car manufacturers using JAP engines, which can be summarised as follows:

BAT	6 and 8hp
British Excelsior	8hp
Campion	5-6hp
DOT	8hp
Enfield	6hp and some 8hp
Matchless	8hp
Morgan	JAP or MAG air-cooled or water-cooled
New Imperial	8hp
Royal Ruby	8hp
Zenith	8hp
LSD	8hp
LJ four-wheeler	8hp air-cooled or water-cooled
LM	8hp water-cooled

Much to everyone's surprise, the decision was taken to hold an end of year show at Olympia; a show in which JAP engines figured quite prominently, even though the company itself followed its usual practice and refrained from taking exhibition space on its own. An analysis of the exhibitors shows that no less than 22 had at least one model in their 1920 range that would be fitted with a JAP engine of some kind, the majority of them comprising the better-known names.

In order to keep abreast of the times and maintain their lead as independent engine manufacturers, the JAP factory announced several improvements that would be included in their 1920 engine range. These included lightening of the distribution and tappet gear, so that the components affected would be only half their previous weight. Henceforth, all valves would be made from special steel and as far as lubrication was concerned there was to be an increase in the size of the oil chamber cast integral with the crankcase. Pistons would carry narrower and lighter rings and the gudgeon pin bearings would be increased in diameter from ½ inch to fractionally below ⅝ inch. Special attention had been given to the 2¾hp single, so that the timing gear case would be more oil-tight and so that the cam wheel spindle ran on two bearings. Other modifications would comprise an internal valve lifter and adjustable tappets, obviating the need for shims, and the use of enlarged bearings. The complete 1920 engine range was listed as follows:

2¾hp 70 x 76mm single
4hp 70 x 64.5mm twin

4hp 85.5 x 85mm single
5hp 70 x 85mm twin
6hp 76 x 85mm twin
8hp 85.5 x 85mm twin, air-cooled or water-cooled

The year closed with what appeared to be a revival of interest in the overhead camshaft type of engine, with particular reference to the Metric design, made in France. Although by no means an innovation, it was beginning to be realised that this type of engine layout had certain advantages and was worthy of exploration.

During the year, John Prestwich had been approached by a pencil manufacturer who required assistance in finding the best method of painting lead pencils on a mass production basis. It was a problem that intrigued him and in arriving at a satisfactory solution he found he could devise a much more efficient plant for the manufacture of pencils than that commonly in use. Trials proved that his new machines offered a far higher standard of efficiency and when the original enquirer found himself in financial difficulties, John Prestwich decided to go into pencil manufacture himself by forming a subsidiary company on the Northumberland Park site. As a result, Pencils Limited was registered in 1920 and housed in premises adjacent to the machine shops. Using only half the average size and amount of machinery normally associated with pencil manufacture, it was found that each of the new machines had an output from three to ten times greater than the equivalent machine of any European competitor. The new company thrived and by 1951, the occasion of the parent company's 50th anniversary, output had risen to 1,500,000 pencils a week, making Pencils Limited the leading manufacturer of its kind in Europe. Pencil making is quite an art, as the following description of the process will show. It was provided by Mrs. E. Oldfield (neé Howard) who worked for nine years in the Works Office with Roland Prestwich, the fourth of John Prestwich's sons who was born in 1909 and subsequently became a director of Pencils Limited.

Cedar wood used for the manufacture of pencils was delivered to the works in sacking parcels, pre-cut to the standard 7¼ inch length and in widths ranging from 7 to 3 pencils wide. When required, the sacks were slit open and stacked in a criss-cross fashion so that the content would dry. In later years the water content could be measured by means of an instrument resembling a cocktail shaker. A wood shaving placed inside, with a measure of carbide, would give a reading on an external dial, when shaken up.

The Moulding Shop grooved the woods so that the leads or crayon inserts would fit, the woods being fed into hopper machines that stacked them and then pushed them out, one by one, at high speed on to a moving belt. This was accomplished by the clawing action of the cutters. From this point the grooved woods passed to the Glue Room, where again they were stacked, this time in pairs so that they arrived in twos, the glued surface uppermost. Girls sitting in a row dropped the leads or crayon inserts into position and made a sandwich of the two halves, holding them together under pressure by means of clamps, an operation later superseded by machine laying. The next day they were end-sanded, then passed back to the Moulding Shop where machines formed them into round, hexagon or oval section, according to orders or work cards. The next operation was that of painting or polishing the outside surface, according to requirements.

The colours used for painting were made and matched to order, two grinding machines, each with two girls in charge, mixing the pigments. Each pencil received two coats of a sealer, then a number of undercoats, before the top polish was applied. Whenever a pure white finish was required, these undercoats needed to be dark blue. Painting was accomplished by shooting the pencils through paint pots at high speed, *117*

Right: Top to bottom:

A typical cedar wood block for pencil making.

The block after grooving, with provision for seven separate pencil leads.

In the Moulding Shop, the individual pencils were formed into round, hexagonal or oval sections by machines, according to requirements, before being separated.

Below:

The grooved blocks were glued together after the leads had been inserted and held under pressure until the glue had set.

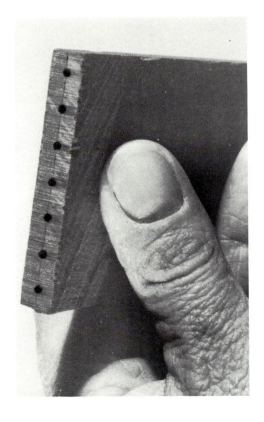

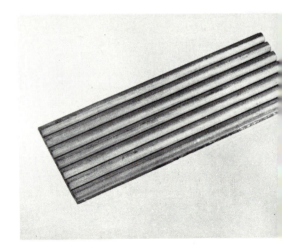

Five separate stages in the making of a pencil.

rubber washers being used to remove any surplus. The pencils then travelled along long belts and dropped down on to a moving bed that returned them to the operator, who needed to be sufficiently strong to lift the heavy trays and feed them into the big hopper for the next coat or polish. The next stage was that of pointing, sharpening the pencils in large machines located in a room next door. The best pencils were left unpointed, only the ends being sanded to remove the paint. Some were printed with customer slogans or names in a special machine. Others were stamped in gilt or silver, only the very best being stamped in 22ct gold from rolls of foil about the size of a toilet roll. Wastage of this precious metal was kept to a minimum by returning the used foil for remake. After this treatment the embossed pencils were cleaned with either damp sawdust or flannel, depending on their quality, by girls sitting at benches.

Some pencils needed to have their ends rounded, in which case they were pegged out on boards and the ends dipped in a contrasting colour. Others had metal ferrules with rubbers affixed. The girls in the dipping shop were given an extra pint of milk each day to help offset the possible harmful effects of the paint fumes. Not all could be persuaded to drink it, whilst some took it home! It was the high quality, top class work that caused the

119

most anxiety in terms of quality control, as excess dampness in the atmosphere would cause the paint to 'bloom'. When this happened the work had to be abandoned until better conditions prevailed. Roland Prestwich kept an hygrometer in the Works Office so that he could monitor the humidity of the air to prevent a recurrence of the 'blooming' problem.

The dirty work took place in the Lead Mill, the area that contained the milling machines being staffed by elderly men, some of whom qualified for a special 'dirty bonus'. The ingredients to tbe used in the formula for making the pencil lead were weighed and mixed with water in big tubs, graphite and french chalk being the most commonly used components of the mix. From this stage they went through a grinding and milling sequence several times, so that eventually big 'nuggets' were formed. These were fed by women operators into extruding machines, from which the strips of lead or crayon were laid on to ridged blotting paper and placed in an oven for a set period of time. They were then cut into 7¼ inch lengths, placed in cans and boiled in paraffin wax. Black lead went to the furnace room, where the colour of the fire indicated whether the lead was receiving the correct treatment.

With so many different processes being employed in pencil making, Pencils Limited had its own first aid facilities in the Works Office, most problems relating to cuts and splinters. The women machine operatives had to wear protective hats to prevent their long hair from being caught in the machinery and resulting in an involuntary scalping — at least one such incident being on record when the person concerned failed to take this very necessary precaution. Factory safety regulations ensured the machines were fitted with correct guards, but even these needed to be checked from time to time as their unauthorised removal could help speed up production. The JAP factory intself had a very good First Aid Room in later years, but as far as Pencils Limited was concerned, they did the initial 'patching up' before passing any more serious incidents to the main centre.

Returning to the main business of the Tottenham factory, 1920 was also a notable year in so far as Val Page returned, this time in the capacity of Chief Designer. In the five years that he remained with the company, before he moved on to the Ariel factory in Selly Oak, Birmingham, he made a massive contribution to the JAP design and development programme. To many, the years 1920-1925 became the most memorable in the company history, adding greatly to the prestige of the JAP engine and the unending record of successes enjoyed in competition events of all kinds.

Despite the early setback of an increase in the price of petrol, which raised it to 3/10d per gallon as the result of a tax increase of 9½d, competition events were soon making the headlines in the motorcycle weeklies. Kaye Don, riding a 5-6hp Zenith fitted with a vee-twin JAP engine won the Paris-Nice trial in convincing style, although his success was short-lived when, like so many other continental events, the results were subsequently annulled. At home, Eric Williams won the Colmore Cups Trial riding a 3½hp NUT, to be awarded with a Gold Medal, a permanent victory for JAP as far as this event was concerned.

Eyes were now turning towards Brooklands, with the knowlege that the necessary track repairs had been completed by the end of March. The opening meeting was held on the Easter Monday, but it had to be postponed as the result of heavy rain that fell all

Facing page:
A photograph of some of the employees of Pencils Ltd, with John Prestwich seated in the centre of the front row and Roland Prestwich behind him.

morning. A re-run on the following Saturday, 10th April, went off according to plan. The one significant JAP win went to E. B. Ware, who walked away with the three lap handicap race for three-wheelers. He was in form as usual with his Morgan-JAP. When *The Motor Cycle* made an assessment of British motorcycle records later that month, JAP engines showed up particularly well. In Class I (solo up to 275cc) Harry Martin held 5, in Class B (solo up to 350cc) Hugh Mason held 10, and in Class E (solo up to 1,000cc) the Collier brothers held 6. In the two sidecar machine categories, E. B. Ware held 8 in Class H (up to 750cc) and in Class I (up to 1,000cc) Ware held a further 2, Freddie Barnes 2 and G. F. Hunter 1.

As may be expected, Ware also held the Cyclecar to 750cc records for JAP, his score being 6 in this, the Class J category. All these records had been set up between 1909 and 1914. And it was not only in speed events that JAP engines excelled. In the Junior Car Club's Fuel Consumption Trial, for example, a Tamplin cyclecar powered by an 8hp JAP engine emerged the winner, by recording the quite remarkable average of 102 miles per gallon!

Left:
E. B. Ware in his racing attire, photographed during 1920. (Photo: Dr. J. D. Alderson)

Right:
Arthur Church, who assisted Ware with his development work after the Great War. (Photo: Dr. J. D. Alderson)

News of JAP participation in the 1920 Junior TT broke during May, when it was announced the DOT entry would be fitted with a lightweight vee-twin engine from Tottenham, the machine having a two-speed countershaft gearbox and chain-cum-belt transmission. Of 348cc capacity, the ohv engine had bore and stroke measurements of 60 x 61.5mm. The valve seats were cast integrally with the cylinder heads, and ball bearings were used extensively throughout the engine, even in the rocker gear. Another departure from standard JAP practice was the use of ball and socket tappets. The only vee-twin in the race, the DOT JAP performed well, and finished 5th. In the Lightweight Class, the Diamond entry had decided to forsake their allegiance to the JAP engine and used instead a new four valve engine of their own design. But they must have experienced more than their fair share of problems during practice, as one of their team of three riders reverted to the use of a two valve JAP engine at the last moment. Unfortunately, he suffered the fate of his two colleagues, the entire Diamond entry having to retire. The lightweights were run concurrently with the Junior race, there being no separate event for them.

The early part of July brought forth the announcement of a new make of motorcycle to be fitted with a JAP engine — the Massey Arran — which commenced production in Delbarn Road, Brimingham. Their first machine was a 2¾hp lightweight, using the side valve single cylinder engine, but relatively few were made. The company remained in business for about five years, using six different addresses in Birmingham during this period and finishing up in Blackburn. In consequence the reasons for limited production are only too apparent!

Meanwhile, post-war racing successes at Brooklands mounted. At the MCC's 7th Annual Meeting held on 10th July, Vic Gayford enjoyed a runaway win in the 3-lap 560cc-1000cc race. Starting as limit man on his 6hp Zenith-JAP, he won by more than two miles, at a speed of 62.6mph. But it was during the BMCRC meeting that followed a week after that a man whose name would become synonymous with the larger capacity vee-twins throughout the whole of his illustrious racing career, achieved his first win at this famous track. He was E.C.E. Baragwanath, known more familiarly as just 'Barry', who entered an 8hp ohv Zenith JAP sidecar outfit, fitted with a Zenith carburetter. Against stiff opposition in a field that included Freddie Barnes and Reuben Harveyson, he brought the Zenith home first, winning by as much as a mile at 61.22mph. It was an imposing success too, for in so doing he broke the record for this class of machine set by Freddie Barnes in 1913 at 58.78mph. Towards the end of the day, E. Remington won the last of the scratch races, a 10 mile event for machines of up to 1000cc. Riding a NUT JAP twin, his winning speed was 75.44mph. Oliver Baldwin took second place, on a Matchless JAP of similar capacity.

During that same meeting it is interesting to find that E.B. Ware rode a 349cc NUT JAP twin in the up to 350cc event. For once his luck ran out, a displaced valve cotter causing his early retirement from the race.

At the end of the month, Baragwanath came into the news again, when he won the 1000cc class in the speed trials held at Luton Hoo Park, and went on to a third place in the up to 1000cc sidecar class. Meanwhile, Douglas Hawkes was busy winning the Three Wheel Cyclecar Class at the South Harting Hill Climb, with his Morgan JAP. But this success had taken its toll of the engine. In the 1000cc Racing Car Class he suffered the indignity of having a complete cylinder depart from the crankcase!

JAP advertising seems to have adopted a more subdued approach by this time, as it was not easy to make direct reference to successes that were only just starting to build up. The main theme was 'British and Best', with mention of medals won in events such as the Lands End and Victory Cup trials. There was also reference to the good fuel economy achieved by the Tamplin cyclecar.

In the Speed Trials that formed part of the BMCRC Members Meeting held during mid-August, Baragwanath won the class for up to 1000cc sidecars, whilst Remington took the Allcomers Handicap on his solo NUT JAP. Almost a month later, on 11th September, the big twins once again figured prominently in the results. L. Openshaw won the Closed Handicap for members of the Public Schools MCC at 61.8mph on a Zenith JAP. In the 10 mile Solo Scratch Race for up to 1000cc machines that followed, Remington left all behind him to win at a record speed of 79.71mph, his 998cc NUT JAP twin setting a new Class E record in the process. Harveyson was second, on the big Indian twin, and Oliver Baldwin third, on his Matchless JAP. In the earlier smaller capacity classes, E. Longden had won a 3-lap Allcomers Solo Handicap at 56.55mph on a DOT JAP. Included in the entry was Vivian Prestwich, riding as a member of the Public Schools MCC. Making his debut at Brooklands on a 350cc NUT JAP, he finished a very creditable 2nd.

The JAP factory continued to use this somewhat aged Renault truck for transporting their machines to race meetings long after the end of the Great War. Arthur Church is seated next to the driver, and Stan Greening is seen standing on the running board.

(Photo: Dr. J. D. Alderson)

The offside view of an experimental NUT JAP, the engine of which had been fitted with three-valve cylinder heads. This machine was on display on the NUT stand during the 1920 Motor Cycle Show. (Photo: Peter Sparkes)

The nearside view of the same machine. The modification did not prove successful and the machine never went into production in this form, probably because it was the exhaust valves that were duplicated. (Photo: Peter Sparkes)

Amongst the new models listed for the 1921 season was the FEW JAP, a new 6 hp twin made by F. E. Waller in works at Kew Gardens, on the outskirts of London. The machine described in *The Motor Cycle* seemed a little basic in specification, having direct belt drive and no gearbox. But there was mention of what was described as a novel friction drive that was being developed. JAP advertising now adopted another slant, by promoting factory repair and overhaul facilities, the repair department at Tottenham having been greatly expanded. It seemed a wise move, as the high cost of the new post-war models had forced many to continue using their older machines for longer than they had anticipated.

As racing began to wind down for the year, Oliver Baldwin managed to beat Harveyson's Indian in a Senior Motorcycle Handicap race at Brooklands. It was certainly a race to be remembered, for the finish was quite dramatic after Baldwin and Harveyson had crossed the finish line close together. Unable to slow sufficiently, Harveyson found he had no alternative other than to ascend the Member's Banking, and go right over the top, to the horror of the onlookers. Miraculously, he survived the incident, despite his severely damaged Indian twin being found some 100 yards or so from the point where he left the track. He got away with a dislocated shoulder and torn ligaments in one leg. According to the report in *The Motor Cycle,* the accident was caused because the Indian had no brakes, and it was alleged he had crossed the line around the 90mph mark. Other reports suggested his ignition cut-out had failed, a vital necessity on a machine running with a fixed throttle. Irrespective of whatever the true reason may have been, it raised the question whether some of the older machines without brakes should be allowed to compete in speed events. The day ended with another JAP victory, when Remington won at 79.15mph after a challenge by Baldwin had failed when the latter was forced to retire.

At the BMCRC Championship Meeting held at Brooklands on 9th October, Vivian Prestwich took second place in the 350cc Championship Race, being beaten by Kaye Don riding a very advanced AJS that had been used in the 1920 Junior TT. Prestwich again rode his NUT JAP, but on this occasion he also had with him a 272cc 2½hp Diamond JAP, on which he finished second in the Class A event for solos not exceeding 275cc. An Indian twin ridden by Bert Le Vack evened the score in the 750cc-1000cc race, Remington having retired with plug trouble. Baldwin was second, and Harry Reed, on a DOT JAP, third.

It is interesting to record that T. Eve was third on a Martin JAP in the Class A event that was mentioned earlier. According to Jack Bindley, who has a good knowledge of racing at Brooklands during this period, the machine he rode was almost certainly the one and only 64.5 x 76mm 249cc side valve JAP-engined model which Harry Martin himself had ridden in the 1921 Junior TT and also in the 500 mile race of that year. The Martin works had built three machines in all, the other two being identical to the machine ridden by Martin, apart from the fact that they were fitted with a 70 x 90mm 346cc side valve JAP engine. Built for the 1921 TT, these machines had been ridden by A.G. Millar and Eve.

Announcements about new machines for the 1921 season continued, amongst them being two new manufacturers who intended fitting a JAP engine. The Armis Cycle Manufacturing Co., of Heenage Street, Birmingham, intended to market a 2¾hp solo bearing their name, fitted with a two-speed Burman gearbox and chain-cum-belt drive. The other newcomer was the P and S JAP, of similar capacity, made at the Norfolk Engineering Works in Worthing, Sussex. Only a matter of a week or two later, the department at Scotland Yard that dealt with the licensing of taxis agreed to license the first sidecar taxi, thereby suggesting another market for the large capacity sidecar outfit.

Almost simultaneously, Coventry-Eagle announced a new 5-6hp vee-twin, powered by a 70 x 85mm side valve JAP engine, as well as a single powered by a 2¾hp side valve JAP. If desired, spring frame options were available, at extra cost. A few lightweight four wheel cars were fitting JAP engines at this time too, such as the AV Bicar (8hp air-cooled JAP engine, with a 2-speed epicyclic gear), the Richardson (8hp JAP or 10hp Precision engine, with friction-cum-chain drive, the LM (8hp water-cooled JAP engine, with a three-speed and reverse gearbox), and the Tamplin referred to earlier (8hp air-cooled JAP engine, with three-speed chain-cum-belt transmission).

The 1920 Show was preceded by attempts to break records, so that the successful manufacturers could achieve maximum publicity when motorcycles were very much in the news. Amongst the successful participants was Vivian Prestwich who, at Brooklands on 11th November, used his Diamond JAP to break the Class A 5 and 10 Mile Records for 250cc solos at speeds of 56.67 and 55.97mph respectively. He also took the Class A One-Way Flying Start Kilometre and Mile Records at 63.91 and 63.60mph respectively. The engine he used had been specially prepared by Val Page, who was experimenting with a new, over-square 249cc side valve design that had bore and stroke dimensions of 70 x 64.5mm. In an interview, he claimed he could not understand how JAP engines had managed to achieve so many successes, using what he considered to be such absurdly small port and valve sizes. Current practice dictated the use of an exhaust valve with a diameter larger than that of the inlet valve, which to him did not make sense. He believed engine breathing would be improved significantly if the inlet valve had the larger diameter of the two. He put his theory into practice, and using the revised valve sizes in the new 249cc engine, he found the breathing was so improved that the engine could be run up to 8000rpm with safety — an unheard of figure at that time. By the end of the month, some further long distance record breaking attempts by Vivian ensured he held the Class A records from 100 to 250 miles, and over periods ranging from 2 to 6 hours. A summary of his records is as follows:

Class A 100 miles	55.22mph
Class A 150 miles	49.75mph
Class A 200 miles	46.46mph
Class A 250 miles	47.02mph
Class A 2 hours	53.91mph
Class A 3 hours	47.75mph
Class A 4 hours	47.03mph
Class A 5 hours	46.87mph
Class A 6 hours	47.24mph

The first set of record-breaking attempts, made with the same 2½hp engine on 11th and 25th November, had already secured the following records:

Class A Flying Kilometre (one way)	63.91mph
Class A Flying Mile (one way)	63.60mph
Class A 5 miles	59.40mph
Class A and A1 10 miles	58.30mph
Class A and A1 50 miles	55.81mph
Class A and A1 1 hour	55.55mph

In short, Vivian Prestwich took all the Class A and A1 lightweight records during these two separate attempts at Brooklands.

Here it should be mentioned that prior to the opening of the 1920 racing season, the FICM and the A-CU introduced mean speed records over the flying start and standing start kilometre and mile distances, both runs to be completed within a time period of ten minutes. One-way runs over these distances became National Records, and soon disappeared from the records list.

The lessons learnt from competition and similar high speed events are frequently used to good effect on the standard production models, which serves to emphasize the oft-mentioned statement that 'racing improves the breed'. Certainly this was so when the JAP engine modifications were listed for the 1921 season. The shape of the cylinder fins had been modified to give a more effective profile, and the Apex oil union discarded in favour of a direct oil feed to a union on the front cylinder of the twins. The 5 hp vee-twin was fitted with simplified timing gear, which was similar to that used on the 8 hp twins, the camwheel carrying two cams for the operation of all four valves. The position of the compression taps had been changed too. No longer at the centre of the cylinder, they had been moved to a new position opposite the inlet valve cap. A straight induction pipe joined the two unions between the front and rear cylinders.

The new side valve racing engines could be distinguished by their long, 'fir cone' aluminium alloy exhaust valve caps, used to dissipate the heat more rapidly. The 8 hp water-cooled twin now had a larger and improved water jacket. All engines were fitted with a new design of piston, having two thin piston rings at the top, and one oil scraper ring. The gudgeon pins were made a drive fit, and featured brass end-caps.

The 2¾ single had more fins, those on top of the cylinder being arranged longitudinally. One engine was seen to have three valves — one inlet and two exhaust, whilst a similar-looking side valve engine was fitted with an aluminium alloy piston, roller bearing big-end and a ball bearing crankshaft. This was the engine used so successfully by Vivian Prestwich for his record breaking attempts at Brooklands. Also seen was a six valve twin cylinder engine of 500cc, which was designed with racing use in mind.

Rival proprietary engines were still being made, although Precision no longer offered a serious challenge. Whilst some manufacturers were now making their own engines, others had a choice of JAP, MAG, Blackburne and Villiers, the last specializing in two-strokes. A cleverly designed two-page advertisement in the 2nd December Show Report issue of *The Motor Cycle* displayed the logos of the 24 manufacturers who had at least one JAP-powered machine in their range. In point of fact, 27 manufacturers were listed, but three of them had been duplicated to help give the display a more balanced effect.

Of most concern to riders was the introduction of new licensing regulations that would come into effect at the beginning of 1921. The calculations were made on a weight basis, so that a solo machine weighing not more than 200 lb would carry a tax of £1.10s per annum. If it was required to draw a trailer or be hitched to a sidecar, a payment of £2.10s was required. In the case of a bigger machine, £3 would have to be paid to keep a solo on the road, provided the weight did not exceed 8 cwt. The addition of a trailer or a sidecar raised this payment to £4. Tricycles not exceeding 8 cwt in weight were also taxed at this latter rate.

One machine that should have made its debut at the Motor Cycle Show was the Brough Superior, made by the son of the manufacturer of the horizontally-opposed Brough twin. But sadly it could not be finished in time, with the result that the first official announcement about its existence was delayed until the December 23rd issue of *The Motor Cycle*. A very handsome-looking machine, with its own individual shape of petrol tank, it sported a 90 x 77mm ohv vee-twin JAP engine — the so-called '90 bore' —which it was claimed would give from 8 - 80mph in top gear. A great deal more would be heard about this marque in the coming years, particularly at Brooklands and other speed venues.

When *The Motor Cycle* published their annual review of British Motor Cycle Records early in January 1921, it was seen that the Class A records claimed by Vivian Prestwich during his record breaking attempts at Brooklands a couple of months previously had been ratified. That is, all except one — the Flying Kilometre. This had subsequently been broken by D. R. O'Donovan on a two-stroke Velocette, who had raised the one-way speed to 66.97mph on December 1st, 1920. Prestwich also held the

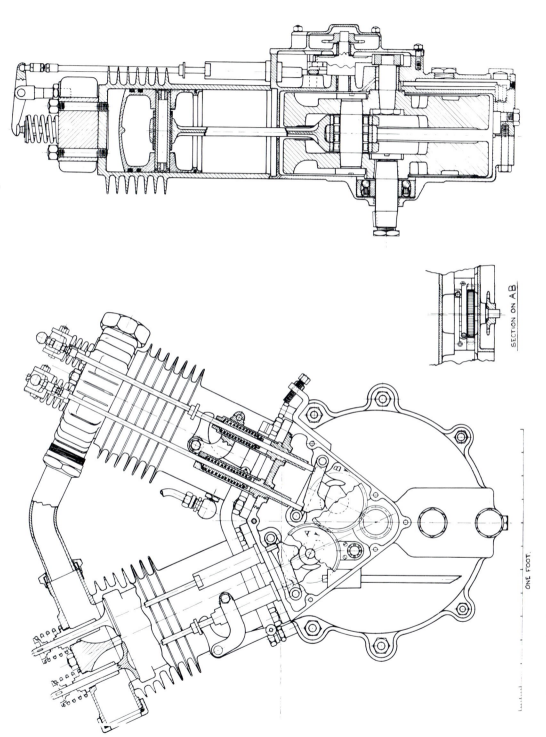

Fig. 7.1 The famous '90 Bore' engine, specially made for Brough Superior. (*Courtesy Ronald H. Clark*)

majority of the Class A1 records, with three exceptions. O'Donovan had taken the Flying Kilometre record in this class, too, during his December 1st record breaking session. The Flying Mile and Five Mile Records were still standing from 1911, when Harry Martin had claimed them on his Martin JAP. Hugh Mason held about 50% of the Class B records with his NUT JAP, whilst a considerable number of the large capacity class records could now be attributed to Bert Le Vack, riding an Indian twin. It was only in Class J, for cyclecars not exceeding 750cc, that E. B. Ware held every record with his Morgan JAP.

The price of new and second-hand motorcycles remained high, that of new models being partly due to the fact that manufacturers now had available machines to offer that represented a considerable advance on the updated versions of their pre-war designs. As an aid to readers, *The Motor Cycle* published at regular intervals an analysis of second-hand prices for individual makes, based on information taken from their classified advertisements section. Supply had yet to overtake the demand for both second-hand and new models, and until this occurred prices were likely to remain firm or even increase in some cases. Probably the only manufacturers to profit from a substantial upsurge of sales during the early part of 1921 were those who had added a license holder to their range of accessories. With the necessity to pay tax on a machine before it could be taken on to the public highways there was need to have a convenient means of displaying the new tax disc on the machine, so that it was both clearly visible and waterproof. Prices ranged from 3/- to 9/9d, depending on the quality of the fitting.

The first road test of a Brough Superior to be published in *The Motor Cycle* appeared in their 20th January issue. The machine was hailed as Britain's answer to the American big twins, and the only criticism that could be levelled was the noise of the valve gear of the JAP engine at high speeds. This criticism, however, may have been influenced by the fact that the test machine was hitched to a sidecar, from which mechanical noise could have been reflected. The outfit had the registration number HP 2122, a number that was subsequently used on many 'works' models of one kind or another, to the confusion of historians in later years!

JAP advertisements at this time drew attention to their 2¾hp side valve engine (272cc), described as the engine that broke 27 World's Records. The Tottenham factory were anxious to draw attention to the fact that their standard, over-the-counter engines, were capable of providing high performance with good reliability, without need for special preparation. But it would seem unlikely that this could be applied to the record-breaking engine used by Vivian Prestwich, which must have been very carefully prepared at the works.

The Monopole Cycle and Motor Co. Ltd of St. Mary Street, Coventry, who had commenced the manufacture of motorcycles before the Great War, decided to add a model powered by a 5-6hp JAP twin to their range during March. The specification included a three-speed Sturmey Archer gearbox, complete with clutch and kickstarter. Martin JAP announced a new lightweight model at the same time, a 2¾hp machine that weighed only 165lb and would therefore qualify for the 30/- per annum tax class. If desired, it could be purchased with a sidecar attached, the respective prices being £86.19s and £108.19s. Meanwhile, I. P. Riddoch was making Fastest Time of the Day with an 8hp Zenith JAP at the Inter 'Varsity hill climb, which was held at Aston Hill, near Tring, during the first weekend of March. His was another name to become closely associated with the Brooklands track during its heyday.

An analysis of makes that had at least one model in their range powered by a JAP engine amounted to a total of 25, the individual names being as follows — Acme, Armis, BAT, Brough Superior, Calthorpe, Campion, Coventry-Eagle, Diamond, Edmund, Excelsior, Francis Barnett, Gough, Hazlewood, Martin, Massey-

Arran, Monopole, New Imperial, P & S, Ready, Rover, Royal Ruby, Victoria, Viper and Zenith. The Portland formed a last minute addition to this list that related only to motorcycles.

From this analysis, it also became obvious that Blackburne were now the JAP factory's main competitors; they were in a position to offer 349cc and 499cc singles, as well as a 998cc vee-twin.

Vivian Prestwich about to start up at Grimsthorpe Park during the Easter Monday meeting on March 28th, 1921. (Photo: Dr. J. D. Alderson)

The Massey-Arran referred to earlier was joined by a second JAP-engined model during April 1921 when an announcement was made about a new 5hp machine powered by a 70 x 88mm vee-twin, using chain-cum-belt transmission via a Sturmey Archer three-speed gearbox. But a machine that created much more interest at that time was the new Francis-Barnett sporting lightweight. Apart from its rakish look, the machine was distinctive on at least two counts. The cylinder barrel of the 293cc sv JAP engine had no fins on its lower portion, whilst the exhaust system took the form of a long, flexible exhaust pipe that was supported by brackets, and carried no silencer.

When the BMCRC held their first meeting of the 1921 season at Brooklands on 16th April, it was Kaye Don who set the pace in the Class A Speed Trials by raising the Flying Kilometre (one-way) Record to 69.62mph, using a Diamond powered by a   *131*

249cc ohv JAP engine. Vivian Prestwich, riding a machine of similar make, relied upon the 249cc side valve engine and finished second. His machine drew attention as he had an additional, hand-controlled oil pump, fitted to the rear of the oil tank. Furthermore, the engine had an inlet valve cap made of aluminium alloy, and an exhaust valve cap of the 'fir cone' type. Later in the day, he beat Don in the 250cc Solo Race, setting up a new Class A 5 mile Flying Start Record at 60.95mph in the process. As seemed to be the custom in the 1100cc cyclecar category (Class H), the honours went to E. B. Ware and his Morgan JAP, but without a record being broken in this instance.

Towards the end of April, when thoughts were beginning to turn towards the 1921 TT, the Tottenham factory announced that it was their intention to use only standard side valve engines. For the Junior Race, their 70 x 90mm single would be fitted with new valve gear in which the tappets would be adjustable and the valve guides a push fit in the cylinder barrel. The timing gear had been simplified by having only two pinions, the camwheel carrying the inlet and exhaust cams, and the crankshaft pinion having a keyed and taper fit on the crankshaft. Three keyways were cut in the pinion, so that the valve timing could be finely adjusted. Other engine improvements included the use of a ballrace on the drive side of the engine, and a big-end assembly comprising two rows of caged roller bearings. Built along similar lines was a 249cc engine, with bore and stroke dimensions of 64.5 x 76mm. It was anticipated that the engines would be used in conjunction with Diamond cycle parts, as in the case of the machines raced at Brooklands.

This announcement about TT plans coincided with a press visit to the factory, and also shown on this occasion was an experimental six valve ohv vee-twin engine. Having a 50° angle, this engine utilised double finger rocker arms to actuate the valves, and featured detachable cylinder heads surmounted by a ribbed aluminium alloy cap to aid cooling. It was stressed that this was an experimental engine, and that the works were pinning their faith on a much simpler design for the TT. An indication of the care and attention with which engines were assembled was underlined by the sight of a special machine used for checking the firing angle of magnetos fitted to the twin cylinder engines.

Competition successes were not so frequent during this period, especially now that the American twins were beginning to dominate the larger capacity classes. JAP advertising copy preferred to refer to world opinion of their engines, reprinting testimonials from satisfied users in England, South Africa and Australia.

Once again Kaye Don made the headlines, this time at the BMCRC's first Open Meeting at Brooklands, held on 7th May. Despite inclement weather, he won the Junior Open Handicap Race on his 249cc Diamond JAP, overhauling A. A. Prestwich (348cc DOT JAP), E. B. Ware (349cc NUT JAP), Vivian Prestwich on another Diamond JAP, Harry Martin (Martin JAP) and W. J. Lord (Hobart JAP), representing the JAP-engined entry. Vivian Prestwich took 3rd place.

More news about the TT came from the manufacturer of the Coulson, who intended using for the first time a 2¾hp ohv JAP twin in the machine that was to be ridden by Eric Longden in the Senior Race. This engine was similar to that which he had used in a DOT JAP in the 1920 Junior Race, in which he had finished 5th. He used his TT mount to good effect during the BMCRC Members Race Meeting held at Brooklands on 21st May, when he won the Junior Brooklands TT Race at an average speed of 54.67mph, with the new 60 x 61mm vee-twin engine fitted. Third place was taken by A. G. Miller, riding a 347cc Martin JAP.

New Imperial announced they would be using side valve JAP engines in their 250cc and 350cc Junior TT entries, the capacity classes being run concurrently as in the past. Meanwhile, yet another manufacturer decided to include a JAP-engined model in his list of standard, road-going machines. This was the Slade-JAP, now a forgotten name, but the creation of Whittle's Motors, of Slade Lane, Longsight, Manchester. Fitted with a 2¾hp side valve single and having a two-speed gearbox with kickstarter and chain-cum-belt transmission, this newcomer retailed at £65. A mediumweight BAT JAP was announced at more or less the same time, utilising a 64.5 x 70mm vee-twin engine of 496cc capacity. With a gearbox and all-chain drive (employing the strange-looking Brampton spring chain), the new BAT JAP retailed at £120 less electrics, an indication of the way in which the price of new machines still remained high.

A major success was achieved in the 250cc class of the Junior TT, when D.G. Prentice brought his New Imperial into 1st place (10th overall), to win *The Motor Cycle* Cup. In all, JAP engines took 4 of the first 20 awards in the Junior Race and were able to claim in their advertisements that 'standard production again scores'. Altogether, a very good achievement.

During July, Bert Kershaw dominated the 250cc class of a 500 Mile Race organised by BMCRC at Brooklands. Destined to become more closely associated with Villiers in later years, he rode a 249cc New Imperial JAP on this occasion, winning his class at an average speed of 50.34mph and covering the first 100 miles at 55.79mph. His performance was such that he broke the 1 - 9 Class A hour records during his winning ride.

Vindec announced a new mid-year model, an 8hp sidecar outfit fitted with a 976cc vee-twin JAP engine, thus continuing a long-established link with Tottenham. This was soon followed by the re-emergence of the Trump JAP, this time in the guise of an 8hp sporting model and a 4hp single using a new 550cc JAP single. This latter engine incorporated a modified crankcase release valve, which was located with the timing gear, to blow oil directly on to the valve stems.

Brough Superior was now starting to come to the fore, having notched up quite a few minor competition successes with riders such as Harold Karslake, Jack Watson-Bourne, Handel Davies and George Brough himself. Meanwhile, Stan Greening was quietly fitting a 500cc side valve twin into his own privately-owned Sunbeam.

Towards the end of August, L.P. Openshaw made fastest time of the day on an 8hp Zenith JAP at a hillclimb held at Kingsdown Hill, Bath, winning the John Bull Cup. Successes by JAP-engined machines were once again beginning to mount. Within a matter of a week or two, no less than 11 medals were won in the Scottish Six Days Trial, and first places gained in the 250cc class of the French Grand Prix and the 350cc class of the Belgium Grand Prix. Prentice and Kershaw followed up with Gold Medals in the A-CU Six Days Trial, New Imperial being awarded the Class A Team Prize (3rd member. L. Horton). JAP-engined machines gained a total of 6 Gold Medals in the A-CU event, and were also credited with best performance in the cyclecar class.

Another old association was renewed when during October Matchless announced their intention to market a rigid frame twin with the option of either a 7hp MAG engine or a 976cc JAP. It had come to their attention that there were very few British big twins suitable for solo riding. At last production had caught up with demand, so that there was every prospect of cheaper motorcycles for the forthcoming 1922 season. Already, some manufacturers had considered it prudent to announce their price reductions, without waiting for the now imminent 1922 Show.

Record breaking again became the name of the game, and at the BMCRC Championships held at Brooklands on October 8th Vivian Prestwich won the 250cc Championship Race on his 249cc Diamond JAP at 62.16mph, establishing in the process new Flying Start 5 Mile and standing Start 10 Mile Class A records at 63.40mph and 62.28mph. By now, advance information about new 1922 models was   *133* becoming available from most manufacturers, quite a few of whom were continuing to fit at least one model with a JAP engine. For example, the Sirrah range was being extended by the addition of 5-6hp vee-twin with all-chain drive, and a 2¾hp model with a choice of JAP or Blackburne engine. Wolf intended to market a Wolf JAP 350cc single, whilst the New Imperial range was to include an entirely new 293cc loop frame model, based on their highly successful 1921 TT machine. Fitted with a three-speed gearbox and all-chain drive, this model had the engine and gearbox assembled as a complete unit, prior to installation in the loop frame. Other JAP-engined machines included 250cc and 350cc Sports models fitted with a clutch but having no kickstarter, and an 8hp side valve twin. Hazlewood had two models, a 293cc single with a Sturmey-Archer two-speed gearbox and chain-cum-belt drive, and a 4hp model with a three-speed gearbox. Bown announced a 2¾ (293cc) single with an Albion two-speed gearbox fitted with a kickstarter, and chain-cum-belt drive. Francis-Barnett retained their 2¾hp Sports Model, which used a three-speed Sturmey Archer gearbox fitted with a kickstarter and having all chain drive. Finally, there was an 8hp vee-twin engined Sunbeam.

Increased competition was forthcoming from the manufacturer of Blackburne engines, four singles and four twins now being available. The singles comprised a 2¾hp ohv, a 4¼hp side valve, a 2¾hp standard side valve and a 4hp with a similar valve configuration. In the twin cylinder category there was a 5-6hp (96cc), an 8hp (998cc) and a big 1098cc available in either air- or water-cooled form. All were 60° twins and all of the side valve type, but in number they were no match for the very much wider range of engines available from JAP.

For the 1922 season, the Tottenham factory had available ten different types of side valve engine, listed as follows:

250cc single
293cc single
350cc standard single
350cc sports single
550cc single
500cc twin
680cc twin
986cc standard twin
986cc sports twin
986cc water-cooled twin

The 350cc sports single featured the new location of the pressure release valve, as mentioned previously in connection with the new 550cc single. The new arrangement comprised a pipe with a flattened end that had two narrow openings each side, about ¼ inch in length, to direct oil spray to the valve stems. Die-cast aluminium alloy 'fir cone' valve caps were fitted to both valves and the location of the sparking plug was changed to that used so successfully in the TT engines. Roller bearings were employed in the big-end assembly, and a roller bearing was also used on the drive side of the crankshaft. New and more robust timing gear of the two pinion type followed the practice adopted for the 70 x 90mm side valve TT engine. Other changes in specification included the use of a mild steel magneto platform and valves of 1⅝in diameter. For competition use an aluminium alloy piston was specified; for normal road use, one of cast iron.

The new 550cc single (85 x 95mm) followed a broadly similar specification, but was of low compression, with close pitch fins cast on the cylinder barrel. It had a cast iron piston and large diameter flywheels.

The 986cc sports twin was another engine to have the modified pressure release valve, and specially cast fins to help keep the timing chest cool. Valves of 1⅛in diameter demanded large ports. Ball bearings were used to support both ends of the crankshaft assembly.

The engine that created most interest was the 250cc engine, similar to that used by Prentice when he brought the first 250 home in the Junior TT. A similar engine had also been used very effectively in the Paris-Nice race, too. It was claimed this engine was good for 80mph — at 10,000rpm! Perhaps more to the point, this speed was equal to what one could expect from the 8hp twin.

Although not described in detail, the other engines now had caged roller bearing big ends, whilst the 500cc twin used two 250cc cylinder barrels of 44.5 x 76mm dimensions.

By now it had become easier to identify JAP engines due to the fact that a very simple alphabetic code had come into effect during 1920. By taking the word 'PNEUMATICS' and using one letter for each manufacturing year, the year of manufacture was readily apparent by referring to the engine number on the crankcase. Hence 'P' indicated 1920, and 'N' 1921, etc. Additional letters in the coding enabled the capacity to be identified, the valve configuration, whether the engine was of the sports or racing type, and if it was water-cooled. The table in Appendix 1 gives details of the coding arrangement. Exactly why the word 'PNEUMATICS' was used for the date of manufacture coding is no longer known, or for that matter why 'WHYZDRVFOG' succeeded it when it came to covering the years 1930-1939, except that none of the letters in the latter had been used before. The JAP production year always started on 1st September.

An internal view of the Northumberland Park Works taken during the twenties. (Photo: Dr. J. D. Alderson) 7/15

At the 1921 Show, quite a few manufacturers had available at least one JAP-engined model, the list comprising: Omega, Ready, LSD, NUT, Edmund, New Imperial, Verus and Sirrah, Sun, Olympic, Calthorpe, Matchless, Morgan, Francis-Barnett, Zenith, Coventry-Eagle, Brough Superior, PV, Sparkbrook, Diamond, Massey- Arran, DOT and Wolf. Often, there was the option of a JAP engine or another of proprietary make, such as MAG or Blackburne. The company itself made a welcome reappearance at this Show, and could be found on Stand 192.

At the end of the racing season, and after the usual pre-Show record breaking activities at Brooklands, the picture had changed yet again, especially in Class A. Now Vivian Prestwich held only the World Mile and 50 Mile records, Bert Kershaw having annexed the 100 to 600 Mile records with his New Imperial JAP, as well as the 1 - 6 Hour records. There were no records in Classes B, C and D for JAP engines, whilst in Class E it was the old 700 Mile and 24 Hour records established by Harry Collier in 1909 that still held good. Fortunately, the records in Class H2 (two-seater cyclecars not exceeding 1100cc capacity) were still relatively safe. E.B. Ware held 7 with his Morgan JAP, which accounted for exactly ⅓ of the total.

As the year closed there came news that the Tamplin cyclecar had been redesigned with a wider track, so that the driver and passenger could sit side-by-side behind the 8hp JAP engine. Another of the more obscure makes made its debut too. This was the Wigan-Barlow, made by Wigan Barlow Motors Ltd, of Lowther Street, Stoke, Coventry. This now completely forgotten make used a 293cc JAP engine in conjunction with a two-speed Albion gearbox that had both a clutch and a kickstarter. Characteristic of the period, chain-cum-belt transmission was specified.

JAP advertising had changed its theme yet again. The latest advertisement in *The Motor Cycle* dated December 21st, 1921 related to what they described as the 'new lightweight engine', the 70 x 76mm 293cc side valve unit that weighed only 32lb.

Chapter Eight

Bert Le Vack revives the big twin

JAP ADVERTISING copy took on a changing pattern during the first three months of 1922. The first advertisement to be published related to the new 293cc side valve engine, which was claimed to have four outstanding attributes — Efficiency, Reliability, Speed and Economy. But when the results of the London-Exeter-London Trial were announced, no opportunity was lost to proclaim that 25% of the Gold Medals were awarded to riders of JAP-engined machines. Rather as an afterthought, attention was drawn to 'The Combination Single', the 85 x 95mm 550cc. Only a matter of a few weeks later, a prophetic advertisement appeared, which proudly announced 'Britain's Reply — The Super Big Twin', an allusion to the 986cc 85.5 x 85mm ohv sports engine. It had not escaped the attention of motorcycle enthusiasts that the American big twins were now making most of the running at speed events in the larger capacity classes. Something was needed to restore British supremecy.

The first positive step to be taken in this direction was made towards the end of March, when a small announcement in *The Motor Cycle,* accompanied by a photograph, confirmed that Bert Le Vack would henceforth be associated with the JAP marque as development engineer. The photograph showed him astride a Brough Superior fitted with a 976cc vee-twin JAP engine, the machine on which he had competed at the recently-held Essex MC's Kop hill climb. This particular meeting is worthy of special mention because the star of the event was Stan Greening. He made five ascents on a 250cc Francis-Barnett JAP, all five times varying by not more than 0.5 second, a quite remarkable feat of consistency. He won the 250cc and 350cc Touring Classes outright, was second in the 500cc Class, and first in the 750cc Class. Vivian Prestwich also rode a the same meeting, using a machine fitted with a 2¾hp JAP engine. He was second in the 250cc and 350cc Touring Classes, 6th in the 500cc Class, and 3rd in the 750cc Class. he was also placed 5th and 6th respectively in the Any Machine up to 500cc and 1,000cc Classes. Once again, JAP engines had made their mark in no uncertain manner.

The acquisition of Le Vack's services was a brilliant move, for although he remained with the company for less than four years, he accomplished so very much during this relatively short period. Yet for all that, he was an enigmatic character, such that what little is known about him has been told by his nephew, Wal Phillips. He hero-worshipped his uncle and managed to get a job at the factory to be near him.

Although Bert had a formal engineering training, the amount of knowledge and skill that he had managed to acquire was quite staggering. His expertise as a fitter was

Stan Greening astride a 1922 Sunbeam JAP twin. Apart from handling technical enquiries at the factory, he achieved numerous competition successes with JAP-engined machines of all kinds. (Photo: Mrs. C. May)

A factory group, photographed during 1922. Left to right: *Vivian Prestwich, Edward Ware, John Prestwich, Stan Greening and Arthur Prestwich.* (Photo: Mrs. C. May)

unparalleled and he later became renowned as a blender of potent fuels. He kept to himself and preferred to work in his own workshop within the Tottenham factory, behind closed doors. To assist him he had two skilled mechanics, one of whom, his former business associate, Sid Moram, he had brought with him. He also had a boy assistant and a frequent visitor in the form of Vivian Prestwich, who shared his love of racing and his enthusiasm for tuning engines.

He was a quiet spoken man, who went his own way and found it difficult to make friends. In a short feature about Le Vack in *Motor Cycling*, the late Dennis May recounts how Le Vack came home from work one evening to find his house full of relatives and an impromptu party in full swing. Rather than intrude, he let himself in quietly, crept upstairs and went to bed undetected. This, more than anything else, sums up the very nature of the man — a quiet, unassuming introvert who richly deserves his place in the pages of motorcycling history.

Le Vack's first appearance at Brooklands under the JAP banner took place during the First BMCRC Members Meeting of 1922, held on Saturday, 8th April. Riding a new 980cc side valve Zenith JAP, he finished second to Claude Temple's Harley-Davidson, relegating Kaye Don to third place on his Indian and thereby splitting another potential 1 - 2 for the American twins. This marked the first appearance of the KTC engine, designed by Val Page. It retained the KT-type bore and stroke dimensions of 85.5 x 85mm, but featured improvements in the form of aluminium alloy pistons and larger valves, the latter of which necessitated the use of 1¾ inch diameter exhaust pipes. A single camshaft operated the four valves and the 'fir cone' valve caps were a distinctive feature. This engine was first announced officially at the 1921 Olympia Show. At this same meeting, E.B. Ware drove his 1098cc Morgan-JAP in the 600cc - 1000cc 3-lap Passenger Machine Race, to finish third — a somewhat unusual and lowly position for him.

Early in the year it had been announced that the lightweight class of machine would have its own separate race in the 1922 TT programme, instead of being merged with the Junior Race and starting concurrently. D.G. Prentice announced he would defend his lightweight title in the new race, whilst R.W. Longton declared his intention of riding a 250cc Francis-Barnett that would be fitted with a 65.5 x 76mm engine identical to that used in the New Imperial that had won the 1921 Lightweight Class. Soon came the news that Le Vack had planned to enter both the Junior and Senior Races, using an as yet unspecified machine fitted with an entirely new 350cc engine. But there could be no doubt about the origin of the engine! Whilst all kinds of rumours abounded, DOT announced a new sports twin for road use, powered by the 8hp ohv sports JAP engine. Just a week later, New Imperial revealed that henceforth their machines would have mechanical lubrication, dispensing with the old and familiar hand pump.

During the BMCRC's Second Members Meeting at Brooklands held on 6th May, which provided an opportunity to test some of the TT entries, Vivian Prestwich won the Class A category in the Junior Brooklands TT Race. Riding a New Imperial, he averaged 56.83mph over the 26 laps. In the 3 lap 1000cc scratch race that followed, Le Vack again took second place, there being only three starters. As previously, it was Claude Temple's Harley-Davidson that won, Le Vack's 998cc Zenith JAP overhauling R. Stewart on a Trump-Anzani.

Back at the Tottenham factory, work was continuing apace. During mid-May, a redesigned version of the standard 349cc side valve single made its debut. Its main features were more generous finning and a 1¼ inch diameter exhaust port — identical in size to that of one of the cylinder barrels of the 998cc twin. But it was towards the end of the month that the greatest surprise of all came about, when the new 350cc TT engine was unveiled. To be housed in New Imperial cycle parts, it was of the double overhead camshaft type, with the camshafts driven by bevel pinions. Nothing quite like this had been seen before and although JAP cannot be credited with having the first dohc engine, it is unfortunate that details of a much earlier 4 valve ohc design, probably originated around 1910, have become lost with the passage of time. Certainly an engine of this type reached the experimental stage, for it is alleged a chain drive was used in preference to a vertical shaft and bevels.

The new dohc engine had a detachable, cast iron cylinder head, with twin exhaust ports and a hemispherical combustion chamber. It was retained to the cast iron cylinder barrel by a five stud bolt-through arrangement, direct to the crankcase. Generously finned, like the cylinder barrel, it gave the engine a somewhat lopsided appearance, due to the fact that one of the 1¾ inch diameter exhaust pipes (right-hand) faced forward, whereas the left-hand pipe emerged sideways. The valves were inclined at 90°, and the engine had bore and stroke dimensions of 74 x 80mm, giving a cubic capacity of 344cc. Surprisingly, the compression ratio was only 5:1.

Although only these basic details were available at the time of the announcement, it subsequently became apparent that the drive to the overhead camshafts was by means of five bevels and an exposed vertical shaft, the two camshafts being driven off the top bevel pinion and operating the valves by rockers that ran parallel to the crankshaft. The whole of the valve gear operating mechanism was fully enclosed within an aluminium alloy casting on the right-hand side of the engine, leaving the cylinder head and valves unmasked in the cooling airstream. Engine lubrication was by means of a hand pump, working on the total loss principle, but the valve gear was lubricated independently by gravity drip feed from an extra oil tank mounted on the top tube of the frame. All bearings were of the ballrace type, with the exception of the small end. The piston was of aluminium alloy and fitted with a conventional gudgeon pin assembly. The engine number was EXP 1.

It has been said that the idea of a dohc engine came from John Prestwich and that Val Page commenced work on the design as late as February. The first engine was assembled by Sid Moram, under the close supervision of both Page and Le Vack, and when complete it was taken straight to the test bench. It showed such promise that the same three set about preparing it for the 1922 TT, working late almost every night for six weeks solid.

In the Junior TT Race, Le Vack led on the first lap, with a 3 second lead ahead of the second man, Harris, on an AJS. He increased his lead on the second and third laps, but just when it seemed he had the race in his pocket, a gearbox seizure forced him to retire, at Windy Corner, by which time he was 1 minute, 48 seconds ahead. There was no locking device on the screwed-on gearbox sprocket and in consequence the sprocket unscrewed itself on the over-run. Having spent every waking hour working on the engine to get it ready in time, Page, Le Vack and Moram had entrusted the preparation of the rest of the machine to the New Imperial works. Their only reward was a new lap record, Le Vack having covered the first lap from a standing start in 40 minutes, 7 seconds (56.46mph). This was one second faster than the previous year's 500cc record!

In the Senior (500cc) Race that followed, Le Vack was 12th on the first lap, but managed to work his way up to 8th position on the 3rd, 4th and 5th laps, after a brief spell in 7th position on the 2nd lap. But it proved to be too much for the magneto platform, which came loose on the 6th lap and forced him to retire. The Island was never a happy hunting ground for Le Vack, this being a typical example of the kind of misfortune that befell him.

It was ironic that the new engine itself had performed satisfactorily when so much had been expected of it yet had been let down by such minor defects from supporting

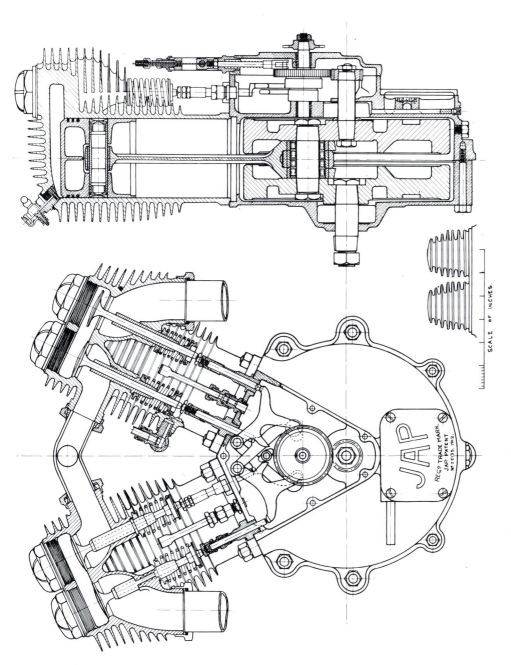

Fig. 8.1 The 1922 JAP 1,000cc side-valve vee-twin. *(Courtesy Ronald H. Clark)*

components. During practice it had given no trouble at all and if anything, had tended to run too cool. When dismantled after three laps of the TT course, the internals looked just as though they had just come from the machine shop, according to contemporary accounts. Fortunately, it was not long before it showed its true capabilities. Of the other JAP-engined entries, the best performance was achieved by D.G. Prentice, who finished 5th on his New Imperial in the new 250cc Lightweight Race. Only one machine fitted with a vee-twin JAP engine had been entered for the Senior Race, a NUT which was forced to retire before completing the course.

To the delight of many, Le Vack entered his 344cc TT New Imperial-JAP in the Third Monthly Race Meeting held by the BMCRC at Brooklands on 10th June. Surprisingly, they went away disappointed, as he was nowhere in the running. An unusual machine, a Coulson B, took the honours. J.J. Hall, a legendary figure who created such an interest in old machines after World War 2, came third in the 500cc-1000cc Solo Handicap Race, riding a 744cc Trump JAP, after leading the field on the first lap. Stan Greening won the 2 lap Passenger Machine Handicap Race at 54.05mph, with his 346cc Francis-Barnett JAP sidecar outfit. There was a JAP-engined machine somewhere in the running at most meetings.

In the 200 Mile Sidecar Races held at the same venue on 17th June, Le Vack had the opportunity to shine on his other mount, a 988cc ohv Zenith JAP sidecar outfit. The more observant noticed that he had replaced the original carburetter with an American-made Schebler, similar to that fitted to the Indian twins he had ridden before he changed allegiance to JAP. Clearly he intended to profit from his past experiences. Despite a pit stop, when it became necessary to change the rear wheel of the Zenith, he set up three new Class G records — 200 miles at 64.84mph, 2 hours at 67.13mph and 3 hours at 64.53mph. He finished second in the race at an average speed of 64.88mph, a very creditable performance taking into account the delay for repairs at his pit. The race winner was D.H. Davidson who, theoretically, should have been awarded the international records. But he could claim the British records only, as the diameter of his sidecar wheel did not meet the requirements of the FICM. JAP-engined machines finished in 2nd, 4th and 6th positions in the 200 mile event, and were the only British manufactured machines to complete the course. Ironically, the report in *The Motor Cycle* quite erroneously lists Le Vack as riding a Zenith-Blackburne.

It was not until the Motor Cycling Club's meeting held on 8th July that Le Vack had another opportunity to enter his 344cc dohc New Imperial JAP. But before his turn came, George Brough made a surprise appearance on one of his own machines in the Over 560cc Solo Handicap, a 976cc Brough Superior fitted with a side valve vee-twin JAP engine. Given a 1 minute, 3 second start over Claude Temple and his all-conquering eight-valve Harley-Davidson, George made the most of his opportunity and won at 82.08mph, Le Vack taking second place with his 998cc Zenith JAP. This was one of many victories achieved by the old Brough Superior side valver, which was a racing version of the SS80 model. Originally dubbed 'Spit and Polish' on account of its appearance, it was later re-christened more affectionately as 'Old Bill'. Still in existence today, it has 51 firsts to its credit, in succession, out of 52 entries. Even on the 52nd occasion the machine crossed the finishing line first, though on this occasion without its rider in the saddle! It has the distinction of being the first side valve machine to lap Brooklands at over 100mph.

In the 350cc Solo Scratch Race, Le Vack found himself in good company, with Cyril Pullin alongside him on the start line, the latter riding a 349cc ohv Douglas. This time, there was no doubt about the capabilities of the dohc New Imperial JAP, when Le Vack led from start to finish, winning the race at a speed of 71.31mph. Later, he brought out his 998cc Zenith JAP once more, to contest the Over-560cc Solo Scratch Race.

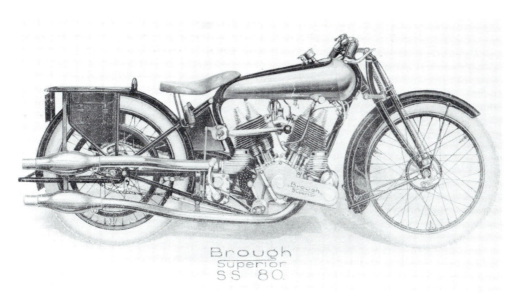

The 1922 SS80 Brough Superior, fitted with a 988cc side valve vee-twin JAP engine.

George Brough in the Paddock at Brooklands on his original SS80 racing model that was nicknamed 'Spit and Polish'. This photograph was taken during an MCC meeting in 1922. (Photo: Dr. J. D. Alderson)

143

But he had to concede victory to Claude Temple's Harley-Davidson and take second place. The American big twins were still proving invincible, and it was time for something to be done about it.

As may be expected, these regular race meetings at Brooklands, many of which were of long duration, were causing a severe noise problem for local residents. Similar car events and various long distance record breaking attempts helped exacerbate the problem, such that a successful lobby was mounted against the track authorities, making it abundantly clear that unless they themselves took positive steps to reduce noise levels, the residents would seek an injunction to get the track closed. Colonel Lindsay Lloyd, the Clerk of the Course, took immediate action and warned competitors that unless they silenced their machines in an effective manner they would be barred, not only from taking part in future race meetings, but from the whole of the Brooklands Estate. Unknowingly, the foundations were being laid to what eventually would become known as the 'Brooklands Can', a special design of silencer that became a compulsory fitment early in 1924. But until then, it was a question of finding some means of reducing the noise level to a tolerable level, with the minimal possible effect on performance. Unfortunately, it was mainly the motorcycle contingent that had been responsible for the complaints.

Mid-year announcements about new models brought to light the Kingsway-JAP, made by the Kingsway Motor Cycle Co. of Much Park Street, Coventry. Of simple design, using the 293cc side valve engine, it was in production for little more than eighteen months. Coincident with this announcement was news of a new Francis-Barnett, using a similar engine. A touring version of the sports model, it was fitted with a three-speed gearbox and provided with both a clutch and a kickstarter.

It was during the two-day period 19th/20th July that history was made when a lady, Mrs. G. Janson, attempted the Double 12 Hour Record at Brooklands on a 249cc Trump JAP. The date had been scheduled for S.F. Edge, the well-known car driver, to try to improve upon his own 24 hour record of 65.09mph which he had set up during 1907, but because of the noise lobby, the original itinerary had to be changed so that Edge could drive only from 8am to 8pm on two successive days. The car he intended using was a Spyker, made in Holland, and it so happened that the Managing Director of the British Spyker Co. Ltd — the UK importers — was Lt Col S. Janson, who also had a financial interest in Trump Motors Ltd. It occurred to him that if his wife Gwenda, herself a motorcyclist and a holder of shares in Trump Motors, were to attempt a Double 12 record at the same time as Edge, use could be made of the timing apparatus that otherwise would have proved expensive to hire. So with no worries about what make of machine to use, J.J. Hall was entrusted with its preparation. A decision was made in favour of using a lightweight Trump powered by a 249cc side valve JAP engine, it being considered that a machine of this type would prove more reliable and easier to control by someone of slight build. Hall was especially thorough in his preparation, using 'about 20 rolls of insulating tape and half a gallon of shellac to see that nothing moved' to quote his own words.

The attempt went well and Gwenda got her record, which provided a more than adequate testimony to the stamina of the 249cc JAP engine. According to the account published in *The Motor Cycle,* the only problems experienced were the need to change the rear wheel on the first day and the necessity to clean oil off the contact breaker points whenever the machine came in for a checkover and refuel every two hours. Yet Hall is reputed to have claimed that he had fitted the front wheel the wrong way round, so that the hub bearings came unscrewed during the first hour, causing delay and unnecessary tension whilst the problem was rectified. No doubt the incident was overlooked when the record had been gained and everyone was in a happier frame of mind. On the first day,

Gwenda covered 556 miles at 46.33 mph, and on the second day, at just over 44 mph, 515 miles giving her the record for 1071 miles, 1180 yards at 44.65 mph in 24 hours. She also took two world's records in Class A, 11 hours at 46.03 mph and 12 hours at 46.33 mph. In all, a quite remarkable performance for a motorcycle 'first'. At the finish, spectators lifted her out of the saddle and carried her, shoulder high, to join Edge, who also had set a new record. His problem had been that of boredom, whereas Gwenda had to contend with cramp and the constant pounding of the uneven track surface, with its notorious bumps.

Gwenda Janson gets off the line with a Trump-JAP, 249cc side valve single similar to that on which she gained her 'double twelve' record. (Photo: Dr. J. D. Alderson)

On 21st July Bert Le Vack took his 344 dohc New Imperial JAP to the track for an attempt on some Class B records. He too was successful, taking the 10 mile and 50 mile records at 73.52 mph and 74.00 mph respectively, 100 miles at 72.81 mph and 1 hour at

74.17mph. The last of these was a quite remarkable achievement, because it represented an advance on the 500cc record that two years previously had been set at 72.4mph. Le Vack's successes almost overshadowed those of E.B. Ware, who had taken the 50 mile Class H1 and H2 records at 77mph in his Morgan JAP. JAP advertising made the most of these recent achievements, claiming, 'What use is speed without reliability?'.

With such frequent references to Brooklands, it is easy to convey the impression that it was only at this venue that serious racing took place, or that most JAP successes came from this concrete bowl. Yet nothing could be further from the truth. Whilst, admittedly, Brooklands needed to be used for record-breaking attempts in Britain and for long distance races, for which it had been designed, countless other events were being held throughout the country almost every weekend. Often, these required the use of public roads, sea front promenades and, particularly in the north of England, sand on the foreshore — Scotland and Wales having their own equivalents. Sand racing had its own exponents and required special riding techniques. One of the more popular venues in Wales was Pendine Sands where, during August, Handel Davies won the unlimited class on a 976cc Brough Superior JAP in convincing style.

The A-CU Six Days Trial could always be guaranteed to attract some of the big names, who welcomed the opportunity to test their skills in other than high speed events. The 1922 event attracted George Brough, who entered on a 976cc JAP-engined model and also Mrs Janson who, on this occasion, preferred a 350cc Coventry-Eagle JAP. Quite a few riders of JAP-engined machines qualified for Gold Medals, including George Brough, Eric Barnett (of Francis Barnett), Stan Greening, H.F.S. Morgan (of Morgan Cars) and the New Imperial team of Kershaw, Horton and Wilkins. Sadly, Mrs Janson went out of the running when she was forced to retire at Brooklands of all places, during the final stages of the trial.

It now became apparent that racegoers were beginning to tire of the many meetings held at Brooklands, particularly as the season progressed. As one report in *The Motor Cycle* put it, Brooklands meetings are like Ford cars — they are all the same. Late in August, the same magazine published an article headed 'Make Brooklands worth visiting', suggesting the main problems were too few star riders and too many handicap races that made progress difficult to follow. Some races could start with no more than three contestants. But was there really an answer? The same old formula seemed to continue, and the same arguements came up with monotonous regularity.

BMCRC's Fifth Monthly Members Race Meeting held on 12th August proved of interest in so far as Bert Le Vack had entered a 245cc version of his 344cc dohc New Imperial in the first of the 250cc Solo Handicap races. The engine was literally a scaled-down version of its larger brother, having a reduced bore size yet retaining the same stroke (62.5 x 80mm). It too had a five stud fixing between cylinder head and crankcase, and an exposed vertical drive to the cambox. It is alleged a 424cc engine of similar design, having bore and stroke dimensions of 75 x 96mm, was built about the same time, but it does not appear to have been used until the year following.

At the Brooklands meeting the new 245cc New Imperial JAP was unplaced, and no JAP-engined machines figured prominently in the results, a rare occurrence. Of interest at this meeting was the wide variety of silencers used in an attempt to meet the new lower noise level requirements. Some were particularly ingenious, like the design fitted to the Trump-Anzani of Colonel Stewart. According to the drawing in *The Motor Cycle* it was mounted to the rear of the rider's seat, so that it occupied and resembled the tail fairing fitted to many of the racers of the fifties and sixties.

Switching to the 344cc New Imperial JAP at the Surbiton Club's Brooklands Meeting of 2nd September (organised on behalf of the A-CU), Bert Le Vack had a runaway win in the 350cc Solo Race, winning it at 79.20mph. Stan Greening did well in this meeting too, with his 348cc Francis-Barnett JAP sidecar outfit. He held a comfortable lead, but eventually was passed by C. Volk on a 494cc Douglas outfit, who went on to win.

So far, no record breaking attempts had been made with the 344cc New Imperial JAP harnessed to a sidecar; none, that is, until Le Vack took such an outfit to Brooklands on 6th September. He must have been confident of success, for he came away with the Class B 510 mile record at 62.74mph, which was not ratified and subsequently improved upon by Pullin's Douglas. But it was 12th September that brought the largest collection of would-be record breakers to the track, no doubt as a lead up to the forthcoming Motor Cycle Show at Olympia. By far the best performance was put up by Bert Le Vack who, with the same 344cc New Imperial JAP, this time without the sidecar, set up new Class B solo records. He covered the flying kilometre at 93.79mph, aided by a favourable wind, and his two-hway speed after a return run averaged out at 83.56mph. He took the flying mile at 91.88mph, a British record, under similar conditions, and his return gave a mean of 81.86mph for the two-way run, seemingly more records in the bag. But they were not ratified and subsequently beaten by Pullin on 20th November.

The spate of record breaking attempts made prior to the Motor Cycle Shows in the twenties created problems in so far as the FICM would not be in any hurry to ratify the first claims when they appeared likely to be beaten by subsequent, later claims. Such was the case when Pullin and Le Vack went record breaking during the same period of time in Classes B and B/s, and when Trump made their standing start kilometre and mile claims, as will be seen.

Colonel Stewart set about the Class D records with his 750cc Trump-JAP, taking the standing start kilometre record at 60.59mph, which gave a mean of 58.80mph after the return run. J.J. Hall riding a similar machine took the standing start mile record at 65.86mph, with a mean of 62.96mph after his return run. Then it was a tilt at the Class A records, this time using a 249cc Trump JAP. Colonel Stewart got the standing start kilometre at 48.91mph, with a mean of 46.50. On this occasion Mrs Janson rode the second, similar machine, to claim the standing start mile record at 44.45mph. She could manage only the one-way run, which meant she had to be content with the British record only. Sadly, the 250cc Trump JAP records did not stand for long. A fortnight later they had been claimed by a Levis rider, and later still, on 23rd November, the standing start kilometre classes C and D records fell to Jack Emerson on a 496cc Douglas and the standing start mile classes C and D records to Sheraton on a 490cc Norton.

The 500 Mile Races that were to be held at Brooklands on 23rd September had to be called off due to the anti-noise lobby, a fact that made motorcyclists very angry because they thought they were being made the scapegoats. But that did not mean the track was not being used by motorcyclists. On 28th September, Le Vack demonstrated very convincingly the potential of the new 245cc New Imperial JAP, when he set up new Class A records. He raised the flying start 5 mile record to 76.43mph and the standing start 10 miles to 73.44mph — these speeds being higher than the flying start kilometre and flying start mile records Class A records currently in the Record Book!

In the north of England, a young man by the name of George Tottey had won the 250cc Solo Machines event at the Scarborough MCC's Speed Trials held on 23rd September. Although no significance could be attached to his name at that time, his ride along the sea front on his 250cc New Imperial JAP marked the beginnings of a very successful racing career, about which much has been written. His was destined to become yet another famous name associated with the JAP marque. It is also pertinent to record that George Brough had a field day a week later, when he rode in the Doncaster

Speed Trials and made fastest time of the day with his Brough Superior JAP. Running firstly with sidecar attached, his Brough Superior outfit won at 69.33mph, beating Freddie Dixon's Harley-Davidson. He went on to beat Freddie in the solo class too, never an easy task. In recording 82.57mph, he set a new record for the Doncaster course. These two locally-organised events were typical of so many run throughout the length and breadth of the country, as briefly referred to earlier in this Chapter.

Announcements were now being made about new models for the 1923 season, prior to the 1922 Show at Olympia. Excelsior were one of the first to give details of their new model range, which included a 2¾hp JAP-engined model to the same specification as that already available with a Blackburne engine. It would have all chain drive. In addition, there was to be an 8hp machine with sidecar use in mind, powered by a 976cc side valve vee-twin JAP. The specification included a Burman three-speed gearbox and all chain drive. Shortly afterwards, Francis Barnett gave details of their 293cc and 346cc JAP-engined models which would have all chain drive, using a three-speed Sturmey Archer gearbox fitted with clutch and kickstarter. Sports and touring versions were intended, and a special 346cc TT model would be available, to form the centrepiece of their stand at the Olympia Show.

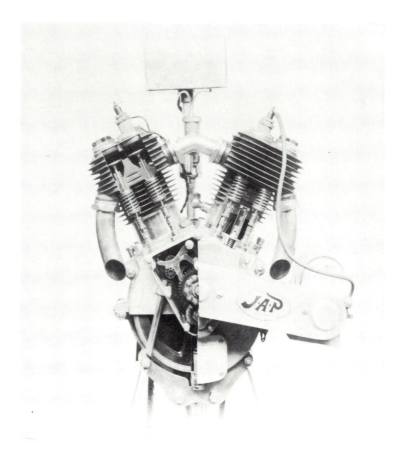

A cutaway vee-twin engine used for exhibitions, showing the arrangement of the valve operating mechanism. (Photo: Douglas Prestwich)

As the Show drew nearer, record breaking attempts at Brooklands intensified, but of more immediate interest was the BMCRC Championship Meeting to be held on 21st October. This prestigious meeting was one in which good performance could result in increased sales, due to its close proximity to the Show itself. On this occasion, Bert Le Vack was on top form, winning four of the championships and coming second in a fifth. He won the 1000cc Sidecar Championship at 71.31mph with his 996cc Zenith JAP sidecar outfit fitted with a prototype 4 valve long stroke, side valve KTR engine which never went into production. The 1000cc Solo Championship at 92.65 with the same machine, and the 250cc and 350cc Championships at 58.84mph and 76.91mph respectively, using the dohc-engined New Imperials. He was second in the 350cc Sidecar Championship. Unlike the 350cc Race, where he faced stiff opposition from Cyril Pullin's 346cc Douglas twin, he found the 250cc event boring. He held such a lead after 4 laps that a contemporary account claims he had time for a chat with his mechanic, Sid Moram, during a pit stop! It is worth recording that second place in the 250cc Championship went to Vivian Prestwich, who was using a 249cc side valve JAP single.

It could be inferred that his quite exceptional performance in the championship meeting encouraged Le Vack to make some further record breaking attempts at Brooklands on 27th and 28th October. Taking only his 996cc Zenith JAP on which he had won the 1000cc Championships, he set up a new Class E flying start 5 mile record at the incredible figure of 100.27mph, his second lap being timed at 100.65mph. Although this record had been achieved in drizzling rain, which made the handling tricky, it was the first time a British motorcycle had established a record at over 100mph, and the first time *any* motorcycle had lapped Brooklands at over 100mph. Along the Railway Straight, the Zenith JAP had recorded over 108mph.

On the following day, Le Vack reappeared with the Zenith, this time with a sidecar attached. In this trim he claimed the Class G/s 1000cc Sidecar Records for the flying start five mile and standing start ten mile distances at 81.72mph and 78.88mph respectively.

In a rare interview conducted soon afterwards by a reporter from *The Motor Cycle*, Bert Le Vack claimed the solo Zenith was not easy to hold on course due to the bumps, especially those near the aeroplane sheds. Yet the machine would steer itself along the Railway Straight, due to the fact that he had designed and fitted a quite effective front fork damper. He found he could even move one hand from the handlebars at this point, to make an adjustment to the carburetter! There was need to slow down on the approach to the banking, otherwise there was no means of holding the machine down. He also needed to watch out for, and avoid, a particularly bad bump by the Vickers shed. The biggest problem was caused by the wind funnelling as he approached the Members Bridge, which caused his eyes to stream and his vision to blur. He came within 20 feet of the top of the banking as a result, higher than he liked. His main wish was to thank his mechanic, Sid Moram, who had worked both early and late to get the engine prepared in time.

One problem that concerned Le Vack, although he did not make reference to it at the time of the interview, was the way in which his lap speeds had been calculated. Motorcycle lap speeds were calculated on a line 10 feet from the inner edge of the track, whereas cars used a 50 foot line measured from the inner edge. Le Vack had spent the whole of his record-breaking run well outside the 50 foot line, which meant that he had covered more ground in the same time than that for which he had been credited. In consequence, his lap speeds should have been higher. He made a formal protest, and as a result the 50 foot line was used for motorcycles from 1923 onwards.

Seemingly still unhappy with his record breaking attempts at the end of October, Le Vack returned again a matter of days later, to make another attempt at Classes E and *149*

G/s. In solo form, his 998cc Zenith JAP raised the British flying start kilometre and flying start mile mean speed records to 102.80mph and 102.91mph respectively, these being the mean speeds for the two-way run necessary to qualify. He also managed a one-way flying start mile at 103.71mph. After attaching a sidecar to the Zenith, he set new Class G/s records with similar runs, at speeds of 86.62mph, 85.40mph and the one-way mile at 85.83mph respectively. He did not compete in the Remembrance Day Meeting of 11th November, however. On that day, Vivian Prestwich was placed 2nd in the 250cc Race, riding his 249cc New Imperial-JAP.

Here it is pertinent to record that the American, E. Walker, had set up World's Class E records over the flying start kilometre, mile and 5 miles at 103.56mph, 103.75mph and 108.68mph respectively, on his 994cc 8-valve Indian at Daytona Beach, Florida, on 14th April 1920. The FICM did not ratify these records until January 1921, which caused strained relations with the Americans and led eventually to their resignation from the Federation in 1923.

The Northumberland Park Works in the twenties. (Photo: Douglas Prestwich)

Facing page:
Vivian Prestwich with one of his racing machines powered by a 249cc side valve JAP engine. (Photo: Douglas Prestwich)

A mass of overhead shafts and pulleys drive the lathes in the Machine Shop. (Photo: Douglas Prestwich)

The view inside the gates, showing the weighbridge and the Number One factory. (Photo: Douglas Prestwich)

The Tool Room, where inspection work was carried out to very high standards of accuracy. (Photo: Douglas Prestwich)

The Electroplating Shop with the plating vats in the background. (Photo: Douglas Prestwich)

154

The crankcase drilling section, with its row of vertical drilling machines. Note the crankcase castings piled on the floor. (Photo: Douglas Prestwich)

Facing page,

Top:
The Final Inspection Shop in which engines were checked prior to despatch. (Photo: Douglas Prestwich)

Middle:
The engine assembly section, with its long work benches. (Photo: Douglas Prestwich)

Bottom:
The Repair Shop. In the foreground are sidecars detached from machines undergoing repair or overhaul. (Photo: Douglas Prestwich)

The cylinder grinding section, showing the ducting which carried away the metallic particles. (Photo: Douglas Prestwich)

The huge Crossley 250bhp suction gas engine used to power the overhead shafts for driving the factory machinery. When this engine was started up each morning, the whole factory used to shake. (Photo: Douglas Prestwich)

Undeterred by the November fog, Bert Le Vack returned yet again to the Brooklands track on 17th November, to try and gain the Class E 50 mile, 100 mile and 1 hour records with his Zenith JAP. Unfortunately, the damp weather conditions played havoc with the machine's carburation, and he was unable to beat the existing 50 mile record. But the 100 mile and 1 hour records fell to him at speeds of 89.92mph and 89.90mph respectively, giving him fresh entries in the Records Book. A day later, when the weather had improved, he returned for another Class E attempt. When the 10 mile standing start record fell at 93.04mph, it looked as though he was going to be successful at last. But when a valve cap blew out, the attempt had to be abandoned. Clearly his luck was out, for when he brought out the 344cc dohc New Imperial JAP with sidecar attached, gearbox problems set in before he could make a serious attempt at the equivalent Class B/s sidecar records.

An interesting feature of Le Vack's Zenith JAP in its latest record breaking guise was the use of a huge 5 gallon petrol tank, one of the largest and best supported ever seen at the track. In effect, it was two 2½ gallon tanks held together by metal straps, supported by a platform that had been brazed to the lower of the two tank tubes of the frame.

With the time rapidly approaching when the Brooklands track would have to be closed for its winter repairs, Le Vack turned up again on 23rd November with his 998cc Zenith JAP, this time sporting a pair of Druid forks. Once again he was forced to abandon any serious attempt at the Class E records when clutch slip set in and could not be remedied. But he was back the next day, and with Vivian Prestwich recruited as his sidecar passenger, he demolished the Class G/s 1 hour and 100 mile sidecar records, taking the former at a speed of 74.87mph. He was lapping consistently at speeds in the mid-70s.

The next day it was the turn of the 245cc dohc New Imperial. With ease, Le Vack took the Class A records for 50 and 100 miles, as well as the 1 and 2 hours, the speeds of the former being 68.61mph and 67.41mph respectively. Now, no more could be done until the track reopened in 1923. His determination had paid off, as reference to the following table of 1922 Records will show. His is the name that figures most prominently in this list of riders of JAP-engined machines.

Class A (Solo motorcycles not exceeding 250cc)

Flying start kilometre	Le Vack 245cc New Imperial	76.55mph
Flying start mile	Le Vack 245cc New Imperial	76.55mph
5 Miles	Le Vack 245cc New Imperial	76.43mph
10 Miles	Le Vack 245cc New Imperial	73.44mph
50 Miles	Le Vack 245cc New Imperial	68.61mph
100 Miles	Le Vack 245cc New Imperial	67.41mph

Class B (Solo motorcycles not exceeding 350cc)

Flying start mile*	Le Vack 344cc New Imperial	91.88mph
5 Miles*	Le Vack 344cc New Imperial	85.75mph
10 Miles*	Le Vack 344cc New Imperial	81.13mph
50 Miles	Le Vack 344cc New Imperial	74.00mph
100 Miles	Le Vack 344cc New Imperial	72.81mph
1 Hour*	Le Vack 344cc New Imperial	74.16mph
2 Hour*	Le Vack 344cc New Imperial	67.84mph

Class D (Solo motorcycles not exceeding 750cc)

Standing start kilometre	Col R.N. Stewart 744cc Trump	60.59mph

Standing start mile	J.J. Hall 744cc Trump	65.86mph
Standing start kilometre*	Col R.N. Stewart 744cc Trump	58.80mph
Standing start mile*	J.J. Hall 744cc Trump	62.69mph

Class E (Solo motorcycles not exceeding 1000cc)

Flying start mile*	Le Vack 998cc Zenith	103.71mph
10 Miles	Le Vack 998cc Zenith	93.04mph
50 Miles	Le Vack 998cc Zenith	91.71mph
100 Miles	Le Vack 998cc Zenith	89.92mph
1 Hour	Le Vack 998cc Zenith	89.90mph

Class G/s (Sidecars not exceeding 1000cc)

Flying start kilometre	Le Vack 998cc Zenith	86.62mph
Flying start mile*	Le Vack 998cc Zenith	85.83mph
Flying start mile	Le Vack 998cc Zenith	85.40mph
5 Miles	Le Vack 998cc Zenith	81.72mph
10 Miles	Le Vack 998cc Zenith	78.88mph
50 Miles	Le Vack 998cc Zenith	75.59mph
100 Miles	Le Vack 998cc Zenith	74.70mph
200 Miles	Le Vack 998cc Zenith	64.84mph
1 Hour	Le Vack 998cc Zenith	74.87mph
2 Hours	Le Vack 998cc Zenith	67.13mph
3 Hours	Le Vack 998cc Zenith	64.53mph

Class J1 (Single seater cycle cars not exceeding 750cc)

10 Miles+	E.B. Ware 744cc Morgan	59.50mph
50 Miles+	E.B. Ware 744cc Morgan	47.52mph
1 Hour+	E.B. Ware 744cc Morgan	47.26mph

Class H2 (Single seater cycle cars not exceeding 1100cc. Max. weight 772lb)

| Flying start mile | E.B. Ware 1096cc Morgan | 82.19mph |

Note: Unless marked otherwise all records listed here are world's records
* British record
\+ Not FICM ratified but regarded as World's Records

During November, more new models for the 1923 season were announced. Hazlewood had two twin cylinder side valve sidecar outfits, powered by either a 976cc or a 770cc JAP engine, with belt final drive in the case of the smaller model, the larger being all chain. There was a tradesmans outfit available too. New Imperial announced no fundamental changes to their lightweight range, available with side valve JAP engine options of 249cc and 348cc. But they had added a new 348cc Touring model, virtually a utility, lower-priced version of their 348cc Sports model. Prices were still falling and manufacturers were finding need to cater more for the lower end of the market.

The DOT range, announced during mid-November, comprised five JAP-engined models. Bottom of the range was a 293cc Touring lightweight, fitted with a three-speed Sturmey Archer gearbox and chain-cum-belt transmission. Next was a 348cc Sports model, with the option of a Touring version built along more or less similar lines to the 293cc model. All these models had all-chain drive, and in the case of the 350cc models, there was the option of 349cc Blackburne or Bradshaw engines. Top of the range was a 976cc twin cylinder Sports model, which could also be obtained in touring trim.

THE JAP BULLETIN.

November, 1922.

Issued by

J. A. PRESTWICH & CO., LTD.
NORTHUMBERLAND PARK, TOTTENHAM, ENG.

Manufacturers of the famous J.A.P. Engines.

J. A. PARAGRAPHS.

"The Matchless J.A.P.", says an announcement. We have always known it.

*   .   *

From a rider who is evidently anxious to collect as many gold medals as possible next season we have received an enquiry for a J.A.P. engine " made throughout of high speed steel."

*   *

Would-be speed merchants who are prone to drill the internal parts of their J.A.P. engines in an endeavour to make the power output more than ever phenomenal are warned that there is a difference between tuning and " chew "-ning.

*   *   *

An objection we have heard raised against the J.A.P. engine is that, the flywheel being internal, the legend " P.T.O." cannot be painted on in order to induce revs. For a slight extra charge, however, we are prepared to stamp these letters on the fly wheel during the assembly of the engine, and it will be obvious to every thinking motor cyclist that this method will ensure much more permanent results than mere paint.

We wish to contradict a rumour that J.A.P. engines run better on alcohol. On the contrary, it is apt to make the pistons tight.

*

Young Hopeful : " I wish you were like the piston of Daddy's new J.A.P. engine, Mother." Mother : " Whatever for ? " Y. H. : " I heard him say it does'nt slap."

*

" Why do you Prestwich people call your motors ' British and Best ' ? " writes " Indignant." " My son, who went to the Brooklands Championship Meeting, told me that nearly everything was won by the Japs." Quite right, " Indignant," but the J.A.P.'s from London north east, not the Far East.

*

A customer who sent his J.A.P. engine in for overhaul " after several years' hard work " writes to tell us that meanwhile he is re-enamelling his machine, and concludes by asking : " When I have lined the tank, can I stick the transfer on myself ? " Of course, he can if he really wants to, but it is more usual to stick it on the tank.

The November 1922 issue of the JAP Bulletin, a factory-issued publication that contained jokes, hints likely to be of use to owners of JAP-engined machines, and news of the latest JAP competition successes. (Ken Hodgson)

THE HOME OF THE J.A.P. ENGINE.—"British and Best."

Telegrams :
Prestwich, Tottlane, London.
Code, A B C, 5th Edition.

Telephone:
Tottenham 1612
(3 Lines).

J. A. PRESTWICH & Co., Ltd. (Contractors to the War Office), Northumberland Park, Tottenham, London, England.

The factory published a comprehensive booklet each year which provided technical information about their range of engines. The issues of the twenties contained this artist's impression of the Northumberland Park Works in Tariff Road. (Douglas Prestwich)

8 H.P.
Brough
Superior
MARK 1.

The Mark 1 Brough Superior of 1922, which was fitted with an 8hp ohv vee-twin JAP engine.

PV offered a 293cc JAP-engined model, which could be ordered with a 350cc Villiers engine, if the purchaser so desired. The 349cc model could be obtained with either a JAP or a Barr and Stroud sleeve valve engine. Coventry-Eagle had three JAP-engined models, 293cc and 550cc singles, as well as a very impressive-looking 976cc Super Sports model. Zenith had on offer a 349cc JAP-powered mediumweight model fitted with a three-speed Sturmey Archer gearbox and a frame that would also accept the standard 293cc JAP single. They, too, had a 976cc Sports model, newly introduced, fitted with the Super Sports vee-twin JAP engine. Last to announce their plans in 1922 was Trump Motors, who claimed their latest 70 x 90mm 346cc JAP-engined model had been developed as a result of Brooklands experience. Their factory was in Byfleet, only just down the road! Also available from Trump was a 488cc JAP-engined model fitted with a close ratio Sturmey Archer gearbox, and two JAP-engined vee twins of 770cc and 976cc capacity.

As the year drew to a close, it was apparent that the British-made big twins were offering a more than serious challenge to the American twins that had made the running in the larger capacity classes for so long. But the smaller, single cylinder JAP engines were having to face up to quite a serious challenge from Blackburne, even the new sports engines with their large diameter valves and ports. The ohv Blackburne design had the edge over the side valve JAP in some speed events, although this situation was due to change in favour of the Tottenham factory, as following events will show.

Indian motorcycles in Springfield, Massachusetts. He joined their London Depot, and to use his own words, he helped 'to lick the eight valve Indian into shape'. It was the struggle between Harley-Davidson and Indian to have the first machine to attain 100mph in England that caused him his greatest disappointment. When the struggle reached its climax during the spring of 1921, he had already made an unofficial run over the kilometre at 103mph, and looked like being able to repeat it whilst officially timed, after Harley-Davidson had failed at their first attempt. But a miscalculation about the expansion rate of vital engine components caused a cam follower to break and smash the timing case during his timed run, shedding a push rod in the process. Although he worked all night to get the engine repaired in time for another run the following day, there was a misunderstanding as to when the time-keepers would be available. The next he heard was that the 100mph record had been taken by his rivals.

The news so upset him that he decided to quit motorcycle racing altogether and concentrate on experimental engineering. But the following morning he was told by his boss, Billy Wells, that the timekeepers would be ready if he would like to attempt the kilometre record. This he did, raising the one-way runs record to 106.65mph, and later to 107.55mph. Yet the machine he used was an old track racer, made in 1912.

It was during the 500 Mile Race at Brooklands held during July 1921 that he realised the British-made big twin had a terrific potential, and that he could help place it at the top, where it deserved to be. In consequence he wrote to John Prestwich offering his services, which the latter gladly accepted. Le Vack claimed it was from a suggestion made by John himself that the dohc engine he used in the TT during 1922 was evolved. It was a last minute decision to run the engine in the TT, such that it was not possible to give New Imperial any indication of what power output could be expected. He went to the Isle of Man with an untried engine and no discredit was due to New Imperial for the unforeseen problem that put him out of the race when he was doing so well.

Le Vack was very much in favour of using alcohol-based fuels in racing and made no secret of the source from which he obtained his supplies, a London distillery. He also stressed the value of racing, with reference to the benefits that eventually passed to the ordinary motorcyclist. He considered Brooklands to be an ideal testing ground.

Finally, it was his wish to acknowledge all the help he had received from his friends, especially his mechanic, Sid Moram, and A.V. Ebblewhite, the never-failing timekeeper.

An announcement made during February by the B.A.T. Motor Manufacturing Co. confirmed their intention to fit engines of JAP manufacture only, the model range comprising a 346cc single and two twins of 678cc and 976cc, the last being a de luxe model designed for sidecar use. Sadly, the company was now on the decline, with only three more years to go before they faded from the motorcycle scene for ever. They still used their distinctive cylindrical petrol tank and were finished in their characteristic grey, but they no longer featured saddle and footrests sprung in unison, to give the comfort of a spring frame.

An unusual feature in the 22nd February issue of *The Motor Cycle* was an account of a visit to the JAP factory, it being considered that a factory in which only engines were made would have special equipment not generally seen elsewhere. The reporter was not disappointed either, for he discovered that newly-completed engines were run in for 8-10 hours at 800rpm from external shafting, after being copiously lubricated with oil. After this stage had been completed, they passed to the test shop where they were brake tested, using either a fan brake or one of the Heenan and Froude type from which readings could be taken. Presumably the latter brake was used for the more sporting type of engines so that a performance curve could be plotted. In such a case, readings were taken at 1600, 2000, 2400, 2800, 3200 and 3600rpm, the engine being run for a few seconds only to enable such readings to be made. Whatever method of brake testing was used, the final stage was to dismantle and inspect each engine, prior to reassembly and dispatch.

For the 1923 season, 22 manufacturers were listed as having at least one JAP-engined model in their range: Brough Superior, Campion, Coventry-Eagle, DOT, Francis-Barnett, Hazlewood, Hobart, Matchless, Morgan, New Imperial, Omega, PV, Rex-Acme, Rover, Sharratt, TB (three-wheeler), Trump, Vindec, Zenith, Mars, Wolf and Le Vack. One assumes the last relates to the machines prepared by Le Vack himself which were ridden by others at Brooklands and similar venues. The Le Vack as such was never a production machine, even in very limited numbers.

At the end of March, Coventry Eagle announced their answer to the Brough Superior SS80 — the Flying Eight. Resembling the Brough in some respects, the Flying Eight also was fitted with a special 976cc side valve vee-twin JAP engine, and guaranteed to have a maximum speed of at least 80mph.

Arthur Church with a side valve vee-twin engine on dynamometer test. (Photo: Dr. J. D. Alderson)

CHAPTER NINE

Little had so far been published about the JAP factory's plans for the 1923 season, so it was with some interest that their first announcement was received during the first week in April. Big news was the introduction of an entirely new 346cc single, designed for use in sporting and fast touring machines. With bore and stroke dimensions of 74 x 80mm, the new engine had a detachable hemispherical cylinder head, with overhead valves made from tungsten steel. The valves were of semi-tulip pattern and used tapered collets with a retaining circlip for safety, to hold the valve spring caps and their double springs in position. The valve springs were kept insulated from the cylinder head by specially-shaped spacers. The rocker arms were one-piece steel stampings, mounted on long sleeves over stationary spindles. They relied upon wicks for lubrication. The push rods were hollow, with brazed-on cupped ends and enclosed return springs. The tappets were hollow too, and the cam followers incorporated rollers in the bearing surface. The big-end assembly was of the roller bearing type, and an alloy piston with domed crown was fitted. The cylinder head and barrel were generously finned, the former being retained to the crankcase by a bolt-through arrangement. The inlet port was arranged at one side, to provide clearance for the down tube of a frame, and the single 1¾ inch diameter exhaust port was slightly offset, too. Valve timing was; Inlet 10/40° and Exhaust 45/15°. Ignition advance was 3/8 inch BTDC, fully advanced.

Although neither Stan Greening or Bert Le Vack had one of the new engines in the machines they used at the Essex MC's Kop Hill Climb held during early April, they had an unparalleled run of success, Stan winning 9 classes with a 248cc Francis-Barnett and a 348cc Coventry-Eagle, each with a sidecar attached. Bert rode what was listed as a 249cc JAP and a 349cc Zenith JAP, both dohc and using a Zenith diamond frame, to win a further 5 classes. But that was not all. E.B. Ware had entered a 980cc Morgan JAP, too, and he won all three 1100cc events.

A road test of an SS80 Brough Superior and sidecar made interesting reading, even if such tests were always cautious in offering serious criticism, for fear of losing advertising revenue. The tester claimed he liked the riding position and the location of the controls, and found the exhaust note 'not loud but reassuring'. Unfortunately a baulked run up Porlock Hill caused the clutch to burn out, necessitating emergency repairs at Pikes Garage in Exeter. But this setback seemed not to discourage him, such that he reported the machine was very comfortable to ride, thanks to the Brooks cantilever saddle and the Brampton forks. The brakes were excellent too, the only criticism being levelled at the fuel consumption which was described as 'fairly heavy'.

The Public Schoolboys Meeting held at Brooklands on 14th April marked the debut at the track of another of John Prestwich's sons — E.S. Prestwich, known more familiarly as Teddy. Riding a 349cc Le Vack JAP, he won the first handicap race of the day at 57.71mph. In the 350cc scratch race he finished second on a 349cc New Imperial JAP, being one of only 5 starters. He also rode in the one lap handicap race for machines with a top speed exceeding 50mph, in which he finished 3rd on the same machine.

About this time, New Imperial announced a cheaper version of their very successful Light Tourist model, which would be recognizable by an all-black petrol tank finish, revised silencing arrangements and abbreviated mudguards. They, too, recognised the need to market an economy model, and this was reflected in the retail price of the new machine, which was listed at £55.13s.

The 26th April issue of *The Motor Cycle* published a road test of the New Imperial 976cc vee-twin, fitted with a sidecar. The tester considered the steering qualities to equal those of many lightweights and found that best results were achieved when carrying a 10 stone passenger in the sidecar. The outfit was good at hill climbing and possessed a good rear brake. But the front brake was not quite up to expectations, no doubt due to its somewhat small diameter. The JAP engine had an output of 30bhp and, not unsurprisingly, proved quite powerful. At the other end of the scale, it would tick over evenly at quite low speed. When cold, the valve gear proved noisy and there was some piston slap, unwelcome noises that fortunately all but disappeared when the engine had reached normal working temperature. Typical of the tests conducted during the twenties and indeed the thirties it was very bland and devoid of any really harsh criticism. In consequence, readers learnt to 'read between the lines' and regard the comments much as one would when reading an estate agent's description of a house.

The Heenan and Froude Dynamometer at Northumberland Park. Note the motor driven fan used to prevent engines on test from overheating. (Photo: Dr. J. D. Alderson)

Massey Motorcycles announced the addition of a 293cc JAP-engined model to their range, fitted with a two-speed Sturmey Archer gearbox having both a clutch and a kickstarter. Webb front forks formed part of the general specification and there was no front brake, two independently operated brakes being arranged to share the rear brake rim in order to comply with legal requirements. The machine was to retail at £45, but it is doubtful if many were sold as the company was still inclined to move premises at frequent intervals.

Another road test of a machine powered by a large capacity vee-twin JAP engine was published in the 3rd May issue of *The Motor Cycle*. In this instance the machine concerned, a 976cc Zenith JAP, was retained in solo form, which must have given the tester a quite exciting ride. Despite favourable comment on the riding position and the abnormally low petrol consumption recorded, criticism was levelled at quite a number of *167* items. For example, the rear brake was not too good and heavy to operate, this being of the dummy belt rim type. Gear changing was not too easy either, the quadrant being mounted low down on the saddle tube so that it was too low for hand change and too high for foot operation. The front brake made up for the deficiencies of the rear brake, but apart from this, the controls were stiff to operate, whilst the Amac carburetter seemed incapable of providing a satisfactory tickover. One wonders whether Zenith Motors did not spend much on advertising in the magazine concerned, in view of the fact that the tester was less hesitant that usual in offering criticism.

The so-called Century Races were held at Brooklands on 5th May, the name being coined from the 100 mile Junior and Senior Races intended to attract those who wished to try out their TT mounts in advance of their departure to the Isle of Man. Few were tempted, yet although Bert Le Vack turned out, he had a not too successful day. Having worked up to second place in the Junior Race, his 344cc New Imperial JAP developed unspecified trouble, which forced him to retire. In the Senior Race, he brought the 424cc New Imperial JAP to the line, one of its rare appearances before it was decided to abandon further development of this larger capacity dohc engine. It had bore and stroke dimensions of 75 x 96mm and had little more power than the very successful 344cc engine. He was unable to make any impression on the Douglas twin ridden by Vic Anstice, and had to be content with second place. In the 250cc Solo event, Bert Kershaw upheld JAP honours by finishing second on his 248cc New Imperial JAP. W. Weaver was third, on a Sirrah JAP.

As far as the 1923 TT was concerned, the news of most interest was the inclusion for the first time of a sidecar race, which attracted some interesting entries. The Montgomery works decided to enter two outfits, one to be ridden by W.J. Montgomery and the other by J.A. Scally. Their specification included a 599cc side valve single JAP engine, a development of the standard 550cc side valve single brought about by lengthening the stroke by 11mm to give dimensions of 85 x 104mm and the desired increase in capacity. Fitted with ball race main bearings, a roller bearing big-end and an aluminium alloy piston with a fully floating gudgeon pin, the new engine produced maximum power at 3,600rpm. It was used in conjunction with a close ratio, three-speed Sturmey Archer gearbox, the two machines being built to an identical specification.

A fortnight later, the Tottenham factory disclosed their plans for their 250cc and 350cc TT engines, which were to be based on the new ohv design described earlier in this Chapter. The most fundamental change was the substitution of a twin port cylinder head on which the rocker spindles were supported in roller races, rather than being mounted on long sleeves over stationary spindles. Not so obvious was a change made in the specification of the steels from which the valves were made. Tungsten steel was now specified for the exhaust valve, and steel with a high chromium content for the inlet valve. These engines were fitted with a 9 ounce aluminium alloy piston with a domed crown, to give a compression ratio of 6:1. Furthermore, the timing gear had been modified to use a single camshaft with two roller-ended cam followers. In most other respects the TT engines resembled the production sports engines, in having a roller bearing big-end, a ball bearing on the drive side of the crankshaft, and a plain bearing for the timing side. With bore and stroke dimensions of 62.5 x 80mm and 74 x 80mm respectively, they produced peak power at 4,800rpm.

Whilst preparations were going ahead in the Isle of Man, Zenith Motors announced two new singles, one of which would feature the new 344 ohv JAP engine. This machine would be classified as their Fast Tourer. The other model was named the Zenith Three, and used the 346cc side valve engine, in conjunction with a three-speed Sturmey Archer gearbox. The weight of this latter machine had been pared down to 190lb, which meant it would be eligible for the concessionary 30/- tax.

On Friday, 18th May, Le Vack took his 344cc New Imperial JAP to Brooklands for a record breaking session. His bid was successful too, as he was able to claim the following new records:

50 miles at 78.61mph
100 miles at 77.87mph
200 miles at 77.71mph
1 hour at 77.68mph
2 hours at 77.59mph

These records were all the more remarkable when it was discovered that his new 2 hours record exceeded the speed of the existing 500cc record, giving him the unexpected bonus of yet another record to his name. But he was not so lucky at the Third Monthly Race Meeting held at the track on 26th May. He was forced to retire in the 350cc Solo Scratch Race in which he had entered his 344cc New Imperial JAP, and also in the later 1,000cc Solo Scratch Race when his 998cc Zenith JAP failed too. It was Stan Greening who put up the best performance of the JAP-engined riders at this meeting, when he took two second places with his 346cc Francis-Barnett JAP in the 350cc Solo Handicap, and with sidecar attached, in the 600cc Passenger Handicap race. At this meeting, E.B. Ware was observed with a new 90° air-cooled JAP twin fitted to his Morgan three-wheeler.

The Essex MC's meeting at Brooklands on 2nd June had only three motorcycle races in the programme, this being a combined car and motorcycle event. Despite the fact that Oliver Baldwin and Claude Temple took part in this meeting, both were unable to overcome their handicaps, which was fortunate for Vivian Prestwich, who won the 1,200cc Solo 3 Lap Handicap on what was described in the programme as a 344cc Le Vack JAP. Le Vack himself was not present at this meeting as, like most of the other big names, he was already in the Isle of Man for the now imminent TT races.

Having again entered his dohc New Imperial JAP, now listed as having a cubic capacity of 346cc, it was expected that he would be up amongst the race leaders in the Junior Race. And he did not disappoint the spectators either. At the end of the first lap he was lying third, working himself up into second place by the end of the second lap. He then stormed ahead to take the lead on the third lap, which he held until unspecified mechanical troubles put him out of the race during the fifth lap, just beyond Ballacraine. Once again his luck has deserted him. In consequence, the first JAP-engined finisher in the Junior race was George Tottey, who finished eighth, with Bert Kershaw in fifteenth place and T. Cordiner in twenty fourth — all riding New Imperial JAPs. Fortunately, it was quite different story when it came to the Lightweight race, when Le Vack appeared on his 245cc New Imperial JAP, using the smaller version of the dohc engine. After lying sixth on the first lap, he started to work his way up amongst the race leaders and eventually finished second, the winner being Jock Porter on a New Gerrard. It proved to be the only occasion on which Le Vack finished in a TT race on the Isle of Man, whilst riding a machine fitted with a JAP engine. L. Horton finished sixth, C.F. Edwards sixteenth and M. Isaac eighteenth, all on New Imperial JAPs, which tended to suggest the superiority of this marque when it came to staying power. Unfortunately, neither George Tottey nor Bert Kershaw were lucky on this occasion, neither managing to complete the course.

When interviewed after the Lightweight race, it was obvious that Bert Le Vack was not in the best of health. The onset of 'flu had resulted in blurred vision and then a splitting headache as the race progressed. Fortunately the machine caused him very little worry, apart from a tendency to misfire in the mist on Snaefell. He had 'two near goes' during the race, one when his head very nearly hit the wall at Ballacraine. It was quite remarkable that he managed to finish in second place when he felt so poorly and was unable to concentrate, which may explain why he never offered a serious challenge to the race leader. Certainly his machine went well. The engine had never been run on the road before he left for the Island, yet he had averaged 51.014mph in the race and had put up some very fast times during practice. Obviously he was in no fit state to start in the Senior race, for which he had also entered his 346cc New Imperial JAP. By then his 'flu had developed, so he stood down and let D.E. Calder take over his entry. Calder finshed nineteenth, in what can only be described as quite terrible weather conditions. Meanwhile, Le Vack left the Island for France, hoping he would be in better shape to ride a Terrot JAP in the French Grand Prix. But it was not to be and to his disappointment this was another entry he had to scratch.

Bert Le Vack with the 1923 350cc dohc model at a sprint meeting in 1923. Note the offset arrangement of the twin exhaust ports and the hand-operated oil pump on the fuel tank. (Photo: Dr. J. D. Alderson)

The Sidecar race was full of disappointment for the two Montgomery entries, mentioned earlier. Somehow, Scally managed to run into the rear of Montgomery's outfit during the first lap, whilst he was trying to overtake. The collision badly bent Scally's front forks, which brought about his early retirement. Montgomery struggled on with his outfit, which now had a badly damaged sidecar that looked as though it was about to shed its body and the unfortunate passenger within. But the decision whether or not to continue was made for Montgomery when an engine defect caused him to drop out on the second lap.

Looking back on the 1923 TT races, it was interesting to find that a machine fitted with a proprietary engine had won the Junior and the Lightweight races, the engine concerned being an ohv Blackburne design in both instances. Furthermore, it had not escaped Le Vack's observation that an ohc vertical twin Peugeot had offered serious challenge at the French Grand Prix, when it led for thirteen consecutive laps. Designed by M. Antoinesco, it was seen by many as the first real challenge to British supremecy — and an early start to the controversy of whether a single or a multi had the best to offer.

Meanwhile, JAP racing successes continued to mount, not only in the UK but on the Continent and throughout the Commonwealth too. A JAP advertisement in the 12th July issue of *The Motor Cycle* announced the following achievements:

North London MCC Hill Climb
Fastest time (solo)
N.W. District
Fastest time (sidecar)
Great German Road Race
1st (Amateur Class)
Easter Trials of the MCC of South Australia
100 Mile Race: 1st, and South Australian Championship

As the advertising slogan said — 'Universal and World Wide are the Performances of the World's Best'.

Back from the TT, it was George Tottey's opportunity to show his tuning and riding skills, when he put up an outstanding performance in front of a crowd of 5,000 in the 50 Mile Race Meeting held on Southport sands during July. Riding his 350cc New Imperial JAP, his name figured prominently in six of the classes, as follows:

Class 4 350cc Novice 1st
Class 5 350cc General 3rd
Class 6 500cc Novice 2nd
Class 7 750cc General 1st
Class 8 750cc Novice 2nd
Class 10 Unlimited Novice 2nd

George was an interesting character who at one time was studying at Manchester University so that he could take up employment in the dyestuffs industry, gaining a B.Sc. with Honours. But difficulty in getting a job after he left University led to him joining Zenith Motors, where initially he worked in the Assembly Department. Soon, he graduated to working on Freddie Barnes' own bikes, which in turn led to an interest in racing. Eventually, he returned home to the Wirral, where he opened up his garage during early 1922. He developed a natural aptitude for racing and was a frequent visitor to Brooklands, as well as to other speed venues, always riding New Imperials. He remained faithful to the marque and visited the JAP factory in Tottenham on a number of occasions, sometimes staying at the home of John Prestwich. He knew Bert Le Vack quite well too, and received some welcome assistance from him. An interesting account of his racing career is given in the book *Brooklands: Behind the Scenes* by Charles Mortimer (Haynes/Foulis), based on a taped interview he gave the author a few years prior to his death.

Just a week or so after Tottey's Southport successes, N.P. Metcalf won the Leinster 100 on a 976cc Brough Superior. He enjoyed an epic battle with Norton-mounted Graham Walker, and was fortunate enough to finish 12 seconds ahead of this famous rider, which was no small feat. Whilst this was happening, B.S. Allen was thrilling the crowds with a similar mount at the Brighton Speed Trials, where he won three classes.

Saturday, 21st July marked the occasion of the 200 Mile Solo Race Meeting at Brooklands, organised by the BMCRC. The proceedings opened with the 250cc Solo Race, in which Bert Kershaw finished third on his New Imperial JAP. The 350cc Solo Race proved much more exciting when Le Vack, who had led from the start on his 344cc New Imperial JAP, had to ride to his pit on the wheel rim when his rear tyre burst during the 7th lap. Undeterred, a new tyre was fitted and Le Vack re-entered the race, lapping at over 80mph and slowly carving his way back through the field. Despite losing two more laps out on the circuit whilst changing a plug and clearing a blocked jet in the carburetter, he eventually passed the race leader, George Tottey, to win at an average speed of 72.66mph. But his best performance was yet to come. In the 200 Mile 1,000cc race, Le Vack appeared on a new 996cc Brough Superior JAP. Completed only just in time, and with little opportunity to practice, the Brough lapped consistently at over 88mph. Despite a serious challenge from Freddie Dixon and his Harley-Davidson, the Brough Superior crossed the line first, well ahead of his rival, to record a race average of 83.34mph. Not so lucky in this race was J.E.G. Harwood, who crashed his Zenith JAP.

Interviewed soon after his 200 Mile Race victory, Le Vack disclosed he had not collected the Brough Superior frame from Nottingham until the Monday before the race meeting, such that it had been necessary to work all week to get the machine prepared in time. The engine he was using was an 80 x 99mm KTR side valve twin of 996cc capacity, fitted with 1¾ inch diameter valves, undrilled aluminium alloy pistons fitted with only two rings each. A two-speed Sturmey Archer gearbox gave gear ratios of 3:1 and 6:1. It is alleged the Brough Superior was prepared by Sid Moram, aided by Bill Tilby, Le Vack's other mechanic. Le Vack himself was busy getting his New Imperial ready, which was fitted with the 344cc engine he had used in the 1923 Junior TT.

Having ridden each machine in a 200 mile race, Bert Le Vack had covered 400 miles in just 5 hours, 9 minutes faster than the Class E record for this distance — not bad when one considers the bumpy nature of the track and the need for regular pit stops to refuel and replenish the oil. On rare occasions like this, it is a great relief not to have to worry about developing faults, although in the case of the 350cc race, some slick work had been called for to get the rear tyre replaced and the New Imperial back into the race without losing too much time.

The 9th August issue of *The Motor Cycle* contained a road test of the spring frame 976cc Matchless, which had a sidecar with a sprung wheel attached. This was another of the large capacity twins to be fitted with the Super Sports vee-twin JAP engine. The tester claimed the outfit served as a reminder that Britain had not lost the art of making big twins and that the Matchless had the ability to maintain high average speeds in reasonable comfort. He could not be sure whether some unpleasant drumming in the footboards could be attributed to an out of balance engine, or by the construction of the footboards and the legshields that were fitted to this particular machine. Most other

Left:
The 74 x 80mm 350cc dohc engine with which Bert Le Vack won two 200 mile races in one day on July 21st, 1923. It is now owned by an Austrian enthusiast. (Photo: Dr. H. Krackowizer)

Right:
The cylinder head, vertical coupling and bevel drive assembly of the 1923 350cc dohc engine. (Photo: Dr. H. Krackowizer)

comments applied to the outfit as a whole rather than the JAP engine, although there was mention of the somewhat novel linking of the valve lifter with the kickstarter.

Also in the same issue was a mention of the Mohawk JAP, a single cylinder machine fitted with a 293cc side valve single. Made by the Mohawk Cycle Company, of North London, this name was no newcomer to the industry, having made motorcycles soon after the start of the century. After fading from the scene they reappeared with this new JAP-engined model, but by 1926 they had disappeared again, this time for good.

Another somewhat rare make — the P&P — was also given some space in this issue, with a brief description of two models. One was fitted with the 293cc side valve JAP single and the other featured the new 344cc ohv single, the engine being mounted in a forward sloping position. The P&P had a particularly good duplex frame and a rather unusual rear end, in which the rear wheel spindle ran 'live'. The gearbox was a three-speed Moss, and a distinctive feature was the use of a flanged casting to join the exhaust

173

pipe to the cylinder head of the engine, thus obviating the use of the very large nut used by most other manufacturers. As far as possible, the nut sizes on the machines had been standardized, so that maintenance and overhauls would require only a small tool kit. One further unusual feature was an oddly-shaped cast aluminium alloy silencer, with a detachable side plate to allow access to the baffles for cleaning. Yet for all this, the P&P sold in quite small numbers and is today one of motorcycling's curiosities.

Towards the end of August, the JAP factory announced they were to make a small capacity two-stroke engine to augment their range, in the hope that they would be able to sell to the lower end of the market. To be marketed under the trade name Aza (from whence the name came is a mystery), the engine was of the three-port, deflector piston, type with bore and stroke dimensions of 55 x 62mm, giving a cubic capacity of 147cc. Of simple construction, it had an overhung crankshaft, the connecting rod having a roller bearing big-end and a plain bush small end. The piston was held by a gudgeon pin that was retained by two split pins. Marketing was to be handled by the Aza Motor Co, of Capel House, 62, New Broad Street, London, E.C.2.

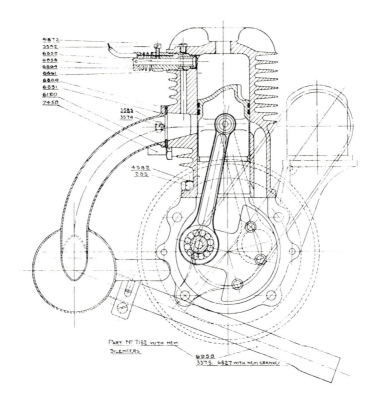

A sectional line drawing of the Aza two-stroke engine, showing its general arrangement. (Peter Sparkes)

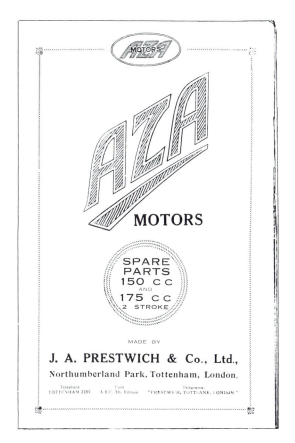

The cover of the catalogue for the Aza two-stroke engines that were announced towards the end of August 1923. Initially, only the 150ccc engine was available. (Peter Sparkes)

Saturday, 25th August marked the occasion of the 200 Mile Sidecar Races organised by the Ealing and District MCC at Brooklands. In the 350cc race, V. Baxter brought his Rex-Acme JAP outfit into second place at a speed of 54.53mph, with J.A. Bowles taking third place on a 344cc Zenith JAP at 50.93mph. Stan Greening finished fifth with a sidecar attached to a P&P JAP, a make of machine not usually associated with his name. Earlier troubles had slowed him up during the opening stages of the race. It was the 1,000cc race that drew the most attention, when Le Vack came to the line with a sidecar attached to his 996cc Brough Superior JAP, this being the machine he had ridden so successfully in the 200 mile solo race just over a month previously. Never seriously challenged after taking the lead on the third lap, and lapping at a consistent 76mph, he won at an average speed of 75.32mph, some 5mph faster than Claude Temple who brought his Harley-Davidson outfit into second place. In so doing, he set new Class G records for 1,000cc sidecars for 50 - 200 miles, and for 1 - 2 hours. His results can be summarised as follows:

50 miles 79.37mph
100 miles 77.82mph
200 miles 75.32mph
1 hour 77.73mph
2 hours 75.93mph

It is worth recording that R. Charlesworth came fourth on a Zenith JAP. He was   *175* the first amateur to finish, and received a special award.

On 9th September, Le Vack and Moram took the two dohc New Imperial JAP machines to France at the invitation of one of the French clubs, for some record breaking attempts. Riding the 245cc machine in the Bois de Boulogne, Le Vack raised the flying kilometre record to 83.16mph, which sadly was not ratified by the FICM as a World's Record and stood as a British Record only. Transferring to the 346cc model, he raised the 350cc record to a staggering 96.5mph — these being the mean speeds for two-way runs. Fortunately for Le Vack, this Class B record was subsequently ratified by the FICM as a World's Record.

A fortnight later at the Luton Speed Trials, a very wet meeting, Bert Kershaw won the 250cc Expert class, the runner-up being A. Swan, both riding New Imperial JAPs. In the 350cc General class the honours went to C.W.G. Lacey, on a 348cc Cotton JAP, R.G. Hickman taking second place on an OK JAP. When it came to the Sidecar class, Stan Greening won both the 350 and 600cc Expert categories, using what was classified as a 350cc JAP. On that very same day, in Northern Ireland, Jimmy Shaw won the 350cc class of the Ulster Grand Prix on a 348cc Zenith JAP, at an average speed of 60.02mph. He also put up the fastest lap in the 350cc class, the event taking the form of a handicap race with the 250cc, 350cc and 500cc classes being run concurrently.

An interesting photograph appeared in the 20th September issue of *The Motor Cycle,* which showed the 346cc Coventry-Eagle JAP Stan Greening had ridden in the recently-held ACU Six Days Trial. A collision with a car during the event had bent the front forks quite severely, so that the wheels were six inches out of line. Yet Stan continued to ride and even managed to average 40.9mph during the speed test! His determination to see the event through was rewarded by winning a Gold Medal.

The 1923 Olympia Show had quite a number of JAP-engined models on display, as the following list will show. The figures in brackets indicate the number of JAP-engined models in the manufacturer's range, all of them not necessarily being on view during exhibition time:

Omega (1), Grindlay-Peerless (1), Wolf (4), Matchless (2), Excelsior (3), New Imperial (6), Zenith (4), Diamond (20), Calthorpe (1), Hobart (2), DOT (1), Mohawk (2), Coventry-Eagle (3), Verus and Sirrah (3).

Just prior to Show, a new Brough Superior JAP was announced, which was fitted with a new 976cc side valve Super Sports engine that had twin camshafts. It featured mechanical lubrication and used a frame similar to that used by Le Vack for his recent record breaking attempts.

When plans were announced for the 1924 season by the Tottenham factory, it was explained that all engines would henceforth use a new mechanical lubrication system, with the exception of the old 293cc side valve single. The complete range of engines would comprise the following:

64.5 x 76mm	248cc side valve sports single
62.5 x 80mm	248cc ohv sports single
70 x 76mm	293cc side valve single
70 x 90mm	346cc side valve, standard and sports singles
74 x 80mm	344cc ohv sports and racing singles
85.5 x 104mm	599cc side valve single
85.5 x 85mm	488cc side valve, standard and sports singles
64.5 x 76mm	496cc side valve twin
70 x 88mm	680cc side valve twin
76 x 85mm	788cc side valve twin
85.5 x 85mm	976cc side valve twin

There was also a brief note about the new 976cc racing engine — the twin camshaft type that was to be used by Brough Superior. Each timing wheel would have two cams — this being the famous 4 cam side valve twin.

With regard to the new lubrication system, it took the form of a piston-type oil pump bolted to the timing cover and so arranged that the flow rate could be controlled by simple adjustment. The pump delivered oil from a separate oil tank to the crankcase, two large holes in the crankcase walls ensuring oil reached a sump in the timing case by splash feed. The outlet from this sump was arranged so that the main timing pinion ran continuously in oil, oil being forced down the outlet by means of the air displaced by the pistons on their downward stroke. Oil from the outlet passed into the oil box at the base of the crankcase, via four disc valves, and as soon as the air in the box reached atmospheric pressure, and there was negative pressure in the timing case and crankcase, the oil rose to be drawn out of the box through the mainshaft ball bearing to the big-end. If desired, a release could be arranged to blow oil on to the primary chain.

Now that the JAP vee-twin engines were becoming more and more powerful, frame problems were beginning to occur simply because frame design had not kept pace. The advent of the Coventry-Eagle Flying Eight, which could now be obtained with either the Super Sports or Special Sports JAP engine fitted, called for a frame of more substantial construction that would not flex unduly and give rise to handling problems. The Coventry-Eagle design team rose to the occasion and produced an entirely new design in which the upper tubes of the rear chainstays were duplicated as were the lower tank tubes. Apart from the big twin, their range now included four mediumweights, with the options of a JAP or a Blackburne ohv engine, or their side valve equivalents.

Having won the 250cc Solo Scratch Race at the Sixth BMCRC Race Meeting at Brooklands on 22nd September at 64.93mph on a 246cc New Imperial JAP, the 1,000cc Sidecar Scratch Race on his 996cc Brough Superior JAP at 80.72mph, then the two lap 350cc and 500cc Solo Handicaps with his 346cc New Imperial JAP at 64.81 and 82.31mph respectively, Le Vack was back again for the BMCRC Championship Meeting on 20th October. In the 350cc Sidecar Championship he had to concede victory to one of his greatest rivals, Dougal Marchant, finishing second with what is listed in *The Motor Cycle* as a 349cc New Imperial JAP. Mechanical problems eliminated him from the 250cc Solo Championship, but in the 350 Solo Championship he defeated the legendary George Dance to win at 85.13mph, on the New Imperial JAP.

It was Le Vack's machine that drew most attention when he came to the line for the 1,000cc Solo Championship race. Instead of his usual Brough Superior, he had a Zenith, fitted with one of the new 80 x 99mm ohv racing engines. Unfortunately, a bout of plug trouble relegated him to third place, but he made amends in the 1,000 Sidecar race that followed, which he won at 83.70mph. Interviewed after the race, Le Vack was able to give a more detailed description of the engine, which embodied quite a number of interesting features.

The engine was fitted with detachable cylinder heads, each having ball bearing supports for the rockers. Both cylinder heads and barrels were generously finned and were retained to the crankcase by long holding-down bolts. They did not, however, thread into the crankcase. Instead, they screwed into 'T' pieces inside the crankcase mouth, which eliminated the possiblity of the bolts pulling out. Hollow cup-ended tappet rods were fitted, their lower ends encompassed by supplementary springs that worked against a bridge piece bolted to each cylinder base. The interior of the engine was standard, with two valves per cylinder and alloy pistons. The crankcase was, however, stiffened slightly on the primary drive side. A mechanical oil pump was fitted, and the characteristic JAP oil box dispensed with. The front forks, of standard Harley-

Le VACK
96 cc ZENITH
1923

Bert Le Vack with the ohv-engined 996cc Zenith JAP he rode in the BMCRC Championship Meeting at Brooklands on October 20th, 1923. Plug trouble relegated him to 3rd place in the 1,000 Solo Championship Race.

Davidson design, had Le Vack's own stabiliser fitted, and the frame was specially built for racing, with an extra stay from the bottom of the steering head to the top of the front down tube. A Schebler carburetter was fitted to the engine. Transmission was via a Sturmey Archer three-speed gearbox.

It was now possible to discover more information about the JAP oil pump, which was mounted on the magneto drive cover. It was driven off one of the cam wheels by a reduction worm, which gave one working stroke of the pump per 40 revolutions of the engine. The pump itself comprised a direct acting plunger, which drew oil from the separate oil tank and delivered it via a sight feed to the engine, whence it was circulated by the JAP automatic system. Delivery was regulated by an adjustable eccentric and a hand pump was retained for use during temporary burst of speed or in an emergency.

In the South East Clubs Meeting at Brooklands on 3rd November, an event organised by the Preston MCC and LCC of Brighton, the Club Secretary, H.A. Johnston, took part, riding a single port ohv 344cc Zenith JAP. He won the 350cc Solo

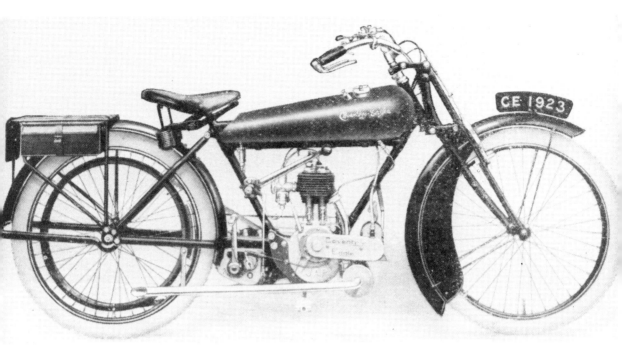

A catalogue illustration of the 1923 2¾ hp Coventry-Eagle fitted with the JAP side valve engine of that period.

At the other end of the scale in the 1923 Coventry-Eagle range was this 998cc vee-twin, fitted with a leaf spring front fork.

Scratch (Expert) and 350cc Solo Scratch (Expert Barred) races, the Sidecar Handicap and 1,000cc Solo Scratch (Expert Barred) races being won by A.T. Koehler on a 998cc Zenith JAP. E.S. Prestwich (246cc Zenith JAP) rode in this meeting too, finishing second in the 3 lap General Handicap event.

With Brooklands due to close for the customary winter repairs, Bert Le Vack took his 998cc Zenith JAP to the track on 9th November, to make a successful attempt on the standing start kilometre and mile records. He set up new Class E records for the kilometre at 73.34mph, and the mile at 82.27mph, making two-way runs on each occasion to qualify for a World's Record. There was still one day left before the track closed, so the Sunbury and District MCC made the most of it by running a meeting in near arctic conditions. E.S. Prestwich was third in the 250cc race, riding his 248 Zenith JAP. Joe Wright, another legendary name having a long association with the track, won the Unlimited Sidecar Handicap and Winners Handicap races, with a 344cc Zenith JAP sidecar outfit.

At the end of the month, a JAP advertisement was proud to proclaim that Bert Le Vack had again been awarded the Brooklands Aggregate, the most coveted award in the motorcycle world for gaining the most points in speed events at that famous circuit. It had gone to him for the second year in succession.

Another road test of the SS80 Brough Superior was published in the 6th December issue of *The Motor Cycle*, the machine having the 976cc Super Sports side valve JAP engine fitted. Again the tester found the low riding position and general balance gave a feeling of extreme confidence. A novelty was the use of a twist grip throttle instead of the usual twin levers, which seemed to blend in well with the smooth transmission and much smoother clutch. The machine, ridden in solo form, proved perfectly safe at speed, with no back wheel bounce or tendency to wobble. It was remarkably silent, due to a modification to the valve gear of the JAP vee twin engine and an improved silencer. The JAP engine liked to rev, yet the remarkable consumption of 90mpg was recorded during the test!

An analysis of the 1923 World's Records, as they applied to riders of JAP-engined machines, shows just how much they were dominated by Bert Le Vack. They were listed as follows:

Class A *(Solo motorcycles not exceeding 250cc)*

500 miles	B. Kershaw 249cc New Imperial	50.07mph
2 hours	H. Le Vack 245cc New Imperial	67.84mph
12 hours	Mrs. G. Janson 244cc Trump-JAP	46.33mph

Class B *(Solo motorcycles not exceeding 350cc)*

Flying start kilometre	H. Le Vack 344cc New Imperial	96.50mph
50 miles	H. Le Vack 344cc New Imperial	85.09mph
200 miles	H. Le Vack 344cc New Imperial	77.71mph

Class C *(Solo motorcycles not exceeding 500cc)*

200 miles	H. Le Vack 344cc New Imperial	77.71mph

Class E *(Solo motorcycles not exceeding 1,000cc)*

Standing start kilometre	H. Le Vack 996cc Zenith	73.34mph
Standing start mile	H. Le Vack 996cc Zenith	82.27mph
50 miles	H. Le Vack 996cc Zenith	91.71mph
100 miles	H. Le Vack 996cc Zenith	89.92mph
200 miles	H. Le Vack 996cc Brough Superior	83.34mph

| 1 hour | H. Le Vack 996cc Zenith | 89.90mph |
| 2 hours | H. Le Vack 996cc Brough Superior | 83.25mph |

Class B/s *(Sidecars not exceeding 350cc)*

| Flying start kilometre | H. Le Vack 344cc New Imperial | 77.40mph |

Class G *(Sidecars not exceeding 1,000cc)*

Flying start kilometre	H. Le Vack 996cc Zenith	90.38mph
Flying start mile	H. Le Vack 996cc Zenith	90.91mph
5 miles	H. Le Vack 996cc Zenith	88.27mph
10 miles	H. Le Vack 996cc Zenith	86.14mph
50 miles	H. Le Vack 996cc Zenith	79.37mph
100 miles	H. Le Vack 996cc Zenith	77.82mph
1 hour	H. Le Vack 996cc Zenith	77.73mph
2 hours	H. Le Vack 996cc Zenith	75.93mph

Class J1 *(750cc single seat cyclecars)*

10 miles	E.B. Ware 744cc Morgan	59.50mph
50 miles	E.B. Ware 744cc Morgan	47.52mph
1 hour	E.B. Ware 744cc Morgan	47.26mph

In addition to the World's records listed, Le Vack also held the following British short distance records:

Class A *(Solo motorcycles not exceeding 250cc)*

| Flying start kilometre | 249cc New Imperial | 83.16mph |

Class B *(Solo motorcycles not exceeding 350cc)*

| Flying start kilometre | 344cc New Imperial | 97.60mph* |
| Flying start mile | 344cc New Imperial | 91.88mph |

Class B/s *(Sidecars not exceeding 350cc)*

| Flying start kilometre | 346cc New Imperial | 77.94mph |

Class G *(Sidecars not exceeding 1,000cc)*

| Flying start kilometre | 998cc Zenith | 90.86mph |
| Flying start mile | 996cc Zenith | 92.68mph |

* *World record also*

The records held previously by the American big twins had been whittled down quite substantially, and of the few that remained, some could be attributed to Le Vack himself, who set them up before he joined JAP at Tottenham. There was now ample proof of the superiority of the British-made vee-twin when it came to out-and-out speed events, and of the JAP side valve and overhead valve designs in particular.

The single cylinder engines had also begun to offer a serious challenge, too, specially with the introduction of the new overhead valve designs from the JAP factory. According to Eric Corneliusen, a one-time sand racer who had his own JAP agency at Crosby, 12 miles from Southport, the sports singles from about 1920 onwards were well made and capable of high rpm. But good as they were, with their large valves and ports, and a light bi-metal piston, they lacked the good pulling power of their contemporaries and were not quite up to the challenge of the overhead valve Blackburnes. In consequence they had to be content with places only and rely on Castrol R as a lubricant, otherwise the cams and their followers would turn blue with heat and score badly, 100lb valve springs being in use at that time. But the introduction of the two-port ohv JAP single changed all that, to emerge as the dominant force. In two years his own 344cc engine won him 17 first, 6 seconds and 3 thirds, yet never broke a valve spring! And he was just one of many who put their faith in JAP, and helped the company achieve a level of success that has no parallel.

Chapter Ten

1924 – higher speeds and more records

HAVING SUCCESSFULLY introduced the new ohv engines to the racing fraternity and those who rode in events of a more sporting nature, there remained the need to have a similar type of engine available for the motorcyclist who might never ride in competitions, yet desired to have that little extra in road performance. In consequence, it was during January 1924 that the Tottenham factory announced what amounted to a 'cooking' version of the 344cc ohv single, which was capable of good performance yet was not necessarily intended for racing. In other words, an engine manufactured to a price the enthusiast who required better road performance could be expected to afford.

Having bore and stroke dimensions of 70 x 90mm, which gave a cubic capacity of 346cc, the engine comprised an ohv cylinder head and barrel mounted on the crankcase of the standard side valve engine. A modification proved necessary to the mouth of the crankcase assembly, to recess slightly the top baffles so that there would be sufficient clearance for the piston when it was at the bottom of its stroke. Apart from this, the crankcase contained the flywheels and timing gear of the side valve engine, which helped ensure its ohv counterpart was only 2⁹/₁₆ inch taller.

The rockers were of more simple design, wicks providing their means of lubrication. The valves in the detachable cylinder head were inclined at 34° and both were made from cobalt steel. The cylinder head was retained to the barrel by four bolts in the conventional manner, and the cylinder barrel to the crankcase by an additional four holding down bolts. Within the timing chest the timing gear was also of simple design, the crankshaft pinion being keyed to the mainshaft and secured by a locknut. Three separate keyways were provided so that the valve timing could be set with complete accuracy, the best position being punch marked. The cams were located at the rear of the camwheel, and employed cross-over followers. An internal valve lifter was fitted. The engine was supplied as standard with the JAP automatic oiling system, but if desired, a mechanical pump could be fitted. The engine produced 10-11bhp at 4,000 rpm and would give a claimed 60mph maximum solo, or 51mph with a sidecar attached.

Brief details were also given of a new 80 x 99mm ohv vee-twin, which was similar to that used so successfully by Bert Le Vack at the end of the previous year. The specification included ball bearing rockers and roller and ball bearings throughout the engine. It developed 31bhp and would be available for £100.

Described as the second most expensive motorcycle on the market, a road test in the 31st January issue of *The Motor Cycle* related to the latest Coventry Eagle Flying Eight, fitted with the redesigned frame, Druid front forks, wider mudguards and the

183

Super Sports JAP vee-twin engine. Steering was pronounced perfect at all speeds, and there was no harsh exhaust crackle or noisy valve clatter from the engine. The riding position proved quite acceptable, too, 'astonishing speeds' being obtainable quite effortlessly when the machine was ridden solo. With a sidecar attached, the machine still handled well and 65 mph could be reached with ease. It was even possible to achieve 65 mpg with the sidecar attached, when hard driven. The only items that received criticism from the tester was the inadequate clearance between the handlebars and the petrol tank, and the need for a stronger kickstarter crank. In the same issue there was mention that the new 996cc (80 x 99mm) ohv vee-twin engine would henceforth be known as the 8-38hp engine, to differentiate it from the 8-30hp two camshaft side valve design.

Zenith were the first to announce a machine fitted with the new 346cc ohv touring engine, the model concerned being listed at £62.10s. Others would soon follow suit, for the latest edition of the annual buyer's guide listing showed that 28 manufactureres were fitting a JAP engine into at least one of their model range. The list comprised the following names:

BAT, Bramham, Brough Superior, Calthorpe, Campion, Coventry-Eagle, Francis-Barnett, Grindlay-Peerless, Hazlewood, Hobart, Holroyd, Invicta, LSD, Massey, Mohawk, Monopole, Montgomery, Morgan, New Comet (Aza engine), New Imperial, P & P, Seal, Sharratt (Aza engine), Sirrah, Verus, Victoria, XL and Zenith.

Some were only minor manufacturers or those who made three-wheelers. Two intended using the new Aza two-stroke engine in a lightweight model of the utility type.

Bert Le Vack with a prototype JTOR engine on dynamometer test at Northumberland Park. (Photo: Dr. J. D. Alderson)

Some seemed to find it difficult to use the name Aza for a two-stroke engine that originated from the Tottenham factory, Montgomery in particular referring to their 150cc model as a Montgomery JAP. Possibly because relatively few would-be purchasers identified the Aza engine with the much more familiar JAP motif caused the factory to think again and revert to the JAP name only a matter of months later.

Nothing has been said so far about the export of JAP engines to motorcycle manufacturers on the Continent, yet it would seem there was a quite considerable potential. *The JAP Story,* an official history put out by the factory during 1951 in the form of a 48 page illustrated booklet, mentions that after the 1914-18 war Germany soon became once again the big customer, placing an order for 35,000 engines a year. There is little evidence today, however, of Continental machines fitted with a JAP engine that sold in sufficiently large numbers to justify this large, annual order. Only occassionally JAP advertisements drew attention to Continental successes, such as one that appeared early in 1924. It would seem that an SS80 Brough Superior JAP took the Championship of the Rhine Province in Germany and also the Championship of the Cologne Club, the rider in the case of the latter championship being E. Zundorf. JAP-engined machines had done well in the Paris-Nice Trial too, winning the Coupe Patino (best team performance) and gaining a total of 7 Gold Medals. 3 of these were won in the 175cc class by riders of Rovin-Azas, 2 more in the 350cc class by Terrot JAPs and the remaining two in the same class by Sphinx JAPs. The Coupe Patino award had been made to the Terrot JAP riders.

One of the more interesting road tests related to the somewhat unconventional P&P JAP, which was ridden solo and reported upon in the 13th March issue of *The Motor Cycle.* The smooth running 85 x 85mm 976cc four cam, side valve engine received very favourable mention, the tester being deceived by its speed. Special mention was made of the jockey wheel used to tension the final drive chain and the way in which it could be adjusted by the provision of a large handwheel. BTH electric lighting was included in the specification of the machine being tested, which also featured a new design of silencer which could not be commented upon in detail as it was the subject of a patent application still to be granted. Despite the impression that the vee-twin engine was a very tight fit in the frame, it was possible to remove both cylinders without needing to lift the petrol tank or disturb the crankcase. The frame was sturdily built and of the duplex type, with the gearchange mounted by the nose of the saddle. The only criticism was levelled at the front brake, which was too small in diameter to prove really effective.

A week later, a JAP advertisement appeared, which must qualify for the smallest amount of copy ever used. It featured the new 344cc ohv engine, and had only the word 'It!', shades of Clara Bow, the pin-up movie star known as the 'It' girl in the 'twenties. In this same issue it was announced that E. B. Ware had been awarded the Westall Cup in the Junior Car Club's Annual General Efficiency Trial. Open to light cars not exceeding 1500cc, Ware recorded the best petrol consumption and also the best acceleration in top gear, driving a Morgan JAP. This was the second occasion on which he had won this particular award.

When Brooklands opened for the 1924 season on 22nd March, the BMCRC organised meeting attracted quite a few JAP-engined entries, including Bert Le Vack and George Tottey. Le Vack and Tottey came to the line together for the first race, the 350cc scratch, but it was Le Vack's adversary, Dougal Marchant, who won, George Tottey bringing his 344cc New Imperial JAP into second place. Le Vack had struck trouble and was not able to make the running on this occasion. In the later 350cc Handicap Race, Tottey made light of a heavy handicap and won at a speed of 73.35mph. A. T. Koehler, a name that was beginning to become familiar at Brooklands and similar venues, finished second on his 976cc four cam KTR-engined Zenith in the *185*

1,000cc Solo Scratch Race, and won the 500cc-1,000cc Solo Handicap on the same machine.

Frequent mention had been made of the achievements of the New Imperial JAP racing models, which unquestionably were enjoying a quite remarkable string of successes during the mid-twenties. In contrast, it was interesting to refer to the road test of one of the standard, over-the-counter side valve touring models which was published in *The Motor Cycle* dated 27th March. Fitted with the 70 x 90mm 346cc JAP side valve single, the machine gave a good initial impression, mainly due to the smooth transmission, good weight and correct weight distribution brought about by the use of a loop frame. 50mph was reached without difficulty and when the internal expanding brakes were tested on Edge Hill, Warwickshire (familiar to todays riders in the VMCC's annual Banbury Run) they were considered to be very dependable. During the test, the spring link had become detached from the primary chain, which brought the machine to a standstill. Yet the complete replacement task took only ten minutes, such was the accessability to the primary drive. In total, 300 miles were covered during the test, and the only critiicism related to inadequate mudguarding.

The Essex MC's annual Kop Hill Climb, held during late March, drew entries from Stan Greening and Bert Le Vack, the former riding a variety of machines. He won Class 2 (175cc - 250cc) on a 246cc Coventry-Eagle JAP, Class 3 (250cc - 350cc) on a 344cc Royal Enfield JAP, and Class 7 (350cc sidecar) with a 344cc Royal Enfield JAP and sidecar — all these classes being in the Touring category. He also won Classes 12 and 17 in the Racing category, the respective capacity classes being 175cc-250cc and 350cc sidecar, using the same machines in each case. The 350cc Racing class (13) was won by Le Vack on a 346cc New Imperial JAP.

At the same time, the Preston and District MC and LCC staged another meeting at Brooklands, under new regulations that gave the race stewards powers to disqualify any machine they considered to by unduly noisy. The anti-noise lobby was getting active again, after the winter quiet period. Zenith machines were most successful at this meeting, acquiring 5 firsts, 6 seconds and 5 third placings. A.T. Koehler won the 3 lap General Handicap Race with a 976cc four cam KTR-engined Zenith sidecar outfit at 71.76mph, came second in the Scratch Race for Unlimited Sidecars, and riding the machine solo, second in the Unlimited Solo Scratch Race. H.A. Johnston, the Secretary of the Preston Club, came second in the 350cc Solo Scratch Race on his 344cc Zenith JAP, whilst E.A.L. Parker won the Unlimited Amateur Solo Handicap Race at 75.46mph on a 976cc Zenith JAP. E.S. Prestwich also took part in this meeting, riding a 344cc Zenith JAP. He had a quite successful day too, finishing 2nd in the General Handicap Race, 3rd in the 350cc Solo Scratch, 2nd in the 500cc Solo Handicap and Unlimited Solo Handicap races, and 3rd in the General Handicap for Preston Club members.

Morgan three-wheelers made the news during the early part of April when H.F.S. Morgan and G. Goodall tied for the RAC Trophy at the ACU's Western Centre Chatcombe Hill Climb. This was one of several successes achieved by Morgan drivers in similar events during the year, although from the results published in magazines it is not always apparent whether the car was powered by a JAP engine or one from another manufacturer.

H.F. Turner won the West Birmingham Reliability Trial with a 350cc New Imperial JAP and sidecar, at the same time putting up the Best Performance of any sidecar machine in that event. In Germany, Hans Werth took First Prize in the 2500 Miles Trial, Stephan Schlomer coming second. Both rode Brough Superior JAPs, the former a 650cc solo and the latter an SS80 sidecar outfit.

Zeniths had another field day at the Public Schools MCC Race Meeting held at

Brooklands on 12th April. H.A. Johnston was the most successful rider, winning three races and coming second in another on his 344cc Zenith JAP. E.S. Prestwich won the 2 lap 300cc Solo Scratch Race on his 249cc side valve Zenith JAP, although in this instance there were only two starters. The win by D.F.C. Fitzgerald at 71.25mph in the Passenger Machine Handicap proved the most impressive, his 976cc Zenith JAP sidecar outfit easily overcoming the poor track conditions caused by the cold, wet weather. Only a week later, many of the same riders found themselves back at the track, to take part in the BMCRC's Easter Meeting. Zenith once again had things more or less their own way, E.S. Prestwich winning the 350cc Handicap race on his 249cc Zenith JAP at 69.08mph. A.T. Koehler ran his 976cc side valve Zenith JAP in both solo and sidecar form, to take second place in the 1,000 Solo Handicap and also in the 1100cc Passenger Handicap, the latter being won by G.N. Norris driving a 1098cc Morgan JAP. Speeds were high at this meeting, the Morgan averaging 87.22mph. D.F.C. Fitzgerald took a well deserved second place in the Private Owners Handicap with his big Zenith JAP, and G. Maund won the Experts Handicap race on yet another Zenith — a 344cc Zenith JAP — at 73.67mph.

A.T. Koehler won the 3 Lap General Handicap Race at a Brooklands meeting during March 1924 riding this 976cc four cam KTR-engined Zenith with a sidecar attached. He was also 2nd in the Unlimited Solo Scratch Race and 2nd in the Scratch Race for Unlimited Sidecars.

It was on 27th April that one of the biggest successes of the year was achieved, when Bert Le Vack accepted an invitation to some speed trials in the Fôret de Seuart, near Paris, from the Association Motorcyclecariste de France. Taking his 248cc New Imperial JAP and his 996cc Brough Superior JAP, also a sidecar that could be attached to the latter, he came away with 3 World's Records to his credit, and 2 British. The details are as follows:

World's Records
Class A
Flying start kilometre   248cc New Imperial   87.28mph

Class E
Flying start kilometre   996cc Brough Superior   113.61mph

Class G/s
Flying start kilometre   996cc Brough Superior and sidecar   94.90mph

British Records
Class A
Flying start kilometre   248cc New Imperial   87.83mph

Class E
Flying start kilometre   996cc Brough Superior   114.48mph

This JAP advertisement in a 1924 issue of The Motor Cycle *emphasises just how successful the JAP engine was in setting up new records.*

It was interesting to learn that in establishing the World's Records by making two-way runs, it was whilst recording a mean speed of 113.61 mph on the solo Brough Superior that Le Vack attained the speed at which Claude Temple held the one-way British Record. As he was a British rider on a British-made machine, he intended to claim the relevant British record too. But his luck was out on this occasion. His World's Records were never ratified by the FICM, or his British Records by the A-CU.

In view of the high speeds attained by both machines, it may be assumed that the course over which the attempts were made was good, and that the weather was favourable too. But in reality nothing could be further from the truth. According to an account given by Le Vack afterwards, the course was a straight road, not too wide, with an obelisk at one end and a monument at the other, which did not allow much room at either the start or the finish. The surface was badly pot-holed, and it was raining so hard that the holes were full of water. During each run he was blinded by spray and buffeted from side to side by a tornado-like wind, which blew across the track. Yet despite these quite appaling conditions, the track was lined by 80,000 spectators, who had paid for the privilege of being able to watch.

His 248cc New Imperial pulled a gear of 5¾:1 and had an engine that would rev to 6,300 rpm. He attributed the wonderful speeds obtained to hard work, good workmanship and good material, and the skill of Val Page, coupled with the general guidance of the Guv'nor himself, John Prestwich. The Brough Superior used a 996cc ohv engine similar to that described earlier, which he referred to as the 8-45, even though it was known to produce over 50bhp. How much more he did not know, as he claimed it had wrecked the test plant whilst readings were being taken! It was fitted into a standard Brough Superior frame, but had been lowered by two inches. A JAP mechanical oil pump took care of the lubrication. When taken down after the succesful record breaking attempts, it was still clean inside and still had traces of graphite on the valve stems.

Other news at this time related to the inclusion of some JAP-engined machines amongst the displays at the British Empire Exhibition, Wembley, and the fact that the Aza two-stroke engine would henceforth be officially renamed JAP.

When the York Club held a hill climb at Sutton Bank during the last weekend in April, the weather was bad there too. F. Dean managed to win the Unlimited Sidecars class, both Amateur and Trade, on his 976cc Zenith JAP. But it was little more than a token attempt and when it came to the solo classes the weather had deteriorated to such an extent that the meeting was abandoned. On the other side of the country, weather conditions were not quite so bad, and it was possible to hold a sand race meeting on Southport Sands. Len Booth from Wallesey won the 350cc Novice Race, and came second in both the 350cc General and 500cc Novice races too, on a New Imperial JAP. The Unlimited Novice race was won by C.M. Needham on a Brough Superior JAP, during intermittent rain. The course was said to be like a quagmire, which kept speeds well down so that no good times were recorded. A fortnight later at the same venue, Len Booth put up a much better performance with his 344cc New Imperial JAP, raced in both solo and sidecar form. He scored three firsts and four second places, in a meeting at which speeds of 80mph were reached on several occasions.

An early announcement about the 1924 TT brought forth the news that the Twemlow brothers, Ken and Eddie, were to ride New Imperial JAPs in the Junior TT, also H.F. Harris, L. Horton and George Tottey — the last three having Lightweight TT entries in addition. All would enjoy works support. But most interest was focussed on the engines that would be available from Tottenham, such that when a detailed announcement about JAP plans was made only a week or so later, the two weekly motorcycle magazines were able to publish a full report.

It would seem that although a considerable increase in power output had been obtained from the 248cc and 346cc TT engines, it was more a question of attention to finer detail, rather than fundamental redesign. Yet even under these circumstances it was claimed the efficiency of the 248cc engine had been improved by no less than 50%. Starting with one of the smaller attentions to detail, the push rod ends were now lubricated by means of a small chamber that contained cotton wool soaked in oil. There was a small hole in the cup in which the ball end of the rocker works, and it was to this hole that oil was fed slowly. For general lubrication, the engines were fitted with a Best and Lloyd mechanical pump, to maintain a consistent level of oil in the crank chamber. The system relied upon the tried and proven JAP automatic feed, in which pressure was created by the downward stroke of the piston, in a chamber on the side of the crankcase. Pressure in the chamber was arranged to be slightly in excess of that in the crank chamber, so that the oil was forced out of the reservoir and circulated throughout the engine, as described earlier. From the main bearing, oil was forced to the crankpin, and was caught in a recess at the side of the crankcase, protected by a steel oil catcher or ring, which caused oil to pass through the rollers of the big-end.

The cylinder head had been modified internally with regard to the ports. As in the case of the previous year there were two exhaust ports, but the inlet pipe had been modified by external threading so that it could be screwed into the inlet port. The valve guides were a push fit in the cylinder head and the rockers arranged to run on roller bearings. The engine mainshaft retained a plain bearing on the timing side of the crankcase, and a ball race on the drive side. Within the timing chest two cam followers ran on plain bushes, but had roller ends. The engines had higher compression ratios varying between $6.3:1$ and $7.5:1$, which necessitated the use of alcohol fuel.

JAP policy had changed with regard to both piston rings and valves. Instead of buying in, the company had started manufacturing their own piston rings, which were knurled in a special machine to ensure concentricity. This change in policy also applied to valves, which were being made in the factory from nickel steel.

Other attention related to the use of end caps over the valve stems to help obviate indentations from the rockers. Every part of each engine was polished, the cylinder barrel itself being lapped with metal polish, and the crown of the piston highly buffed. The same type of crankcase was used for both engine capacities, the 248cc engine having lighter flywheels. It was claimed that during bench testing the new engines not only held their power output, but also showed and increase after a period of continued running.

At the Clipstone Park Speed Trials held on 18th May, some quite remarkable speeds were recorded. Star of the day was Bert Le Vack who, in the Solo Machines Unlimited class, recorded a speed of 111.11mph on his 998cc Brough Superior JAP. And to prove this was no fluke, he equalled this speed exactly in the Experts class. His main adversary at this meeting was I.P. Riddoch, riding a Blackburne-engined Zenith. This may explain why the 100mph mark was passed no less than six times as they came to do battle with each other.

In the JAP advertisement that followed, Le Vack's speed of 111.00mph took pride of place, but other successes of a more International nature were mentioned too:

IRELAND	J.G. Burney. Fastest Time of the Day in the 25 Mile Championship riding a 350cc JAP
FRANCE	Course Toul — Nancy
	M. Gaudet. Fastest Time of the Day on a Terrot JAP
	Course de Côte des Dunes
	M. Lebrun Terrot JAP 1st

GERMANY   International Solitude Races, Stuttgart
           350cc Haweka JAP
           1,000cc Brough Superior JAP

For Speed, Reliability and Consistency, it must be a JAP

There should have been a BMCRC meeting at Brooklands on 10th May, a wet and rainy day that would have proved anything but ideal from the competitors' viewpoint. But a few days beforehand, the noise problem had come to a head when Dougal Marchant was refused admission because it was considered his machines made too much noise. The problem was that with no firm guidelines to determine whether a machine would prove acceptable to the Brooklands authorities on account of the amount of noise it made, there was every possibility that quite arbitrary decisions would be made, with some riders being barred from reaching the starting line in the races for which they had entered. Negotiations between the riders, the BMCRC and the BARC came to naught, and on the morning of the meeting, the riders went on strike. The meeting was abandoned and it was not until a compromise had been reached that the motorcycle riders returned to make use of the track just under a fortnight later. By this time a Supplementary Regulation had been devised by the BMCRC, which called for the fitting of a silencer of agreed capacity, size and shape, which in effect marked the birth of the so-called 'Brooklands Can'. Cyril Pullin had carried out much of the design work and testing of the finished component, which in the case of his 494cc Douglas twin resulted in a drop of only 4mph of the machine's maximum speed.

The first meeting at which machines with a silencer were run was the occasion of the Ealing and District MC's event, held on 24th May. Armed with a long wire with which to probe into silencers, much as the police sometimes used, Colonel Lindsay Lloyd had the embarrassing experience of losing the wire inside the silencer that had been fitted to one of Le Vack's machines, which Tommy Allchin was to ride. He sought out Le Vack to ask what he should do, whereupon Le Vack saw the funny side of things and said 'Oh, it won't hurt. It will probably come out and shoot the starter!' Once again, it was the Zeniths that made most of the running, when A.T. Koehler won the 1,000cc Solo Handicap at 87.38mph on his 976cc Zenith JAP, ending up the only finisher. He also won the Club Championship at 77.21mph, this time with a sidecar attached to the Zenith, and came second with the outfit in an impromptu mixed handicap race, in which some cars took part, including a Studebaker and a Paige. H.A. Johnston took second place in the 350cc Solo Handicap, with his 344cc Zenith JAP. Tommy Allchin found that luck was not in his favour on this occasion, despite the fact that he had the use of one of Le Vack's own machines. A stiff handicap prevented him from taking a first place in any of the classes he had entered.

Whilst most were making their way to the Isle of Man for the 1924 TT, A. Greenwood broke the sidecar course record at Doncaster with his Brough Superior outfit. Claude Temple made the news too, not because he had set up another record with his fearsome Temple-Anzani, but because he had issued an open challenge to Bert Le Vack, to decide who was the World's fastest motorcyclist. He suggested a match race could be held between the two of them at Brooklands, over a distance of 2-5 laps. His challenge was printed in both of the weekly magazines, and readers waited anxiously for a reply.

It was in *The Motor Cycle* dated 5th June that the first road test of a machine fitted with the 344cc ohv JAP single appeared in print. The machine concerned was a Zenith and it seemed to give the tester some quite favourable initial impressions. He recorded that it was lively, responded to every whim of the rider and held the road right up to maximum speed in an exemplary manner. Its steering was described as 'unimpeachable'   *191* and the result of lessons learnt on the race track. The engine was singled out for special mention, on account of its ability to pull well and smoothly, and to do so at surprisingly low rpm. Thanks to the use of a Wex carburetter, it would tick over like a sewing machine. But from this point onward the tester's mood seems to have changed, for he found the brakes (belt rim at rear, small diameter drum at front) anything but good, the silencing poor, and a tendency for fuel to leak from the filler cap. Further criticism was levelled at the adjustment of the ball-ended ohv rockers, which was 'not easy to carry out'; the position of the gear change lever, too low for hand operation and too high for foot; and the rather low top gear ratio, which caused the engine to labour. By now, one suspects he may have had thoughts about over-stepping the mark, so he made allowance for some of the bad points by adding that the machine he rode was the works' hack. And it did have a nice red and black finish!

The Brooklands meeting held on 24th May had shown that the compulsory fitting of a silencer had little effect on speeds, but if there were still any who had doubts, and considered this to be a fluke, their illusions were shattered by Bert Le Vack when he made some record breaking attempts at the track, only three days later, with two New Imperial JAPs. Using the 246cc model first, he raised the British Class A flying start kilometre and mile records to 91.01mph and 89.19mph respectively, the mean figure for the two-way runs being 85.48mph and 84.71mph, which were ratified by the ACU but not by the FICM. Then with his 344cc machine, he established a new World's mile record at 90.68mph, the mean figure for a two-way run being 89.11mph, a World's Class B Record subsequently ratified by the FICM.

During the weekend that followed, E. S. Prestwich took his 248cc Zenith JAP to the South Harting Hill Climb, organised by the Surbiton Motor Club. He won the 250cc General Class, and was ably supported by H. M. Walters and F. R. G. Spikins who, on their respective 344cc Zenith JAPs, were first and second respectively in the 350cc General Class. Spikins went on to win the 600cc and 1,000cc General Classes, too, as well as the 350cc sidecar class, all with the same machine. He almost won the Unlimited Class too, but the opposition proved just a little too strong in the shape of O. M. Baldwin on his big Matchless. Freddie Barnes won the Unlimited Sidecar Class with his 976cc Zenith-JAP, Tom Allchin being placed third on a similar outfit.

Le Vack had yet another good outing at Brooklands on 7th June, the occasion of the Fourth Meeting of 1924 organised by the BMCRC. He took with him three machines — two New Imperials and his Brough Superior, whilst Tom Allchin had the use of E. S. Prestwich's Zenith, the latter having an injury that prevented him from riding. Le Vack started the day well, by winning the 250cc 3 Lap Scratch Race at a speed of 82.18mph, Allchin coming third, the race having only six starters. In the 350cc 3 Lap Scratch Race that followed, there were only three starters, and this proved another win for the New Imperial rider at 80.98mph. But it was different in the 350cc 3 Lap Handicap Race, which attracted 7 starters. Joe Wright won this on a 344cc Zenith JAP at a speed of 71.66mph. The 1,000cc 3 Lap Handicap Race went to Tom Allchin, who on this occasion was riding Le Vack's own 80 x 99mm 976cc side valve Zenith, the engine being one of only 5 made. His speed was a very creditable 97.27mph. A. T. Koehler was third, similarly mounted. Surprisingly, Le Vack had to concede victory to his greatest adversary, Dougal Marchant, in the 1 Lap 250cc Scratch Race, the latter riding a Blackburne-engined Zenith. But he won the 1 Lap 350cc and 500cc Scratch Races that followed with his 344cc New Imperial, at speeds of 81.37mph and 84.13mph. And for good measure he went on to win the 1 Lap 1,000cc Sprint Scratch Race too, this time using his 996cc ohv Brough Superior JAP, at 94.5mph. Allchin was second, on the big Zenith. Not at all a bad day, but possibly one of disappointment from the spectators point of view as none of the races attracted more than 11 starters.

A nicely-restored 680cc Zenith JAP on display at the 1984 Shepton Mallet 'Wings and Wheels' event, owned by Derek Light.

Just under two weeks later, the ohv Brough Superior added to its continuing string of successes when Le Vack made Fastest Time of the Day at the Blackpool Speed Trials. At this same event. Len Booth won the Experts Barred Sidecar Class with his 344cc New Imperial JAP. JAP advertisements were now proclaiming 'The World's Fastest Engine' — prophetically, as it soon turned out.

The next event to claim attention was the 1924 TT, and it was in the Junior Race that the Tottenham factory got their first taste of success, when Ken Twenlow came 1st on his 344cc New Imperial JAP, with Stuart Ollerhead 2nd on a DOT fitted with a similar engine. To have supplied engines that came first and second in the Junior TT was no small achievement, but what was even more surprising was the fact that the 4th, 5th and 6th finishers in the Junior Race rode machines fitted with JAP engines too. The final results were as follows:

1st K. Twemlow	344cc New Imperial JAP	55.8mph
2nd S. Ollerhead	344cc DOT JAP	54.9mph
4th C.T. Ashby	344cc Montgomery JAP	53.39mph
5th H.J. Willis	344cc Montgomery JAP	52.80mph
6th J. Emerson	344cc DOT JAP	52.11mph

At one time it looked as though Len Horton could be certain of second place on his New Imperial JAP, but problems put him out of the running during the last lap.

Kenneth Twemlow was only 20 years old, the elder brother of Edwin Twemlow, who also rode in the same race on a similar machine, but failed to complete the course. Their father was Managing Director of the Foden Steam Waggon Works. Kenneth had made slow progress during the early part of the race, needing to stop and tighten the throttle lever and also the petrol pipe nuts. But then he got going in earnest and was 12th at the end of the second lap. He managed to work his way up to 4th position at the end of the fourth lap, and eventually to gain time on Ollerhead, who had held a steady 2nd place on the third and fourth laps. He then gained on Horton, who had by then displaced Ollerhead and slipped into 2nd place on the fifth lap.

In the Sidecar Race run a couple of days later, Harry Reed came second on one of his own DOT JAP outfits, the race proving somewhat disappointing in view of the fact that it attracted only ten starters. After the race, it transpired that Reed's machine had been fitted with the actual 344cc JAP engine that P. Bell had used in Monday's Junior Race. Bell had been the last finisher, in 15th place, so his engine had been well tested.

The Lightweight Race was run on the Friday, the idea being that the 21 starters would get under way just before the Senior Race, in the hope that the leaders of both races would cross the finishing line more or less together. No one seems to have given much thought about the hazards caused by the slower machines baulking the riders of the faster machines, a situation that would be quite unthinkable today. But somehow the two separate races were run without any real problems being encountered, which was just as well for Edwin Twemlow, who made it a double for New Imperial and JAP. He finished at an average speed not much less than that achieved by his brother in the Junior Race — 55.44mph. J. Cooke brought his DOT JAP into third place at 52.54mph, and H.F. Harris, on another New Imperial JAP was 6th at 50.50mph. Edwin Twemlow was an even younger winner, for he was but 18 years old. He worked in the Drawing Office of his father's company and was riding George Tottey's machine, the latter being unable to ride as the result of an accident that occurred during the Junior Race.

Alec Bennett had won the Senior Race on a Norton, and as the race-winning machines had been made in Birmingham, the winning riders were duly honoured in that city by a dinner at the Midland Hotel, to which 150 guests had been invited. New Imperial and Norton shared the expense. One interesting fact came to light when the riders were asked how they were kept informed of their progress during the race. The method used by Kenneth Twemlow was simplicity in itself. His pit crew showed a red flag if he needed to ride faster, and a yellow flag if he needed to slow down! One wonders how other riders may have interpreted these signals, in view of their quite different meaning in the widely-accepted flag colour code.

Le Vack had given the TT a miss this year, and instead was preparing his machines for some record breaking attempts at the International Speed Trials to be held at Arpajon on the Paris/Orleans road, on 6th July. Quite a few British speed men were attracted, including Rex Judd and Claude Temple. Vivian Prestwich, now fully recovered from his Brooklands accident, accompanied Le Vack and his faithful mechanic, Sid Moram.

Le Vack was in good form, and with his 248cc New Imperial JAP managed to raise the Class A flying kilometre and flying mile World's records to 88.87mph and 89.25mph respectively. Then, changing over to his 996cc Brough Superior-JAP, he took the Class E World's Records for these two distances at 119.05mph and 118.93mph respectively. It was during one of these runs that he was timed one-way at 122.44mph — the World's fastest speed on a motorcycle, though not acceptable as only a one-way run. So much for Temple's challenge — and Temple was there too, to see it for himself! But there was more to come. After attaching a sidecar to the Brough, the Class G/s Records went too, the flying kilometre at 99.80mph and the flying mile at 99.73mph. Needless to say, all these recent successes made wonderful copy for JAP advertisements and to add to it, they could claim a Sphynx JAP had won the 350cc class in the 2,000 kilometre Liège-Bordeaux-Liège race in a time of 42 hours.

The next event to attract Le Vack was the 50 Mile Races held at Brooklands on 12th July. He won the Class A & B Handicap Race with comparative ease on his 248cc New Imperial JAP, at a speed of 71.38mph. Joe Wright came second on a 344cc Zenith JAP, and R.A. Mallet third, on a similar mount. E.S. Prestwich was the unlucky one on this occasion, a persistent misfire putting his 246cc Zenith JAP out of contention, to finish 5th. When it came to the 50 Mile Classes C, D & E Handicap Race, everyone expected Le Vack to win again, but his Brough Superior was plagued by what at first looked like carburetter or magneto trouble, the machine running very roughly and being reluctant to start after a pit stop. Although he was timed at 93mph on the fifth lap, the uneven firing got worse, and after the 8th lap, he pulled in to retire. He was out again for the 50 Mile passenger Handicap Race, but just when it looked as though the big Brough was getting into its stride amongst the other outfits, the misfiring started all over again. Once again Le Vack suffered the frustration of early retirement, a quick check at the pits showing there was no problem with either the ignition or the valves. Later, it seemed that over-lubrication was the cause.

In the Scottish Speed Championships meeting held on St. Andrews sands on 12th July, George Grinton won the 250cc title on a New Imperial JAP. A fortnight later, the Yorkshire Speed Championships were held on Saltburn sands. Jimmy Guthrie won the 350cc title on a New Imperial JAP over a distance of 20 miles. It was early beginnings for a name that was going to have much greater significance in motorcycle racing during later years.

The Essex MC's annual meeting had to be held mid-week, and it was unfortunate that 23rd July was chosen as the date, for not only was there a small entry, but the weather was exceptionally bad, too. Nonetheless, the meeting was run in conditions where even the Brooklands Paddock was flooded, the honours going to C.W.G. Lacey's 344cc Cotton JAP at 81.89mph in the 3 lap Junior Handicap Race, and to Tom Allchin at 98.62mph in the 3 lap Senior Handicap Race — speeds that belied the conditions of both the track and the weather. Allchin was riding Le Vack's 996cc Zenith JAP, his 200 Mile Race machine.

At the beginning of August, Bert Le Vack had his long-awaited ride in the French Grand Prix, aboard a Terrot JAP. This, too, proved to be a very wet meeting, and matters became complicated for Le Vack when he found that the control cables of his machine were too tight, such that they abraided against the front forks, which eventually cut through them. First to go was the exhaust valve lifter cable, then one of the carburettor control cables. Yet despite this handicap, he managed to keep going, even though he could not catch the race leader, F.A. Longman on an AJS. He finished a very creditable 2nd. It was just as wet at home, too. At the Welsh Championship meeting held on Pendine sands during the Bank Holiday weekend, George Grinton managed 2nd place in the 275cc Championship Race, on his New Imperial JAP.

The first news about new models for the 1925 season was released by Royal Enfield. Although very few changes were to be made in their model range, it was significant that henceforth the engines for their 976cc vee-twin were to be built 'in house'. One presumes this involved a licensing arrangement with JAP, for the engine concerned was the standard 85.5 x 85mm side valve design. This change from using a previously complete 'bought in' engine was significant as it marked the beginning of a trend that would grow during the years to follow. Motorcycle manufacturers who previously had used proprietary engines of one kind or another were becoming more inclined to design and make their own, thereby obviating the need to pay a royalty if they built an engine under license, or making a saving if they designed and built their own engine, using their own production facilities. Prices of new motorcycles were still falling, and it was important to save money wherever the opportunity presented itself, without sacrificing quality. At the BMCRC Meeting on 2nd August, the Brooklands Gazette reported: 'It was good to see C.M. Needham on his Brough Superior JAP win the 3 Laps 1,000cc Handicap Race; races are so often won by men whose names continually appear in the programme that it is refreshing to find a new one amongst the familiar. Needham was the dark horse in the field, and he made the handicappers conspicuous with a runaway win at 83.28mph. T.R. Allchin and H.J. Knight were second and third on their Zenith-JAPs. R.A. Mallet, on his 344cc Zenith JAP was second in the earlier 3 Laps Class B Scratch Race'.

During July, the Gazette had road tested an SS80 Brough Superior, and had reported that the timing gear was of an entirely new type, embodying two camshafts instead of the one usual in JAP practice.

During the early part of August, C.M. Needham won the 100 Mile Race on his Brough Superior JAP at the Pendine sand races organised by the Neath and District MC. A few days later, Len Booth had another good day with his 344cc New Imperial JAP at the Southport sands meeting organised by the North Liverpool MCC. He won the 350cc Expert, 350cc Amateur, 350cc Expert Sidecar, 550cc Expert Sidecar and 750cc Expert Sidecar classes, all on the same machine. As on previous occasions, these races were held on the Birkdale sands. Just a week later, E.C.E. Baragwanath came into the news again when he won the 1 lap Sidecar Scratch Race during the meeting at Brooklands organised by the West Kent MC. His mount was a 976cc P&P JAP. The machine was supplied with a nickel-plated frame, for which he did not particularly care. So he hand enamelled it black! At this same meeting, F. Mighell won the 1 lap Experts Barred Race on his 976cc Zenith JAP.

The Ealing Club's meeting at Brooklands on 23rd August proved to be another wet one, which was a pity as it was the third in the annual series of 200 mile sidecar races. The entry included Stan Greening, E.S. Prestwich and Bert Le Vack, but the first JAP-engined entry home in the 350cc race was that of R.J. Piper on a 344cc Montgomery JAP. In the 1,000cc race, Le Vack appeared with an 80 x 99mm side valve JAP engine fitted into the frame of his Brough Superior, whilst Tom Allchin again rode one of the Le Vack 996cc Zenith-JAPs on which he finished 2nd at 62.87mph. Why Le Vack had made the engine change is a mystery, unless the original ohv engine was still suffering from its persistent misfiring. But it was to no avail. The side valve engine gave rise to problems, too, and Le Vack pulled in to retire, after the 12th lap. On the same day, C.M. Needham won the 50 Mile Race on Birkdale sands, Southport, again riding his Brough Superior JAP. Len Booth continued his winning ways by winning the 350cc General class on his 344cc New Imperial JAP, over a distance of one mile.

In the 4th September issue of *The Motor Cycle*, the Tottenham factory announced additions to their JAP engine range for the 1925 season. A new 70 x 78mm 298cc engine was to be added to the range, which closely resembled the old 293cc side valve design. It used the same crankcase and flywheel assembly as the latter engine, but had longer main bearings, that on the drive side being of the double roller type. There was also a longer plain bush bearing on the timing side. In order to accommodate these longer bearings, it was necessary to dish the inner circumference of each crankcase casting, without need to increase their overall width. The cam wheel journals were of greater diameter, using only two timing pinions, one of which carried the single cam. The timing gear cover and magneto chain cover were now cast in one, two versions being available to permit a front or rear-mounted magneto. Internally, the engine had an alloy piston with a domed, buffed top, and a fully floating gudgeon pin. Special attention was paid to engine balance. Lubrication was by the splash method and the connecting rod had a new type of big-end bearing, comprising two open cages of rollers, separated by a distance washer. The crankcase would also accept a 250cc cylinder, if this latter capacity was desired.

Also of interest was a new 976cc ohv vee-twin, with bore and stroke dimensions of 85.5 x 85mm. It was, in fact, a modified version of the 996cc long stroke racing engine that had been used so successfully by Le Vack in his record breaking attempts. Its reduced height made it easier to accommodate in a standard frame, and it was stated that, henceforth, Le Vack himself intended using this new, 'square', engine. It followed that the production four cam side valve KTR engine and the new ohv KTOR were able to use the same crankcase. The main alterations occurred with regard to the crankcase, which had an oil box (used in conjunction with the JAP automatic oiling system) that formed part of the timing gear casing. The system was, however, slightly modified so that a rotary vacuum valve could be incorporated, a move considered necessary to ensure a vacuum was maintained up to maximum rpm, thereby ensuring sufficient circulation of oil and helping to keep it clean. The twin connecting rod assembly contained no less than four rows of rollers, restrained by separating washers rather than by a cage. Plain alloy pistons were fitted, with buffed crowns and aluminium alloy end caps fitted to the gudgeon pins. The overhead valve rockers ran on ball bearings at one end of their shaft, and on roller bearings at the other end.

The early appearance of the ohv engine had led C.T. Ashby to persuade the Racing Department to use the front cylinder for a single cylinder engine, giving a capacity of 488cc, an unusual size of which little had been heard since the war. This engine would, of course, have its own crankcase, though it used the same piston. His inspiration was rewarded when he won the Class C 5 Laps Championship Scratch Race in October at 87.99mph. This engine became known as 'Ashby's engine'. The same issue of the magazine carried a report on the 30th August meeting at Brooklands, organised jointly by the Public Schools MCC and the Guildford and Woking MCC. It proved to be another field day for Zenith JAP riders, the 'stars' on this occasion being Joe Wright, F. Mighell, H.J. Knight and D.F.C. Fitzgerald. It was a Zenith JAP benefit at the Brighton Speed Trials too, held just a week later. H.A. Johnston won the 350cc and 500cc classes on his 344cc Zenith JAP and the Unlimited class on a 976cc vee twin. Baragwanath took the 1,000cc Sidecar Class on his 976cc P&P JAP. Even the 350cc Amateur Class went to two Zenith JAP riders — F.G. Leaney and D.B. Calder who brought their 344cc machines into first and second places.

Over in Northern Ireland the Ulster Grand Prix had its own following. F. Andrews and W. Andrews finished 1st and 2nd in the 350cc race, riding 344cc New Imperial JAPs. The over 600cc Class was won by Stanley Woods, on an unfamiliar   *197*

976cc New Imperial JAP vee-twin. R. Price was 2nd on a 976cc Coventry-Eagle JAP. In this race, every one of the finishers had a JAP engine fitted to his machine!

After the 200 mile sidecar races at Brooklands came the 200 mile solo races, held on the same day as the Brighton Speed Trials and the Ulster Grand Prix. Entries did not seem to suffer as a result, and there was a quite strong JAP representation. In the 250cc Race, JAP-engined machines filled the first three places, the winner being H.M. Walters on a 246cc Zenith JAP at 67.12mph. Stan Greening and E.S. Prestwich were similarly mounted, finishing 2nd and 3rd respectively. Not unexpectedly, the 350cc Race went to Bert Le Vack, who won at 74.33mph on his 346cc New Imperial JAP. The report on this race in *The Motor Cycle* alleged the JAP engines outnumbered the Blackburne engines by 8 to 6. Le Vack had decided to enter for this race at the very last minute, forsaking his ride in the 1,000cc class and taking over the entry by F.R.G. Spikins. In the 500cc Race, C.T. Ashby rode the first JAP-engined entry home, into third place. Using his Junior TT 488cc Montgomery JAP fitted with the new single cylinder engine he inspired, his speed was 58.52mph. In the 750cc Race, J.J. Hall was 2nd on a 730cc P&P-JAP at 60.88mph, whilst Tom Allchin made sure of the 1,000cc Race on Le Vack's 976cc Zenith JAP AT 87.38mph.

E.B. Ware came back into the news during the Junior Car Club's 200 Mile Race held only two weeks later, though in anything but a desirable manner. His Morgan three wheeler was fitted with a new water-cooled vee-twin JAP engine that closely resembled the 996cc and 976cc ohv twins in outward appearance. He was going quite well too, with Tom Allchin as his passenger. He ran into trouble when he came off the Byfleet Banking at over 90mph, when something went wrong with the rear end of the Morgan that caused the rear wheel to cant over. In consequence, the Morgan rammed the corner of the competitors' lap scoring box, opposite the timing box, throwing both Ware and Allchin on to the track and wrecking the three wheeler. Allchin was dazed and suffering from a dislocated shoulder, apart from minor abrasions, bad enough because he had not long recovered from injuries sustained whilst riding in a grand prix. But Ware lay motionless and unconscious, his injuries being much more severe. Both arms were broken and a leg badly smashed. His skull was fractured, his left eye nearly gouged out and his jaw bone driven through his cheek. At one stage he was taken for dead, and covered with a blanket, until his mechanic realised otherwise. He was rushed to hospital and worked on by surgeons for more than ten hours, after which he made a slow but quite miraculous recovery. But it brought to an end his racing career and JAP lost a valuable member of their experimental staff. Fortunately, Ware retained his interest in motor and motorcycling sport, to join the Auto-Cycle Union and ultimately become a Steward and Speedway Engineer. It was alleged he had not sought permission from his employer to take part in this event and there was talk of him suing the company for not paying his salary during the two years he spent in hospital. He considered racing to be an extension of his employment. As an aftermath of this unfortunate accident, the Junior Car Club barred three-wheeler entries in their next annual 200 Mile Race, and also from their High Efficiency Road Trial, too.

The 9th October issue of *The Motor Cycle* contained details of the newer JAP engines for the 1925 season, and also more information about the timed rotary crankcase release as mentioned in the earlier announcement.

Starting with the 64.5 x 76mm 249cc side valve sports engine, this was henceforth to be available with two patterns of cylinder, one with much deeper fins than normal that would be supplied at extra cost. A standard version of this engine would also be available, with solid tappets, standard valve springs, and the so-called 'plain' standard cylinder. To accompany these engines there was to be a standard 62.5 x 80mm 249cc ohv engine, having a single exhaust port cylinder head and a new cylinder barrel — in

PICTORIAL   SEPTEMBER 21, 1924

SENSATION DURING 200 MILE MOTOR RACE

This illustration of Ware's crashed Morgan was published in the 21st September, 1924 issue of the Sunday Pictorial, together with a graphic account of the incident. (Photo: Dr. J. D. Alderson)

effect, an exact replica of the 1923 TT engine.

Four more side valve engines were described. These included a 70 x 78mm 300cc standard design and a 70 x 76mm 293cc engine that was identical to the 1924 design but fitted with plain bearings throughout. There was also a 70 x 90mm 345cc engine which could be fitted with a standard or a deep finned cylinder, and a so-called 345cc Aza roadster engine, similar to the 70 x 90mm design but with the standard, plain cylinder. The Aza two-stroke engine was to continue unchanged.

With regard to the vee-twins, three basic designs were available, the 64.5 x 67mm 498cc standard side valve, the 70 x 88mm 680cc and the 85.5 x 85mm 980cc 'square' side valve. The 980cc sports version of the last mentioned would have heavily finned cylinders. The 8-30 engine had the same dimensions and also the heavily finned cylinders, as well as the new rotary release valve. Other features included new, straight inlet ports to allow a lower carburetter mounting position, and the combustion chamber of each cylinder head specially shaped for good turbulence. The 8-45 engine would be made to the same dimensions as the 980cc side valve design, but feature overhead valves. In addition, there was to be a standard 85.5 x 85mm 980cc water-cooled side valve engine, mainly intended for cyclecar use. This would have valves of 1¼ inch diameter operated by a single cam and use the sports engine crankcase. There would be a plain bearing on the timing side and a bevel drive to the side-mounted magneto.

The timed rotary crankcase release took the form of a small gear pinion that meshed with one of the larger timing pinions. It was integral with a hollow journal which had a slot cut in it to register with a passageway leading to the crankcase oil box. A negative pressure of 1 psi in the timing case caused oil to be drawn in through a small hole into a pipe leading from the oil box to the timing gear compartment. This fed the main bearing direct, transferring oil by means of oilways to other moving parts. The timing of the rotary crankcase release was arranged so that the valve was closed when the piston reached bottom dead centre. But it remained open for 90° of the crankshaft's rotation. The rotary release was henceforth to be incorporated in the following engines: 249cc ohv racing, 344cc ohv sports, 344cc ohv racing, 490cc side valve, 596cc side valve, 980cc side valve twin (8-30) and 980cc ohv racing (8-45), the last as used by Le Vack. Furthermore, all the above engines would now be fitted with alloy pistons.

The meeting held by the Essex MC at Brooklands on 4th October had only three motorcycle races in its programme. In the first of these, H.M. Walters on a 344cc Zenith JAP took the lead in the closing stages of the 3 lap Handicap for machines of up to 1,000cc, his winning speed being 82.18mph. C.T. Ashby was third, on a 488cc Montgomery JAP. In the 3 lap Passenger Handicap Race, Joe Wright was first home with a 344cc Zenith JAP at 65.70mph, E.S. Prestwich taking 2nd place with a similarly-powered outfit. The 3 lap Mixed Handicap Race went to E.C.E. Baragwanath who, on this occasion, had transferred his affection to an outfit powered by a 976cc Zenith JAP.

During the weekend of 11th/12th October, Bert Le Vack rode in the Grand Prix de France, held at the opening of the new Montlhéry track. He won the 250cc event at 72.45mph, and the 350cc event at 80.11mph, using his two dohc New Imperial JAPs. At home, competitors in the BMCRC Championships meeting at Brooklands were struggling in the rain. The only JAP success went to V. Baxter, who won the 350cc Sidecar Race with a Rex-Acme JAP, before the meeting was postponed until October.

More manufacturers were now making announcements about their 1925 programme, prior to the annual Olympia Motor Cycle Show. New Imperial were to continue their existing range, which comprised 14 different models, all of them JAP-engined, with no modifications other than the fitting of a Best and Lloyd Mark II mechanical oil pump and, on some models, pneumatic footboards. In addition, they were prepared to supply to special order a machine fitted with the 344cc two-port ohv engine, classified as a Super Sports model. Diamond proposed introducing a new side valve model, based on the 490cc JAP single, whilst Montgomery would have available three basic models, each with options. These comprised a 600cc sporting model fitted with a specially tuned side valve JAP engine, a 350cc sports model fitted with either the

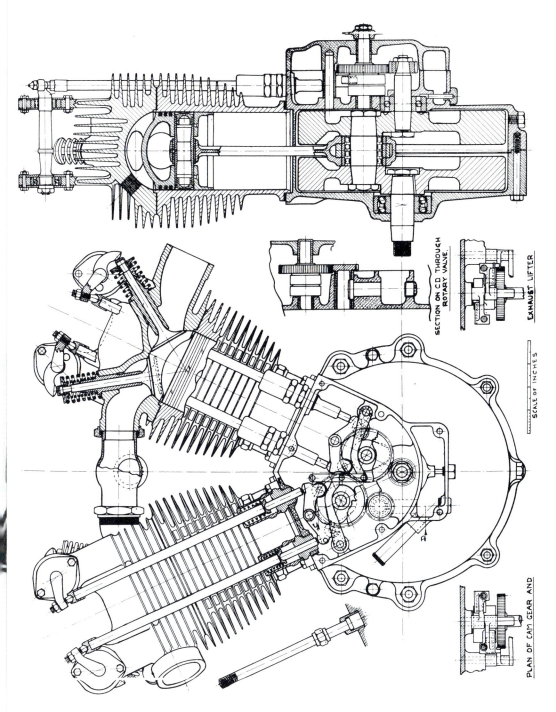

SECTION ON CD THROUGH ROTARY VALVE.

EXHAUST LIFTER

SCALE OF INCHES

PLAN OF CAM GEAR AND

Fig. 10.1 The 1924 JAP 980cc overhead valve 8-45hp engine. (*Courtesy Ronald H. Clark*)

reference to the ever-growing list of World's records achieved by JAP-engined machines. The list was now longer than ever, and can be summarised as follows:

Class A *(250cc solo)*

Flying start kilometre	H. Le Vack	245cc New Imperial	88.87mph
50 kilometre	H. Le Vack	248cc Le Vack	120.93kph
100 kilometre	H. Le Vack	248cc Le Vack	121.37kph
200 kilometre	H.M. Walters	248cc Zenith	106.89kph
300 kilometre	H.M. Walters	248cc Zenith	107.92kph
Flying start mile	H. Le Vack	245cc New Imperial	89.24mph
50 miles	H. Le Vack	248cc New Imperial	75.36mph
100 miles	H. Le Vack	248cc New Imperial	73.63mph
200 miles	H.M. Walters	247cc Zenith	67.14mph
500 miles	B. Kershaw	249cc New Imperial	50.07mph
1 Hour	H. Le Vack	248cc Le Vack	75.43mph
2 Hours	H. Le Vack	248cc Le Vack	73.24mph
3 Hours	H.M. Walters	247cc Zenith	67.14mph
8 Hours	B. Kershaw	249cc New Imperial	50.77mph
9 Hours	B. Kershaw	249cc New Imperial	50.52mph
10 Hours	B. Kershaw	249cc New Imperial	50.07mph
11 Hours	Mrs. R.N. Stewart	249cc Trump	46.03mph
12 Hours	Mrs. R.N. Stewart	249cc Trump	46.33mph

Class B *(350cc Solo)*

Flying start kilometre	H. Le Vack	344cc New Imperial	96.50mph
5 kilometres	H. Le Vack	344cc New Imperial	146.52kph
10 kilometres	H. Le Vack	344cc New Imperial	141.98kph
50 kilometres	H. Le Vack	344cc New Imperial	136.68kph
100 kilometres	H. Le Vack	344cc New Imperial	136.13kph
200 kilometres	H. Le Vack	344cc New Imperial	133.77kph
300 kilometres	H. Le Vack	344cc New Imperial	125.04kph
Flying start mile	H. Le Vack	344cc New Imperial	89.11mph
5 miles	H. Le Vack	344cc New Imperial	91.05mph
10 miles	H. Le Vack	344cc New Imperial	89.13mph
50 miles	H. Le Vack	344cc New Imperial	85.09mph
100 miles	H. Le Vack	344cc New Imperial	83.19mph
200 miles	H. Le Vack	344cc New Imperial	77.71mph
1 Hour	H. Le Vack	344cc New Imperial	84.62mph
2 Hours	H. Le Vack	344cc New Imperial	83.35mph
3 Hours	H. Le Vack	344cc New Imperial	74.34mph

Class C *(500cc Solo)*

400 kilometres	C.T. Ashby and	488cc Montgomery	129.63kph
500 kilometres	H.M. Walters	488cc Montgomery	128.24kph
300 miles	C.T. Ashby and	488cc Montgomery	79.78mph
3 Hours	H.M. Walters	488cc Montgomery	80.54mph
4 Hours	C.T. Ashby and H.M. Walters	488cc Montgomery	79.20mph

Class E *(1,000cc Solo)*

Flying start kilometre	H. Le Vack	996cc Brough Superior	119.05mph
Standing start kilometre	H. Le Vack	996cc Zenith	73.34mph
50 kilometres	H. Le Vack	998cc Brough Superior	149.72kph
100 kilometres	H. Le Vack	998cc Brough Superior	147.35kph
200 kilometres	T.R. Allchin	988cc Zenith	140.86kph
300 kilometres	T.R. Allchin	988cc Zenith	141.58kph
Flying start mile	H. Le Vack	996cc Brough Superior	118.93mph
Standing start mile	H. Le Vack	996cc Zenith	82.96mph
50 miles	H. Le Vack	996cc Zenith	91.71mph
100 miles	H. Le Vack	996cc Zenith	89.92mph
200 miles	T.R. Allchin	996cc Zenith	87.27mph
300 miles	C.T. Ashby and H.M. Walters	488cc Zenith	79.78mph
1 Hour	H. Le Vack	996cc Zenith	89.90mph
2 Hours	T.R. Allchin	996cc Zenith	89.06mph

Class B/s *(350cc Sidecar)*

Standing start kilometre	G.E. Tottey	344cc New Imperial	51.28mph
400 kilometres	S.M. Greening & E.S. Prestwich	344cc Royal Enfield	91.74kph
500 kilometres	S.M. Greening & E.S. Prestwich	344cc Royal Enfield	92.32kph
600 kilometres	S.M. Greening & E.S. Prestwich	344cc Royal Enfield	91.01kph
700 kilometres	S.M. Greening & E.S. Prestwich	344cc Royal Enfield	90.89kph
300 miles	S.M. Greening & E.S. Prestwich	344cc Royal Enfield	57.55mph
400 miles	S.M. Greening & E.S. Prestwich	344cc Royal Enfield	56.77mph
4 Hours	S.M. Greening & E.S. Prestwich	344cc Royal Enfield	56.71mph
5 Hours	S.M. Greening & E.S. Prestwich	344cc Royal Enfield	57.47mph
6 Hours	S.M. Greening & E.S. Prestwich	344cc Royal Enfield	56.28mph
7 Hours	S.M. Greening & E.S. Prestwich	344cc Royal Enfield	56.76mph

8 Hours	S.M. Greening & E.S. Prestwich	344cc Royal Enfield	56.50mph
9 Hours	S.M. Greening & E.S. Prestwich	344cc Royal Enfield	50.22mph
10 Hours	S.M. Greening & E.S. Prestwich	344cc Royal Enfield	45.20mph

Class F *(600cc Sidecar)*

400 kilometres	S.M. Greening & E.S. Prestwich	344cc Royal Enfield	91.74kph
500 kilometres	S.M. Greening & E.S. Prestwich	344cc Royal Enfield	92.32kph
600 kilometres	S.M. Greening & E.S. Prestwich	344cc Royal Enfield	91.01kph
700 kilometres	S.M. Greening & E.S. Prestwich	344cc Royal Enfield	90.89kph
300 miles	S.M. Greening & E.S. Prestwich	344cc Royal Enfield	57.55mph
400 miles	S.M. Greening & E.S. Prestwich	344cc Royal Enfield	56.77mph
4 hours	S.M. Greening & E.S. Prestwich	344cc Royal Enfield	56.71mph
5 hours	S.M. Greening & E.S. Prestwich	344cc Royal Enfield	57.47mph
6 hours	S.M. Greening & E.S. Prestwich	344cc Royal Enfield	56.28mph
7 hours	S.M. Greening & E.S. Prestwich	344cc Royal Enfield	56.76mph
8 hours	S.M. Greening & E.S. Prestwich	344cc Royal Enfield	56.50mph

Class G/s *(1,000cc Sidecar)*

Flying start mile	H. Le Vack	996cc Brough Superior	99.73mph
Flying start kilometre	H. Le Vack	996cc Brough Superior	99.80mph
5 kilometres	H. Le Vack	996cc Zenith	142.07kph
10 kilometres	H. Le Vack	996cc Zenith	136.47kph
50 kilometres	H. Le Vack	996cc Brough Superior	126.99kph
100 kilometres	H. Le Vack	996cc Brough Superior	125.09kph
200 kilometres	H. Le Vack	996cc Brough Superior	122.06kph
5 miles	H. Le Vack	996cc Zenith	88.27mph
10 miles	H. Le Vack	996cc Zenith	86.14mph
50 miles	H. Le Vack	996cc Brough Superior	79.37mph
100 miles	H. Le Vack	996cc Brough Superior	77.82mph
200 miles	H. Le Vack	996cc Brough Superior	75.32mph
400 kilometres	H.R. Harte and S. Glanfield	988cc Coventry-Eagle	107.64kph

500 kilometres	H.R. Harte and S. Glanfield	988cc Coventry-Eagle	106.09kph
600 kilometres	H.R. Harte and S. Glanfield	988cc Coventry-Eagle	106.75kph
700 kilometres	H.R. Harte and S. Glanfield	988cc Coventry-Eagle	106.27kph
800 kilometres	H.R. Harte and S. Glanfield	988cc Coventry-Eagle	105.88kph
900 kilometres	H.R. Harte and S. Glanfield	988cc Coventry-Eagle	105.75kph
1 hour	H. Le Vack	996cc Brough Superior	77.73mph
2 hours	H. Le Vack	996cc Brough Superior	75.93mph
4 hours	H.R. Harte and S. Glanfield	988cc Coventry-Eagle	66.92mph
5 hours	H.R. Harte and S. Glanfield	988cc Coventry-Eagle	66.16mph
6 hours	H.R. Harte and S. Glanfield	988cc Coventry-Eagle	66.44mph
7 hours	H.R. Harte and S. Glanfield	988cc Coventry-Eagle	66.09mph
8 hours	H.R. Harte and S. Glanfield	988cc Coventry-Eagle	65.60mph
9 hours	H.R. Harte and S. Glanfield	988cc Coventry-Eagle	65.66mph
10 hours	H.R. Harte and S. Glanfield	988cc Coventry-Eagle	60.31mph
11 hours	H.R. Harte and S. Glanfield	988cc Coventry-Eagle	54.83mph

Articles and race results published in the two weekly motorcycle magazines often quoted incorrect engine capacities for the various JAP engines, both singles and twins. Even the factory were not entirely reliable in this respect! The more observant will have seen there was a marked lack of consistency regarding Le Vack's dohc engines in particular, so whilst the following explanation is inconclusive, it will show that even the FICM were not always correct either.

Throughout the life of the 250cc engine, its bore and stroke remained unchanged at 62.5 x 80mm, which gives a cubic capacity of 245cc. Yet although this figure was quoted correctly in reports throughout 1922, it was changed to 248cc in 1923 and listed as such thereafter, for no apparent reason. The formula $\Pi R^2 H$ confirms a figure of 245.43cc.

The 350cc engine initially had bore and stroke measurements of 74 x 80mm, until 1925 when they were revised to 70 x 90mm, which changed the original cubic capacity of 344cc to 346cc. Yet reports gave the engine capacity as 344cc until 9th September, 1923, after which 346cc was substituted until late in 1924, when a reversion to the original 344cc figure was made.

The FICM World's Record Lists have always been regarded as the most reliable source of information on engine dimensions, and both they and the BMCRC Race Programmes agreed on the 344cc figure until 25th August 1925. On that date, Le Vack used the same engine to record 99.46 and 98.66mph respectively, over the Flying Start Kilometre and Mile, to claim both the Class B and Class C World's records. So it is surprising to find the FICM recorded the engine capacity as 346cc for the Class B attempt, and 348cc for the Class C! Using the same formula as in the previous paragraph, the calculated capacity of the 74 x 80mm engine is 344.06cc and that of the later 70 x 90mm engine, 346.36cc.

The 424cc, 75 x 96mm engine, does not enter into the controversy. It was never a success and when it failed to show sufficient promise, all further development work was abandoned.

Chapter Eleven

The wind of change

HAVING ENJOYED two, perhaps three, very good years, it looked as though 1925 would be a year of climax for J. A. Prestwich and Co. Ltd in terms of both success and prosperity. Yet whilst there was good reason for such optimism, it was an inescapable fact that the whole British motorcycling scene was changing. Some of the more prominent motorcycle manufacturers who previously had been content to buy in and fit proprietary engines were now poised to design and manufacture their own. Others, such as Velocette and Douglas, who had designed and built their own complete machines right from the very early days, had now developed these to the point where they were offering a very serious challenge in speed events of all kinds and in the setting up of many new records. Although JAP had pioneered the overhead camshaft engine, it had not been designed for quantity production, but others who had followed in JAP's footsteps had different ideas. Veloce Limited had a very attractive and advanced design that was already available to the public, and it would not be long before others followed suit. The racing Peugeot twin had shown that development was likely to progress in this direction and that JAP did not possess a monopoly.

The low pressure (or balloon tyre, as it was called initially) had just started to make its appearance, offering the security of a wire bead rather than high pressure to keep it on the rim. Within a year or two, the beaded edge tyre would be on its way out. Internal expanding hub brakes were now the rule rather than the exception, and already manufacturers were fitting the new, more shapely 'saddle' petrol tank that made the 'wedge' tank look dated. Add to this mechanical lubrication, overhead valve engines capable of sustained high performance, and really powerful vee-twins, and it can be seen how 1925 was truly the year of transition. But it was also a year of vicissitudes too, as subsequent happenings will show.

Uncharacteristically, the year opened with a New Year's Day meeting on Birkdale Sands, Southport. It was a gamble on the behalf of the organising club, but in this instance taking a chance paid off. The weather was fine and the whole meeting ran according to schedule. J. F. Ashworth won the Solo up to 350cc General Class on his 346cc New Imperial JAP, and also the Solo up to 350cc Novice and Solo up to 500cc General classes. Len Booth, on a similar mount, was placed in the first and last of these classes. George Patchett, an up-and-coming rider to be reckoned with, won the Solo Unlimited Novice Class on his 980cc Brough Superior JAP. It got the new season off to a good start, and other clubs must have wondered about the following suit in the future.

Good at helping to pass the time when motorcycling was at its most inactive during

Left:
The 350cc dohc engine of 1925 had bore and stroke measurements of 70 x 80mm, a single exhaust port cylinder head and the vertical coupling fully enclosed. This engine, too, is now in Austria. (Photo: Dr. H. Krackowizer)

Right:
Nearside view of the same engine. Note the long holding-down studs from the cylinder head and the heavily drilled engine sprocket. (Photo: Dr. H. Krackowizer)

the winter months, *The Motor Cycle* conducted an open debate on whether a racing motorcycle could be silenced. Prominent racing personalities were asked to express their points of view, amongst them Stan Greening, Freddie Barnes and George Brough. Stan considered effective silencing could not be achieved unless unlimited space was available for a suitable design of silencer. In addition, he considered the question of the extra weight would have to be taken into account. Freddie Barnes believed it was the 350cc and 500cc singles that were the worst offenders, with their high compression ratios. But he considered the fitting of a silencer presented an equal handicap to all. He went so far to suggest that a free hand should be given to silencer design, so that such a fitment would be judged by its efficiency and not by its design features. George Brough suggested the need for further experimentation, claiming a machine fitted with a silencer should be made to pass an audiometer test at maximum speed and one quarter speed. It should then be made illegal to sell any machine that does not comply with this standard. Many others put forward their own points of view, but nothing really conclusive emerged. It was a topic soon forgotten.

At the beginning of February, it was announced that Bert Le Vack had won the Bates Cup, an award presented in recognition of the greatest improvement made in an Hour Record attempt in Classes A, B, C, D and E. During the 1924 season, he had recorded a speed of 84.62mph in Class B on his 350cc New Imperial JAP, which represented an improvement of the Class B record by 4.38%. A road test of the 680cc Zenith JAP was published in the same issue of *The Motor Cycle* that contained the announcement about the Bates Cup. This machine was fitted with the 70 x 88mm side valve vee-twin, but the report itself proved to be of little value as the engine was still being run in. Even so, the tester managed to climb Glen Lea Hill, near Haslemere, in top gear. It was claimed this showed the flexibility of the engine — a strange statement in view of the way in which the engine was so clearly being abused. Little else of any consequence was reported, apart from the fact that the machine 'handled well'.

Anyone accustomed to reading about the success of the Zenith JAPs at Brooklands and other high speed venues would have been surprised to read about a quite different form of achievement during mid-February. P. Cranmore won the Colmore

The Seal was an unusual three-wheel design in so far as the driver and passenger sat side-by-side in the 'sidecar', the steering wheel being connected to the front fork by a series of links. This photograph was taken at the start of the Grasshopper Run, organised by the old Kent, Surrey and Sussex Section of the VMCC in 1960. (Photo: Ken Hodgson)

Cup on a 344cc Zenith JAP sidecar outfit, and also the Watson Shield for the best sidecar performance (the two premier awards) in the Colmore Cups Trial. And this on an ohv model, too!

In the issue dated 19th March, *The Motor Cycle* published a road test of the latest 980cc Coventry-Eagle Flying Eight fitted with a sidecar. The JAP side valve engine was considered to be delightfully smooth and well balanced, being held by engine plates that completely surrounded the crankcase as though it were on a test bench. Access to the engine was easy, the more so in view of the readily detachable lower tank rails. Mechanical lubrication was provided by a Pilgrim pump and, even with a sidecar attached, petrol consumption of 50mpg could be achieved, driven hard. The outfit would go well beyond 60mph and would cruise all day at 45-50mph. Silencing was considered to be 'admirable' and the only criticism levied was the need to close the carburetter air control when accelerating suddenly, to prevent pinking.

The opening meeting at Brooklands, held on 21st March, attracted the usual contingent of JAP-engined machines, including Bert Le Vack with the 346cc overhead camshaft engine mounted in Coventry-Eagle cycle parts. It may be wondered why the riders of JAP-engined machines changed their allegiance to manufacturers so frequently, although the reason is quite simple to comprehend. It was the manufacturer that offered the best bonus payments that attracted the support from the experts, and as these payments were usually negotiated during the 'closed' season (often during the Show), changes in machine name were usually evident at the start of the new season. Riders were not influenced in any way by the Tottenham factory, being left to make their own decisions. This explains why Greening, Le Vack and members of the Prestwich family did not necessarily all ride for the same machine manufacturer — the common bond of engine was sufficient.

In the 350cc Solo Scratch Race, Le Vack could not get his machine to start. As a result, the best placing by a rider of a JAP-engined machine was that of H.M. Walters on a 344cc Zenith JAP, who came seecond. Joe Wright finished third, on a similar machine. H.J. Knight managed third place in the 1,000cc Scratch Race that followed, riding a 976cc Zenith JAP, but he was no match for Riddoch's winning 998cc Blackburne-engined Zenith. However, he got his revenge in the later 350cc-1,000cc Handicap Race, when he came home first on the same machine at 85.43mph. Joe Wright took third place in the 350cc Handicap Race on his 344cc Zenith JAP, whilst the Experts Handicap Race was won by George Tottey on a 488cc New Imperial JAP at 81.51mph. This was not well received by the makers, who had no 500cc production model! He made a welcome reappearance at this meeting, his first competitive ride since his accident during the 1924 Junior TT.

The same day there was another meeting at Southport, where 350cc New Imperial JAPs took the first two places in the 350cc General One Mile Solo event. First was Len Booth and second, J. Ashworth, both on 344cc Novice One Mile Solo race, and went on to win the 750cc Novice One Mile solo. C. Needham won the Unlimited General One Mile Solo race with his Brough Superior-JAP. It was interesting to note that amongst the competitors at this meeting was Edwin Twemlow, who contested the unlimited class on a 490cc HRD.

The March Buyer's Guide listing in *The Motor Cycle* showed that 26 manufacturers had at least one JAP-engined model in their 1925 range: BAT-Martinsyde, Brough Superior, Cedos, Coventry-Eagle, Diamond, DOT, Grindlay Peerless, HRD, Invicta (Aza two-stroke), Massey, Matador, Mohawk, Montgomery, Morgan, New Imperial, Omega, P & P, Rex-Acme, Royal Enfield, Sharratt (also Aza two-stroke), Sun, Verus, Vindec, Wolf, Zenith.

An early indication of what was likely to happen to many of the currently held

World's records became apparent when R.N.M. Spring, C.S. Staniland and L.P. Driscoll broke quite a number of Class F records with a 490cc Norton and sidecar, towards the end of March. Also about this time came the announcement that Percy Brewster had made his own 998cc ohv vee-twin engine, which he intended fitting into a Zenith frame. Built with competition use in mind, the engine was alleged to develop 48bhp at 5,000 rpm. Only the one engine was made, and it is surprising to find that it has survived the passage of time such that recently the machine has been fully restored to its original specification.

Coincident with the record breaking attempts by Spring and his fellow riders, Le Vack decided to attack the Class B/s sidecar records with an outfit powered by his 344cc Coventry-Eagle. His attempts preceded those by the Norton riders, thus giving him the honour of breaking the first records in 1925. He set new figures for the following:

Flying mile 76.18mph
Flying 5 miles 76.18mph
Standing 10 miles 72.99mph
Flying 5 kilometres 122.83kph
Standing 10 kilometres 114.56kph
Flying kilometre 82.06mph
Flying kilometre 78.68mph (two-way mean)
Flying mile 80.34mph
Flying mile 77.95mph (two-way mean)

The next event of any consequence was the Essex MC's Kop Hill Climb, held on Saturday, 28th March, Stan Greening, this season riding a 346cc Omega JAP, was on form as usual. He scored four firsts, in the Touring Machines, Unlimited, 350cc Sports Machines and Any Solo classes. Also riding at this meeting was E.C. Fernihough on a 249cc New Imperial JAP and C.W.G. Lacey on a 344cc Cotton JAP.

Tom Allchin was another who rode at this meeting, having fully recovered from the Morgan crash in which his driver, E.B. Ware, had been so badly injured. He rode the big twin Zenith owned by I.P. Riddoch, which was fitted with a vee-twin Blackburne engine. Little did he know when he commenced his first ascent of the hill that he would become involved in an incident that was to have far-reaching effects on the future of speed events held on public roads in Britain.

The problem occurred as the result of inadequate crowd control at the top of Kop Hill. A crowd had gathered around Claude Temple's machine, on the corner, and it was this that caused Allchin much anxiety during his ascent as he tried to keep well clear of them. He took the right-hand curve very close, and as a result he shot across the road, running on to the grass. His machine then hit a deep gulley, which caused it to leap into the air (one report claimed it leapt eight feet) before hitting a bush and crashing on the left bank. Fortunately, none of the spectators were hit, but Allchin broke his wrist and was rendered unconscious, with severe bruising. A car driver also experienced a somewhat similar happening, again without causing injury to anyone but himself, but the implications were there for all to see. Good crowd control was essential, and unless it could be guaranteed, future spectator fatalities seemed inevitable.

The whole incident could have passed off quietly, but it seems that great pressure was brought to bear on both the RAC and the A-CU from unspecified high authority. Shortly afterwards, both bodies revoked all permits for future events to be held on public highways and stated quite categorically that they would never again be issued. In consequence, the speed trials held soon after the Kop incident by the Wessex Centre of the A-CU, in Hereford, proved to be the last ever licensed event to be held on a public road. From that moment onward, clubs had to seek suitable off-road venues such as roads on private estates or in parks, or to run grass track or sand racing events as a suitable alternative. The action taken had been so sudden and so dramatic, with no possibility of appeal, that everyone involved with motor sport was temporarily stunned. Ironically, during 1924 there had been signs that the regulations pertaining to the use of public highways for speed events were likely to be relaxed, to the extent that grand prix-type road racing events seemed a distinct possibility.

New Imperial were next to announce a win by one of their machines in other than a speed event. During the weekend that followed the Kop Hill incident, Stan Jones won the MC and AC Reliability Trial on a 2¾ hp New Imperial JAP and was awarded the Dunlop Cup for making fastest time of the day against 62 starters, in a field that comprised motor cars and motorcycles up to 1,500cc capacity. New Imperial won the Team Prize, too; the team comprising Jones, P.J. Williams and R. Turner. During the same weekend, there was a fairly low key meeting at Brooklands organised by the West Kent MC. An interesting innovation was a JAP v Blackburne engine race, which went very much in favour of Blackburne amongst the amateur riders taking part.

Saturday, 11th April marked the date of the Easter Meeting at Brooklands organised by the BMCRC. It had been expected that the ban on racing on public highways would have led to a much greater attendance at Brooklands meetings, but this was not the case at this particular event. Bert Le Vack made sure of the 250cc Scratch Race, which he won with ease on his 246cc Coventry-Eagle JAP at 65.10mph. George Tottey came third on a 246cc New Imperial JAP. In the 350cc Solo Scratch Race that followed, Le Vack had to work harder for his win at 85.56mph, this time aboard his 346cc ohc-engined Coventry-Eagle JAP. He had no starting problems on this occasion. In the 500cc Solo Scratch Race, George Tottey brought his 490cc New Imperial JAP into third place, and in the 1,000cc solo event, H.J. Knight was second on his 976cc Zenith JAP, having to concede victory to Claude Temple. E.C.E. Baragwanath made his debut on an SS100 Brough Superior JAP at this meeting but was unplaced. Towards the end of April, New Imperial announced a new addition to their range, a 350cc side valve that would have the 70 x 90mm JAP engine bolted in unit with the gearbox, as had now become New Imperial practice. The machine weighed only 192lb, which brought it well within the concessionary 30/- tax limit. The overall specification included the New Imperial loop frame and a three-speed gearbox fitted with a clutch and a kickstarter. A retail price of £45 10s was specified; prices were falling and it was necessary to keep up with competitors by having an up-to-date specification.

Before the month had drawn to a close, the death of James Lansdowne Norton had occurred, which caused great sorrow throughout the entire trade. A much respected man, it seemed ironic that he should pass away just when the machines that bore his name were having an unparalleled run of success.

It was about this time that Royal Enfield announced plans for a 350cc racing single that was to be exported to South Africa and also used in the 1925 Junior TT. Powered by a two-port 344cc ohv JAP engine, used in conjunction with a three-speed Sturmey Archer gearbox the engine was to be lubricated by the Enfield system supplemented by a foot-operated pump. Both exhaust pipes were upswept and an ML magneto supplied the ignition. Three 'works' entries were to be made in the TT; these being Stanley Woods, T.G. Burney and G. Reynard, the last the Southport sand racer who was putting up such a good performance on their machines. A smaller, but more significant, announcement stated that henceforth, the company would make its own 70 x 90mm 350cc side valve engine.

The South Eastern Centre's meeting at Brooklands on 25th April made the

The power unit of the 1925 SS100 Brough Superior suberbly-restored by Ken Middleditch. Possibly the most outstanding of all the overhead valve vee-twin JAP engines, and one of its best examples. 11/4

headlines, though not with regard to any JAP engine. It was at this meeting that Jack Emerson won a 3 lap race on Riddoch's Blackburne-engined Zenith at a speed of 100.41mph — an achievement all the more remarkable as Emerson had not ridden at Brooklands for some time. Joe Wright managed second place in the 3 lap 500cc Solo Handicap Race on his 344cc Zenith JAP, and E.C.E. Baragwanath, having successfully changed his allegiance to Brough Superior JAP, won the 3 lap 1,000cc Passenger Handicap Race on a 980cc model, in a field of 11 starters.

In May, New Imperial released details of a special 980cc ohv vee-twin that was being built for the German Grand Prix. Apart from the use of an ohv JAP engine, it featured a large diameter front brake drum, Druid front forks and a separate oil tank. At the other end of the scale, Royal Ruby advertised what they claimed to be the lowest priced machine on the market. Fitted with a 293cc side valve JAP engine, the overall specification included a three-speed Moss gearbox, all-chain drive, Brampton front forks and a Binks carburetter. Weighing in at 186lbs, and therefore eligible for the 30/- taxation rate, this machine retailed at £33 10s. A combined JAP/Mobil Oil advertisement started appearing in *The Motor Cycle*, and Gamages, the famous department store in Holborn, were selling a 293cc Omega JAP for £38 15s, or if desired, on deferred, easy terms.

The 9th May meeting at Brooklands organised by the Essex MC demanded very little attention, there being only three motorcycle races in the programme. Once again, comments were being made in *The Motor Cycle* about the dullness of Brooklands meetings, comments that led eventually to a leader on the same topic. the bone of contention seemed to be the way in which spectators were left completely uninformed about the progress of a race, with no mention of retirements or other happenings that would affect the race leaders' progress. It seemed as though the race officials were determined to keep this information to themselves.

During mid-May, the Tottenham factory made an announcement about engines for the 1925 TT. Very few changes were to be made, the aim being to increase reliability. Four types of engine were listed; 62.5 x 80mm, 246cc, 74 x 80mm, 344cc; 85.5 x 85mm, 490cc; and 85.5 x 104mm, 598cc — the last for sidecar use. All engines would have stronger valve springs, and feature push rod return springs. Big-end bearings would be of the double roller type, and lubrication would be by mechanical means, with an additional hand pump. To facilitate better lubrication, the vacuum in the vacuum box had been increased to 2½ psi. Heavier piston rings would be fitted to an alloy, heat-treated piston in each case, and the flywheels would be of polished steel. The ports would be ground and polished, and the connecting rods sandblasted after stamping.

With regard to the individual engines, the 490cc version would have triple valve springs and longer push rod return springs. The rockers would run in roller bearings on the thrust side and in ball bearings on the other. A full-skirted piston would be used, with a domed crown and three rings. The 588cc engine would have a single-port cylinder head, but be similar to the 490cc version in all other respects. The improvements would henceforth be incorporated in the standard engines, and all would feature a new design of valve lifter within the timing chest that operated on a pawl and pin arrangement.

After quite a build-up in the motorcycling press, the 16th May event at Brooklands, organised by the BMCRC, incorporated a new 100 Mile Handicap Race, to be known as the Hutchinson 100 — the major award being a massive cup donated by the Hutchinson Tyre Company. In the races that preceded the main event, Bert Le Vack won the 350cc Solo Scratch Race on his 344cc Coventry-Eagle JAP at 81.81 mph, C. W. G. Lacey coming third on his 344cc Cotton JAP. H. J. Knight, now becoming a force to be reckoned with, took second place in the Private Owners Handicap Race with his 980cc Zenith JAP. Surprisingly, the Hutchinson 100 Race was described by *The Motor Cycle's* reporter as 'an unexciting handicap race', F. A. Longman being declared the winner on his 989cc Harley-Davidson at a speed of 89.66mph. During the course of the day's racing, George Tottey broke down after passing the 100 mile mark during the 37th and final lap of the race, and had to push in from about ¾ mile from the finishing line. Although Tottey had passed the 100 mile mark in advance of the rest of the field he found, to his surprise, that he had not been awarded the race. He protested

Checking the timing of a single cylinder ohv engine in the factory. Note the glass burette, used for measuring the compression ratio of the engine. (Photo: Mrs. C. May)

his point to the Stewards but as the regulations clearly stated that the winner of the race would be the first to cross over the line having completed 37 laps, he had to be content with his 6th place. A reporter, thinking he had completed an extra lap to be sure of completing the course, asked him to stop and pose for a photograph. Fortunately, George's reply was not quoted, nor did the photographer report any physical harm. But the photograph never got taken, that's for sure! Many thought H. J. Knight stood a good chance of winning the Hutchinson 100 event, but a tendency for his Zenith to run on one cylinder ensured he could not improve upon his third placing.

The same weekend, Edwin Twemlow made another appearance at the Southport sand races, and on this occasion won the 20 Mile Solo Race on a 346cc Cotton JAP. Nearer home, at the North London MCC's speed trials, Stan Greening turned out on his 346cc Omega JAP, to take second place in the 350cc solo class, and third place in the 500cc and 750cc classes, on the same machine. E. C. E. Baragwanath won the Unlimited Solo and Sidecar classes with his 980cc Brough Superior JAP. Shortly afterwards, news filtered through about the German Grand Prix. Held at Solitude, the event attracted 300,000 spectators. It seems probable that the big 980cc ohv New

CHAPTER ELEVEN

Imperial twin mentioned earlier was ridden by someone with the surname Dobler, as a machine answering to this description finished second in the sidecar race. For reasons unknown, surnames only were used when listing the names of successful foreign riders in Continental events.

The Ealing Club's 200 Mile Sidecar Races held at Brooklands on 23rd May attracted only a very small crowd of spectators, partly due to the poor weather. V. Baxter won the 350cc Sidecar Race on a 344cc Rex-Acme JAP at 59.64mph, with Stan Greening second on his 344cc Omega JAP. Most excitement, however, was derived from the 1,000cc race, which was won by C.T. Ashby on his own 976cc Zenith JAP at 72.71 mph. He had fought a race long battle with Le Vack on his 996cc Brough Superior outfit, both having more than their fair share of troubles. Ashby had to replace a primary chain during the race, then have a conflagration put out by firemen when a leaking carburetter sprayed petrol on to the hot cylinders. Le Vack had to cope with a burst rear tyre then, when making up ground, his Brough Superior went on to one cylinder. He managed to finish second, well behind the leader. Even so, speeds attained during the race secured for him four new World's Records in Class F:

> 100 miles at 78.77mph
> 1 hour at 78.71mph
> 2 hours at 77.07mph
> 200 kilometres at 122.97kph

These added to the records that had been set up just three days previously by E.S. Prestwich and J.J. Hall, who shared at 246cc P&P JAP. They broke seven long-distance records:

> 400 kilometres at 92.47kph
> 500 kilometres at 93.25kph
> 600 kilometres at 94.22kph
> 300 miles at 57.92mph
> 400 miles at 58.60mph
> 6 hours at 58.60mph
> 7 hours at 58.28mph

So successful had been the attempt, that Hall was to use the same engine for his 1925 Lightweight TT entry.

A road test of the 344cc two-port HRD JAP, published in *The Motor Cycle* was laced with superlatives, the tester claiming that within five minutes he felt thoroughly at home with the machine and that after twenty minutes was considering a late entry for the Junior TT! He regarded it as a real super sports machine and although no speedometer was fitted, he knew it would reach 60mph with ease and was confident 75mph was possible. The exhaust note was none too quiet, despite the use of a cast aluminium alloy expansion chamber on each pipe and a pepper box fishtail end. Also, there was need to use the ignition control sensibly. But the steering was good and the tick-over slow and dependable, thanks to the Binks carburetter, which averaged 85-90mpg throughout the test. The engine required a petrol/benzole mixture to run satisfactorily, despite the fact that the cylinder barrel had a compression plate below it. The only serious criticism was directed towards the efficiency of the rear brake, which was by no means as good as the front brake, a comment that had been made about a Zenith in an earlier road test report.

The 6th June meeting at Brooklands, organised by the Sutton Coldfield and North Birmingham AC did not attract much attention, mainly because most of the better-known riders were in the Isle of Man, practicing for the TT races. Even so, two amateur riders recorded wins with their JAP-engined machines. T. Morton won the Winners

Handicap Race on a 490cc HRD JAP, and was awarded the Iliffe Cup. M. G. Cantacuzino won the 350cc class on a 344cc HRD JAP. The races at this meeting were hard fought, and it was a pity such a low key meeting did not attract more spectators.

Bert Le Vack was in the Isle of Man at this time, not as a competitor, but fulfilling the role of the Tottenham factory's technical expert. In this position he was available to give advice to riders of machines fitted with JAP engines and, where necessary, to assist with engine prepartation and even rebuilds. Because so many competitors were riding machines fitted with a JAP engine, he found that he needed to be a talent scout too, so that he could decide for himself which riders showed the most promise and therefore demanded the best support. This year, it seemed obvious to him that the man to watch was Howard Davies, who had entered HRD machines of his own manufacture in the Junior and Senior races. He had good experience of the TT course, having taken part in no less than eleven races, his greatest achievement being an outright win of the 1921 Senior TT on a 350cc AJS, a feat not previously accomplished, or, indeed, considered possible. Now he was manufacturing in Wolverhampton machines that bore his initials, production having commenced only about a year prior to the 1925 TT. He fitted JAP engines, and those supplied for his TT machines had been overseen and checked by Le Vack, before they left Tottenham. It is claimed that Le Vack took two weeks to prepare Davies's engine for the Senior TT and it was no doubt due to his assistance during practice that Davies managed to break the Senior TT lap record, held by Freddie Dixon. Some considered that at 32, Davies was over the hill as far as further successes were concerned, but Le Vack thought otherwise, knowing how he had trained during the winter to be at the peak of physical fitness. He made an agreement with Davies to look after his Senior engine personally and to have a 10% share of the prize money if Davies was fortunate enough to win.

The Junior Race gave a foretaste of what was to follow, when Davies came second at 63.87mph, only just over 1mph slower than the race winner, Wal Handley. H. F. Harris finished fifth, on another HRD JAP, Len Horton was sixth on a New Imperial JAP, and C. H. Young was seventh on a Royal Enfield JAP. As shown in the Junior race results, out of the nineteen finishers, eight had ridden a machine fitted with a JAP engine!

The Lightweight race was next, and considerable excitement arose because Twemlow brothers were amongst the starters. During the early stages of the race, it seemed almost certain that Edwin Twemlow was unlikely to repeat his 1924 success, when he oiled a plug on the approach to Governor's Bridge and lost time in fitting a replacement and cutting down the oil supply. Yet, if anything, this delay seemed to spur him on so that by the end of the third lap, he was lying fourth. A signal from his pit urged him to speed up, such that he was in the lead by the end of the fourth lap, a position he retained to the finish at the end of the sixth lap. His winning speed was 57.47mph, and New Imperial had yet another racing success to their credit. Brother Kenneth finished third at 55.83mph on a similar mount and it is interesting to record that there were only two other finishers, who also used a JAP engine. J. Cooke was fourth, on a DOT JAP, and D. G. Prentice was fifth on a P&P JAP.

The race was not without its incidents, as Edwin recalled afterwards. During the race, he lost his steering damper completely, not that it was needed, because the New Imperial handled so well. He also managed to ground his right-hand footrest every time he rounded Governor's Bridge. Surprisingly, he did not realise he had won when he crossed the finish line, as it seemed too much to expect to win for two years in succession, especially after such a poor start. When stripped for measurement, his engine was found to be in perfect condition, apart from a top piston ring broken near to the end gap.

CHAPTER ELEVEN

Once again, all eyes were on Davies, when it came to the Senior race. Le Vack had been so concerned about the preparation of the engine that he would not even allow Davies to ride his machine to the start. Instead, Le Vack rode it there himself, getting Eric Corneliusen, the Crosby JAP agent, to give him a lift back to his hotel.

Inwardly, he had his anxieties. When the Senior engine had been stripped down after the final practice session, he had found a crack in one of the gudgeon pin bosses of the piston. Knowing how well the engine was performing, he decided to refit the piston and take a calculated risk. It proved to be the right decision to take.

That Davies won at 66.13mph is now history, Jimmy Simpson having broken the lap record, then blown up his AJS, in characteristic fashion. It proved to be a trouble-free ride too, the engine being in perfect condition at the finish. There had been only one minor moment of anxiety when Davies experienced a sudden snatch in the chain at Windy Corner on his last lap. A stone had got thrown up into the chain, fortunately without causing it to break. But the evidence remained, in form of a bent side plate. The combination of rider and machine was probably the heaviest in the race, as Davies weighed 11 stone, 8 pounds, whilst the machine itself scaled 325lb. Needless to say, Davies was highly elated by his record in both races, with augured well for his infant company, as well as for JAP engines. In this race, the next JAP-engined machine to finish was the Montgomery JAP ridden by Harold Willis, which was placed 9th.

An advertisement in *The Motor Cycle* dated 2nd July made reference to some successful record breaking attempts at Brooklands by H.M. Walters in a Jappic racing cyclecar. This unusual four-wheeler, designed and driven by Walters, was made to sell for about £150, and could be purchased with the option of either a 344cc or a 490cc ohv single cylinder JAP engine. Its name was derived from JAP and Walters' nickname, 'Pic'. With the larger capacity engine, a maximum speed of 85mph was claimed, and it had been seen that it was capable of lapping the track at about 68mph. Small in size, it weighed 4cwt, and was to have been available to order through Messrs Jarvis and Co., of Wimbledon. On the day in question, Walters had a 344cc JAP engine fitted, and he was successful in breaking five Class I World Records for cyclecars not exceeding 350cc capacity:

Flying start 5 kilometres 111.14kph
5 miles 69.04mph
Standing start 10 kilometres 106.85kph
Standing start 10 miles 67.35mph

The weight of the record breaker was given as 528lbs, but it seems probable that this was the only Jappic to be built. Registered for road use, it bore the registration number MH 3995. The successful attempt took place on 6th June, the day of the Sutton Coldfield and North Birmingham AC's meeting. Eventually, the car was destroyed in a fire.

Soon after the TT, Bert Le Vack set off for Germany, where he had entered a 344cc HRD JAP and also an unspecified 250 for the International Race Meeting to be held at Swinemunde. In the 350cc race he lived up to expectations by leading for six laps, but then ill fortune intervened. Whilst still leading the race, the bottom links of the front forks broke at 80mph, causing his machine to head for a tree. Luckily, he managed to throw himself off at almost the last moment, to suffer only minor injuries that permitted him to return to his hotel after treatment. But they were bad enough to cause him to scratch his 250cc ride. Until his crash, Le Vack had put in the fastest lap at 57.2mph. The race was won by G. Thumshorn on a 346cc Ardie Sport JAP at 51.5mph, so the honours went to the Tottenham factory in the end.

A Hako JAP was third in the 500cc race, and in the 750cc event, a 596cc New

A rare photograph of the Jappic racing car, which broke five Class I World's Records for Cyclecars when fitted with a 344cc ohv JAP engine. (Photo: Douglas Prestwich)

Imperial JAP was second. R. Motz won the 1,000cc class on a Brough Superior JAP at 48.84mph.

A competitor by the name of Zundorf wanted to take over Le Vack's entry in the 250cc race, but could only do so if all the other competitors in this race gave their consent. E.C.E. Baragwanath, who had travelled with Le Vack in the role of mechanic, worked all night to get the machine ready, taking the 344cc engine out of Le Vack's damaged HRD JAP and replacing it with a 250cc engine of the same manufacture. He also had to fit new front forks and straighten out the bent and damaged parts that resulted from the earlier crash, in the hope that Zundorf would get his ride. But the competitors could not agree amongst each other, other than to give Zundorf permission to ride unofficially and not figure in the results. He made the most of this somewhat dubious offer and put in the fastest lap at a speed of 53.3mph, as well as recording fastest time of the day. But the official results showed a rider named Kamer to be the winner on a Horex, at a speed of 48.6mph.

Once again, an issue that formed the centre of much controversy got into print in the pages of *The Motor Cycle*, as the result of a leader that was written by Ixion in their 2nd July publication. It centred around the question of whether or not special fuels should be permitted in the TT, Ixion claiming that their use led to the development of 'freak' machines that had little in common with the 'over-the-counter' production models. He also claimed that the use of these fuels permitted much higher speeds, which would soon cause racing to become very hazardous, putting the lives at risk of all those who took part. In the 9th July issue that followed, a number of manufacturers had the opportunity to express their own comments. The JAP view was that special fuels could be obtained commercially and that even if an engine was set up specially for their use, it could very easily be changed for general road use on petrol by the simple expedient of

other engines during the winter of 1924/5. The Racing Department built several others, including one that was water-cooled.

The Pendine sand race meeting held the following weekend was all but rained off, George Grinton and M. Isaac (both on 246cc New Imperial JAPs) taking first and second places respectively in the 250cc 10 mile race. Grinton was also first in the following 350cc event. Up country, at Southport, the weather was just as bad. R. Thomas on a 246cc New Imperial won the 250cc event, and George Patchett put up a splendid performance with his Brough Superior JAP, to win the 100 mile race with ease. It was during this meeting that 'trailing starts' had to be used. A stationary machine on the start line quickly sank into the wet sand, so that the drag on the wheels would stop the engine. In consequence, it was necessary to be on the move when crossing the start line, the 'trailing start' being a form of rolling start developed at Southport out of necessity.

Abroad, Eddie Meyer was busy winning the Austrian Grand Prix on his Brough Superior JAP, K. Gall coming second on a 344cc New Imperial-JAP. According to the JAP advertisement JAP-engined machines were also first in the 350cc, 250cc, 'Acquiescence' and Youngsters races.

During mid-August, Montgomery announced a new 980cc side valve vee-twin model. Based on the frame used for their Anzani-engined model, it had been adapted to accept the side valve JAP engine, and had redesigned front forks that were fitted with a centre spring, dispensing with the leaf spring arrangement used previously. There was also mention of a special 'speed machine' built for H. Hudson, which was of broadly similar construction, although in this instance the leaf spring forks had been retained, strengthened by side stays. This machine had a 980cc ohv engine fitted, and to allow for its extra height, a smaller 1¾ gallon petrol tank was fitted. Other modifications included the use of an 8 inch diameter front brake, Pilgrim pump lubrication, torque stays to the chainstays and engine plates that completely surrounded the crankcase.

In an early announcement about their 1926 season models, New Imperial stated that henceforth their model range would have engines of their own design and manufacture. These would comprise a 70 x 90mm 346cc side valve, a 69 x 80mm 297cc side valve and a 62.5 x 80mm 246cc ohv. The distinguishing feature of all these engines would be their deep cylinder fins.

The 1925 200 Mile Solo Races were held at Brooklands on 15th August, again organised by the BMCRC. For once, almost everything went wrong as far as better-known riders of JAP-engined machines were concerned. Le Vack made a good start in the 250cc Solo Race, but when he came in to refuel after 40 laps, his Coventry Eagle-JAP refused to start, despite a very long push. This malady often affected machines during long distance races, when everything was running at high temperature and the engine 'gassed up'. On this occasion, Le Vack gave the 350cc race a miss, with the result that the best placing by a JAP-engined machine was made by Kaye Don who was third on a 344cc Zenith-JAP at 74.38mphd. In the 500cc race, Le Vack rode a 498cc HRD JAP, whilst M. McEvoy made an appearance on the new 490cc McEvoy JAP. The engine Le Vack used in his HRD was an 80 x 99mm 498cc prototype, with a single exhaust port cylinder head. The inlet port was at right angles to the cylinder and was not inclined upwards as in Ashby's engines of 1924. Both retired before the race was run; Le Vack with unspecified troubles, and McEvoy with slipped timing. E.W. Guyler rode a 488cc DOT JAP into third place. In the 1,000cc Solo Race, Le Vack had entered Chris Staniland on his own 980cc Brough Superior JAP, which was fitted with an 8/45 ohv engine in place of the 1923 long stroke prototype, but once again his luck was out. Persistent carburetter trouble necessitated Staniland's retirement before the race reached its closing stages. Joe Wright saved the day by finishing second on his 980cc Zenith JAP at 69.56mph.

On the same day, the Southport Club were running another of their regular meetings on Birkdale sands. Len Booth notched up several good placings with his 344cc New Imperial JAP, as did Edwin Twemlow on his 490cc HRD JAP and Syd Gleeve on a 344cc Diamond JAP. Most eyes were on M. E. Davenport who was riding an unusual machine — a 350cc AJS fitted with a 344cc JAP engine. He came second in the 350cc General Class, and won the 350cc Novice Class.

Whilst all this was going on, Claude Temple was at Montlhéry, in an attempt to cover 100 miles in an hour. He came close but missed his target by just a fraction. Even so, he set up new 50 kilometre, 50 mile, 100 kilometre and 100 mile records, as well as a new hour record, beating those set up at an earlier date by Le Vack. Possibly it was this that encouraged Le Vack to take his 248cc Coventry-Eagle JAP to Brooklands on 28th August, to set up new records for Class A. He came away knowing that the 50 kilometre, 50 mile, 100 kilometre, 100 mile, and 1 and 2 hour Class A records were now his and subsequently ratified by the FICM. The next day, he returned with his 344cc model and set up new Class B and C records for the flying start kilometre and mile, his mean speeds being 98.66mph and 99.46mph, respectively. Then, just as if he had remembered it was nearly time for the 1925 Motor Cycle Show, he returned again on 1st September with his 248cc Coventry-Eagle JAP and set up new Class A records for 200 miles and 3 hours, at speeds of 72.31 and 72.37mph respectively. Some you lose, some you gain.

When it came to making an announcement about new models for the 1926 season, Francis-Barnett indicated they would be marketing a larger version of their bolt-up frame model, which would be fitted with a 346cc side valve JAP single. This would necessitate the sue of heavier gauge tubing, of larger diameter. They would also have available a new 175cc model, fitted with a 60 x 62mm 172cc side valve JAP engine. The frame and fittings would be identical to those used by the 172cc two-stroke engined sports model.

The new side valve JAP engine had a large diameter ouside flywheel, a roller bearing big-end and generous plain bearings throughout. Internally, the three-ring alloy piston had a large diameter gudgeon pin of the fully floating type, fitted with alloy end pads. The cylinder head was shaped to promote turbulence, the greater part of the incoming charge being compressed in the valve chamber. 31/32 inch valve ports were specified, and because the timing chest extended below the base of the crankcase, to form an oil well, the camshaft was mounted below the crankshaft timing pinion. It operated the side by side valves through crossover followers, having a single cam. An ML magneto was mounted in front of the crankcase, and the engine was used in conjunction with a three-speed Albion gearbox, a jockey sprocket being employed to maintain correct rear chain adjustment. The retail price of this new model was £34.15s.

The Excelsior Motor Company announced two new JAP-engined models, a 346cc ohv sports and a 300cc side valve. Both would have a Burman three-speed gearbox, Best and Lloyd mechanical lubrication, and a Binks single lever carburetter. Their prices, respectively, were £49 and £36 17s 6d.

At the end of August, Len Booth and George Reynard battled it out during the North Liverpool MCC's meeting at Birkdale sands. The New Imperial JAP and the Royal Enfield JAP were fairly evenly matched, but it was Reynard who won the 10 Mile Sidecar Race. On Hest Bank Sands, near Lancaster, Kenneth Twemlow put in a welcome reappearance, riding a 344cc Cotton JAP and a 490cc HRD JAP, and winning three of the races. JAP were now featuring their standard 350cc side valve engine in their advertisements, with the recommendation: 'Insist on having this trade mark on your engine next season'.

News about more models for the 1926 season was released during early *225*

A 1925 350cc Excelsior fitted with a side valve JAP engine. Machines such as this were light in weight and had a quite lively performance.

September. Montgomery had now decided to make an ohv version of the 980cc side valve vee-twin model they had mentioned earlier. As in the case of the machine prepared for H. Hudson, the taller engine necessitated a smaller capacity petrol tank. Furthermore, it had now been decided to have both exhaust pipes mounted on the right-hand side of the machine. Matchless were to continue their spring frame model, which was fitted with a 980cc side valve vee-twin JAP engine, but from now on, balloon tyres would be fitted. Zenith would have two new models, a 680cc vee-twin fitted with a side valve JAP engine and a 346cc side valve. The side twin valve would be fitted with Lucas Magdyno lighting and have a rev counter and speedometer recessed into the top of the petrol tank, the former being driven off the Magdyno shaft and the latter from the rear wheel. The single would have a long exhaust pipe with a silencer at the end, new pattern front forks and a new petrol tank. The engine itself would have mechanical lubrication. Other models in the range included a 344cc ohv single, with a duplex frame and forks fitted with a shock absorber and a steering damper. Lubrication would be by hand pump, combined with a mechanical pump. There was also a 346cc ohv single with a single-port cylinder head, virtually identical to the racing model but having a dummy belt rim rear brake. A 490cc ohv model would have the latest two-port cylinder head and be similarly equipped to the racing model. Top of the range was the 'Super Eight' 980cc twin, fitted with the side valve sports vee-twin JAP engine, the specification now including internal expanding brakes and a chain lubricator. Only the 980cc ohv vee-twin model would remain unchanged.

JAP engines for the 1926 season would have no revolutionary changes, the range now extending from 175cc to 1,100cc. The 175cc side valve engine described previously had been designed to fit frames that were made to take a two-stroke engine. The transmission side was identical to that of the similar capacity Aza two-stroke engine, as was the large diameter ouside flywheel. The latter was needed because the small internal flywheels were of insufficient weight to provide reliable low speed running. The big-end assembly was also identical to that of the two-stroke. The engine produced 4½hp at 5,000rpm.

A two-port cylinder head had now been introduced for the 490cc ohv engine, which now had a ribbed crankcase on the transmission side. As previously, the rockers had roller and ball bearings. All ports were ground and polished. The small timing pinion on the end of the crankshaft now had five keyways cut in it, to facilitate really accurate valve timing. A domed, slipper piston, weighing 1lb 2oz carried three rings and was fitted with a 13/16 inch diameter gudgeon pin. The lubrication system followed established practice, with oil being led to the neck of the cylinder and to the big-end bearing bearing via the main bearing bush and special channels in the flywheels and crankpin. The roller-ended cam followers were retained.

Improvements to the 680cc twin amounted to having a straight induction pipe, and increased area for the exhaust ports. A boss cast on the neck of the front cylinder and drilled permitted an extra oil feed point. This engine produced 14hp.

New was an 85 x 95mm 1086cc water-cooled vee-twin engine developed primarily for use in Morgans. Closely following the specifcation of the 980cc four cam side valve engine, it differed in having bevel drive to the magneto. If desired, this latter method of drive could henceforth be specified for the air-cooled vee-twin engines too. All engines from now on would have alloy pistons and the patent JAP oil box in the crankcase — with the exception of the 250cc and 300cc side valve singles.

George Brough was another to announce a new model, in this case the Alpine Grand Sports Brough Superior. It was, in fact, the SS100 model in full touring trim, having the 980cc ohv-twin JAP engine. At the same time, he also took the opportunity to introduce what he designated as the SS80-100 model, another variation of the SS100 model which, in this instance, was fitted with the less powerful 980cc side valve vee-twin JAP engine. It could be recognised by its combined fuel and oil tank, and a footrest and rear brake assembly that was identical to that of the standard SS80 model. For those who required a true cross between the SS100 and SS80 models, there was the SS80 de luxe. The specification was identical to that of the SS80-100 model, apart from the fact that the 980cc four-cam side valve JAP engine was used.

The top of the range SS100 model had undergone a number of modifications too, mainly in an endeavour to provide even better handling and a few more refinements. The frame had been lowered to give a four inch ground clearance, which permitted a reduction in saddle height of 1¼ inches. The gearbox was lowered, too, by 2¼ inches, the combined effects of this modification giving a lower centre of gravity. The steering head lug had been modified, by reinforcing it with curving twin webs at the rear to form what was virtually a box section. This gave it much greater rigidity. More noticeable was the larger, 3¾ gallon, petrol tank, which was now deeper at its front end. A separate oil tank had a capacity in excess of ½ gallon. the engine itself was already powerful enough, but in order to conform to current JAP practice, the overhead valves each had triple valve springs. 7 inch internal expanding brakes completed the specification.

Options for the SS100 model included a prop stand, an early example of this now taken-for-granted fitting, special Brooks pannier bags having an inner case for the luggage, and a speedometer and clock mounted on an instrument board, for fitting to a sidecar. A de luxe version of the SS100 could be specified too, with a three-panel Triplex screen.

New Imperial seem to have relented, at least for the time being, in their plans to use only engines of their own design and manufacture. Three JAP-engined models were listed to supplement their 1926 range: a new 680cc side valve vee-twin, a 344cc ohv model that was a replica of their 1924 TT winning model, and their Super Sports big twin, with retained the 980cc four cam side valve vee-twin engine. Like the new SS100 Brough Superior, this model, too, had a frame with a specially strengthened steering head.

The 1925 Ulster Grand Prix brought forth some more successes for JAP when J.G. Burney won the 350cc Class at 65.60mph on a 344cc Royal Enfield JAP. Stanley Woods again rode a 980cc New Imperial JAP in the over 600cc Class, and won for the second year running, at 65.26mph. The cycle parts of his machine again let him down, to delay his progress, although this year it was the mudguards and not the fuel tank that caused the trouble. In the 500cc class, it was the Nortons that made most of the running, and this was a trend that was to continue to the disadvantage of machines fitted with a JAP engine.

The Skegness Speed Trials held during September, organised by the Midland Centre A-CU, heralded another victory by George Patchett on his big Brough Superior. He won the Unlimited Class with his SS100 in brilliant form, but thereafter he was out of action when bad clutch slip set in. On the same day, George Tottey rode in the Colwyn Bay Speed Trials, although this was not his first riding appearance after his TT accident, as was claimed by *The Motor Cycle*'s reporter. He scored several third places on his 490cc New Imperial JAP, and tied with H.J. Sutcliffe (Brough Superior) for the Colwyn Cup, awarded to the competitor who made fastest time of the day and resided not more than 30 miles from Colwyn. Sutcliffe was third in the Unlimited Experts event. The fastest 350cc machine was Davenport's hybrid 344cc AJS JAP. He won the 350cc Class with this machine, J. Cooke coming second on a 344cc DOT JAP, and George Tottey third on a 344cc New Imperial JAP.

Whilst all this was going on, Claude Temple had returned to Montlhéry with his Temple-Anzani, determined to cover more than 100 miles in an hour. This time everything went according to plan, when he recorded a speed of 101.98mph on 7th September.

During mid-September, Coventry-Eagle announced their intention to market a range of Le Vack models. Henceforth, they would have available Flying 500 and Flying 350 models which would be fitted with a single- or twin-port ohv JAP engine, and use a frame that had been developed in conjunction with Bert Le Vack as a result of his Brooklands experience. The frame layout was such that the straight top tube sloped rearward to be joined before the saddle lug by a lower tank rail. The front down tube was curved slightly and at its base carried the front of a duplex tube construction, the cradle so formed being extended back so that it formed auxiliary torque members. Both chainstays and back stays were straight. The front forks were of Webb manufacture, and the nose of the saddle was arranged so that it sunk into the rear of the petrol tank.

Years later, it transpired that a frame maker had been employed in the Racing Department, and that he had been responsible for the building of those designed by Le Vack, including that of the 1924 Brough Superior that had set up World's Records at Arpajon. The reason why was because all prototype engines were jealously guarded factory property, and were kept there with the machines in which they were used.

The main characteristic of a Le Vack cradle frame design was the vertical saddle tube with the gearbox attached to a robust sub-frame, attached in its turn to the saddle tube and rear engine plates. It was this characteristic continued in the New Hudson

Bert Le Vack with the 246cc dohc Coventry-Eagle JAP on which he won the 250cc BMCRC Championship at 73.26mph on 10th October 1924. E. C. E. Baragwanath (extreme left) and Bill Tilby (next to him) are amongst those offering congratulations. (Photo: Dr. J. D. Alderson) 11/9

which led to the belief that those frames too had been built by JAP.

A new 680cc side valve vee-twin was also specified, which would use the Le Vack frame. It was regarded as a fast tourer, for solo or sidecar use. It, too, had a JAP engine Two other side valve models were available, one of 350cc and the other, 300cc.

The top of the range Flying Eight had been modified by eliminating some of the auxiliary tubes used in the frame construction. Gone were the front tube side stays and the double back stays. The engine plates that completely surrounded the crankcase of the engine remained, but they were now reshaped to facilitate the mounting of a Lucas Magdyno, close to the front of the crankcase. The rear of the petrol tank had been cut away, so that the nose of the saddle could be dropped. This permitted the saddle to be lowered 1½ inches á la Brough Superior. Heavyweight Webb forks were fitted and the overall specification now included 8 inch diameter internal expanding brakes. The gearbox was a Jardine 3-speed, and a Best and Lloyd lubrication system was used for the engine, which could be a two or four cam side valve JAP, or the ohv version, depending on the model designation.

Coincident with these announcements was the report of an unusual meeting on

St. Ledger' meeting, but it was here that George Patchett set up new solo and sidecar records with his Brough Superior JAP. One can only assume the weather on the eastern side of the country proved much more favourable.

Two more new models were announced during October. Coventry-Eagle added to their range a 350cc model powered by a side valve JAP single, which retailed at 42 guineas, or could be obtained on hire purchase for £11 6s down. Carfield Ltd, of Windmill Lane, Smethwick introduced their Carfield JAP at the same time. This was a 300cc single, which retailed at £35 10s.

The postponed Brooklands Championship meeting was held on 10th October, and it was Le Vack who won the 250cc Solo Championship at 73.26mph, after putting in a lap at 81.24mph. His main adversary on this occasion was Wal Handley, and they clashed again in the 350cc Solo Championship, which again was won by Le Vack, this time at 88.62mph. An indication of the struggle for race leadership occurred during the last lap of the race, which Le Vack covered at 95.41mph. In both races he was using the overhead camshaft engines, in Coventry-Eagle frames. When it came to the 1,000cc Sidecar Championship, it was Joe Wright who set the pace on his 980cc Zenith-JAP, beating Riddoch's very fast Zenith-Blackburne outfit and breaking four records held by Le Vack in the process. As a result, he now held the Class G/s flying start 5 kilometre and 5 mile records at 90.53mph and 90.48mph respectively, as well as the standing start 10 kilometre and 10 mile records at 86.26mph and 87.76mph. His race average was 88.46mph.

Factory policy for 1925 had dictated that Le Vack would further develop the Page-designed 245cc and 346cc dohc engines, and later, the prototype 80 x 99mm 498cc engine with the single exhaust port cylinder head. This was vindicated by Le Vack's three wins at the BMCRC Championships Meeting, whilst in addition, he established lap records in Classes A, B and C during the season. Unfortunately, the need to implement this policy left little time for the preparation of the Brough Superior, which will account for its relatively poor showing at its few appearances in Class E and G Races.

Le Vack experienced trouble during the 350cc Sidecar Championship race and had to make an early retirement. But when it came to the 500cc Championship he struck brilliant form with his 498cc HRD JAP. Despite strong opposition from Victor Horsman and Bert Denly, he won at 97.02mph, setting a new Class C standing start record in the process at 96.02mph. he became the first rider of a 500cc solo machine to lap at over 100mph during a race, his lap speed being 102.48mph, and he was awarded the Buckley Cup. The 1,000cc Solo Championship proved to be the most exciting race of the day, being keenly fought out all the way. Joe Wright proved to be the eventual winner with his 980cc Zenith JAP, his speed being 102.90mph. He, too, had put up much higher lap speeds during the race.

The results achieved by riders of JAP-engined machines at this Championship meeting were almost certainly the best ever. How many other manufacturers could claim that in one single meeting they had won the 250cc, 350cc, 500cc, 750cc, 1,000cc and 1,000cc sidecar classes — and broken a World's Record, too?

When the results of the German Grand Prix were announced, it was found that C.T. Ashby had won the 250cc race on a 246cc Zenith JAP, at 57.5mph. Ratzner was third, on a New Imperial JAP. Surprisingly, Ashby had made the more customery run and bump start with a dead engine, whereas the remainder of the entry had made a clutch start with engines running. Even so, Ashby had carved his way through the field to take the lead on the third lap, a position he held until he crossed the finish line. Another success had been scored in Ireland, where J. Brown won the 100 Miles Championship Race (350cc class) on a 344cc DOT JAP, and also the 100 Miles Championship of

Ulster. He rode the same machine in the 100 Mile Unlimited Race that followed, to finish only two minutes behind the winner and beat many 500cc and 1,000cc machines into the bargain. This too was a quite remarkable achievement.

Bert Le Vack returned to Brooklands on 14th October, bringing with him what was described as a 348cc Le Vack Special. Fitted with an overhead camshaft JAP engine, the machine broke the flying start 5 kilometre and 5 mile records at 152.72kph and 94.84mph respectively, and also the standing start 10 kilometres at 146.51kph.

The final meeting of the year was held at Brooklands on 24th October, but the day before, H. Harte and S. Glanfield set out again on their 988cc Coventry-Eagle JAP sidecar outfit to see if they could better the Class G/s records they had set up a year earlier. They were successful too, setting new records from 4 to 11 hours, and for 400-900 kilometres.

At the Brooklands meeting, E. S. Prestwich won the 3 lap All-Comers Handicap Race at 66.85mph — a good speed for a 344cc DOT JAP sidecar outfit. The 3 lap 1,000cc Solo Handicap Race was won by Oliver Baldwin who, on this occasion, had changed his allegiance to a 980cc Zenith JAP.

Joe Wright visited Brooklands on 27th October with his 980cc Zenith JAP in solo trim. With his sights on the Class E records, he broke the 50 kilometre and 50 mile records at 163.93kph and 102.08mph, respectively. Four days later he returned with a sidecar attached to the big Zenith and set about the same distance records in Class G/s. The 50 kilometre record fell at 140.76kph and the 50 mile record at 87.37mph. But that was not enough! He returned yet again with the same outfit on 14th November, just before the track closed for the winter, to take the Class G/s 100 kilometre, 100 mile and 1 hour records at speeds of 138.66kph, 85.77mph and 85.91mph, to round off a very good year.

As the year drew to a close, the Toreador Engineering Company announced a new 490cc Grand Prix model, which was to be powered by the JAP ohv racing single engine. It would have no kickstarter and be fitted with two brakes that acted on the rear wheel. Shortly after this announcement, *The Motor Cycle* brought out their first British Supremacy Number, an issue extolling the virtues and successes of British-made motorcycles. It was a prophetic move, for within a few years the industry would be in the grips of a deep depression, needing all the export orders it could get to keep the wheels turning.

Looking at the world's records scene as the year closed, it will be observed that once again the overall picture had changed somewhat, due to the fact that there was now much keener competition from other manufacturers. Although quite an impressive number of records were held by JAP-engined machines, they did not number as many as in 1924, and some of them had been standing from the year previous or even earlier. Details are as follows:

Class A *(Solo motorcycles not exceeding 250cc)*

Flying start kilometre	H. Le Vack	248cc New Imperial	88.87mph
Flying start mile	H. Le Vack	248cc New Imperial	89.25mph
50 miles	H. Le Vack	248cc Coventry-Eagle	76.62mph
100 miles	H. Le Vack	248cc Coventry-Eagle	76.76mph
200 miles	H. Le Vack	248cc Coventry-Eagle	72.31mph
400 miles	J.J. Hall & E. S. Prestwich	248cc P & P-JAP	58.60mph
50 kilometres	H. Le Vack	248cc Coventry-Eagle	123.02kph
100 kilometres	H. Le Vack	248cc Coventry-Eagle	123.40kph

200 kilometres	H. Le Vack	248cc Coventry-Eagle	120.72kph
300 kilometres	H. Le Vack	248cc Coventry-Eagle	166.23kph
700 kilometres	J.J. Hall & G. Johnson	248cc P&P JAP	78.06kph
800 kilometres	J.J. Hall & E.S. Prestwich	248cc P&P JAP	78.76kph
900 kilometres	J.J. Hall & E.S. Prestwich	248cc P&P JAP	79.16kph
1 Hour	H. Le Vack	248cc Coventry-Eagle	76.74mph
2 Hours	H. Le Vack	248cc Coventry-Eagle	75.09mph
3 Hours	H. Le Vack	248cc Coventry-Eagle	72.37mph
7 Hours	J.J. Hall & E.S. Prestwich	248cc P&P	58.28mph
8 Hours	J.J. Hall & G. Johnson	248cc P&P	51.87mph
9 Hours	B. Kershaw	248cc New Imperial	50.52mph
10 Hours	B. Kershaw	249cc New Imperial	50.07mph
11 Hours	J.J. Hall & G. Johnson	248cc P&P	78.95mph
12 Hours	J.J. Hall & G. Johnson	248cc P&P	79.40mph
Double 12	Mrs.R.N.Stewart	249cc Trump	44.65mph

Class B *(Solo motorcycles not exceeding 350cc)*

Flying start kilometre	H. Le Vack	346cc Coventry-Eagle	99.46mph
Flying start mile	H. Le Vack	346cc Coventry-Eagle	98.66mph
2 Hours	H. Le Vack	344cc New Imperial	83.35mph

Class C *(Solo motorcycles not exceeding 500cc)*

Flying start kilometre	H. Le Vack	348cc Coventry-Eagle	99.46mph
Flying start mile	H. Le Vack	348cc Coventry-Eagle	98.66mph
5 miles	H. Le Vack	498cc HRD	104.15mph
10 miles	H. Le Vack	498cc HRD	96.02mph
5 kilometres	H. Le Vack	498cc HRD	167.90kph

Class D *(Solo motorcycles not exceeding 750cc)*

5 miles	H. Le Vack	498cc HRD	104.15mph
5 kilometres	H. Le Vack	498cc HRD	167.90kph

Class E *(Solo motorcycles not exceeding 1,000cc)*

50 miles	J.S. Wright	998cc Zenith	102.08mph
200 miles	T.R. Allchin	988cc Zenith	87.27mph
50 kilometres	J.S. Wright	998cc Zenith	163.93kph
200 kilometres	T.R. Allchin	988cc Zenith	140.86kph
300 kilometres	T.R. Allchin	988cc Zenith	141.58kph
2 Hours	T.R. Allchin	988cc Zenith	89.06mph

Class B/s *(Sidecars not exceeding 350cc)*

300 miles	S. Greening and E.S. Prestwich	344cc Royal Enfield	57.55mph
400 miles	S. Greening and E.S. Prestwich	344cc Royal Enfield	56.77mph
400 kilometres	S. Greening and E.S. Prestwich	344cc Royal Enfield	91.74kph
500 kilometres	S. Greening and E.S. Prestwich	344cc Royal Enfield	92.32kph
600 kilometres	S. Greening and E.S. Prestwich	344cc Royal Enfield	91.01kph
700 kilometres	S. Greening and E.S. Prestwich	344cc Royal Enfield	90.89kph
4 Hours	S. Greening and E.S. Prestwich	344cc Royal Enfield	56.71mph
5 Hours	S. Greening and E.S. Prestwich	344cc Royal Enfield	57.47mph
6 Hours	S. Greening and E.S. Prestwich	344cc Royal Enfield	56.28mph
7 Hours	S. Greening and E.S. Prestwich	344cc Royal Enfield	56.76mph
8 Hours	S. Greening and E.S. Prestwich	344cc Royal Enfield	56.50mph
9 Hours	S. Greening and E.S. Prestwich	344cc Royal Enfield	50.22mph
10 Hours	S. Greening and E.S. Prestwich	344cc Royal Enfield	45.20mph

Class G/s *(Sidecars not exceeding 1,000cc)*

Flying start kilometre	H. Le Vack	998cc Brough Superior	99.80mph
Flying start mile	H. Le Vack	998cc Brough Superior	99.73mph
Flying start 5 miles	J.S. Wright	988cc Zenith	90.48mph
Standing start 10 miles	J.S. Wright	988cc Zenith	87.76mph
50 miles	J.S. Wright	988cc Zenith	87.37mph
100 miles	J.S. Wright	988cc Zenith	85.77mph
200 miles	H. Le Vack	998cc Brough Superior	75.32mph
5 kilometres	J.S. Wright	988cc Zenith	90.53mph
10 kilometres	J.S. Wright	988cc Zenith	86.26kph
50 kilometres	J.S. Wright	988cc Zenith	140.76kph
100 kilometres	J.S. Wright	988cc Zenith	138.66kph
200 kilometres	H. Le Vack	998cc Brough Superior	122.97kph
300 kilometres	H. Le Vack	998cc Brough Superior	118.53kph
400 kilometres	H.R. Harte & S. Glanfield	988cc Coventry-Eagle	107.64kph
500 kilometres	H.R. Harte & S. Glanfield	988cc Coventry-Eagle	106.09kph
600 kilometres	H.R. Harte & S. Glanfield	988cc Coventry-Eagle	106.75kph
700 kilometres	H.R. Harte & S. Glanfield	988cc Coventry-Eagle	106.27kph

800 kilometres	H.R. Harte & S. Glanfield	988cc Coventry-Eagle	105.88kph
900 kilometres	H.R. Harte & S. Glanfield	988cc Coventry-Eagle	105.75kph
1 Hour	J.S. Wright	988cc Zenith	85.91mph
2 Hours	H. Le Vack	998cc Brough Superior	77.07mph
4 Hours	H.R. Harte & S. Glanfield	988cc Coventry-Eagle	107.70kph
5 Hours	H.R. Harte & S. Glanfield	988cc Coventry-Eagle	106.48kph
6 Hours	H.R. Harte & S. Glanfield	988cc Coventry-Eagle	106.93kph
7 Hours	H.R. Harte & S. Glanfield	988cc Coventry-Eagle	106.35kph
8 Hours	H.R. Harte & S. Glanfield	988cc Coventry-Eagle	105.57kph
9 Hours	H.R. Harte & S. Glanfield	988cc Coventry-Eagle	105.65kph
10 Hours	H.R. Harte & S. Glanfield	988cc Coventry-Eagle	97.05kph
11 Hours	H.R. Harte & S. Glanfield	988cc Coventry-Eagle	88.24kph

Class J2 *(Three-wheelers not exceeding 750cc)*

5 miles	E.B. Ware	744cc Morgan	61.22mph
10 miles	E.B. Ware	744cc Morgan	59.50mph
5 miles	E.B. Ware	744cc Morgan	47.52mph
1 Hour	E.B. Ware	744cc Morgan	47.26mph

★　★　★　★　★　★　★　★

Looking back over the 23 years that had elapsed since he first commenced the design and manufacture of motorcycle engines, John Prestwich had every reason to be pleased with his achievements. He had designed and made the first overhead valve engine to go into quantity production, a spray carburetter that provided smoother engine control with only one lever to adjust, and a unique tandem three-wheeler with a two-speed epicyclic gear and shaft drive in which both driver and passenger could travel in reasonable comfort. Later, an improved three-wheeler incorporated a very advanced three cylinder side valve engine, by which time he was also manufacturing a number of vee-twin engines, both air- and water-cooled, and building machines to take part in international races.

The pioneering days of aviation encouraged him to take an interest in aircraft and to become associated with A. V. Roe, who later founded a company that became one of the cornerstones of the British aircraft industry. He designed and made a multi-cylinder aircraft engine in a number of variations, one of which was used to power a dirigible that established a record during a flight from Cardiff to the Crystal Palace. Soon, his motorcycle engines were breaking records, too. Made to high engineering standards and with good quality-control, they were used by many of the leading motorcycle manufacturers, both at home and abroad.

During the 1914-18 war, his company continued to make engines, for use by the armed forces and those engaged on war work, as well as munitions of all kinds. During this period, he was awarded a silver medal and a certificate by the Franklin Institute of America for his Fluid Gauge, which permitted the rapid and accurate measurement to very fine limits by an instrument that had no mechanically moving parts.

After the war, his company went from strength to strength, amassing numerous motorcycle speed records and competition successes of all kinds, largely due to the efforts of two men in particular, Val Page and Bert Le Vack. The latter did much to resurrect the vee-twin and make the JAP engine in particular the most successful of its kind. In addition, their combined talents led to the evolution of a series of double overhead camshaft engines that triggered-off an interest in this type of engine and its subsequent commercial production by a number of leading manufacturers. Yet, whilst, all this was going on, John Prestwich remained as active as ever, designing machinery for the manufacture of pencils the culminated in separate, satellite company being formed to produce pencils of all kinds in vast numbers. Although his company had now reached the size where he could have started to relax a little and perform the role of figurehead, he still took a keen interest in the day to day running of the company and was a familiar sight on the shop floor, where he would often stop and talk to his employees, showing an interest in what they were doing.

From outward appearances, it looked as though the company had enjoyed an even better year in 1925, than it had in 1924 but sadly, this was not so. A reduction in orders for engines had started to be felt now that some manufacturers were designing and making their own, whilst the once buoyant market in Germany was beginning to shrink as German industry began to get back into its stride and turned a blind eye to the provisions of the Locarno Treaty. Some reductions in the work force proved necessary to take up the slack, and the worst news of all was the reluctant closure of the Racing Department by the end of the year. This meant Bert Le Vack had to seek employment elsewhere, New Hudson offering him the opportunity to supervise their racing activities, which was gladly accepted. Val Page was another who moved on, in this instance to join Ariel Motors and blossom out with an entirely new range of designs that enhanced his reputation even further. His former employer was not in a position to offer him the salary he required, so the move proved inevitable. Even so, both Le Vack and Page left the Tottenham factory on the best of terms, albeit with a tinge of sadness on both sides.

Despite these happenings and the period of depression that was to hit industry in the forseeable future, it was by no means the end of the JAP story.

Nonetheless, it was during the period covered that the company reached its peak, to enter into the so-called 'Golden Years' of the late vintage era at a time when one motorcycle in every eight was fitted with a JAP engine, in the days when JAP had a very different connotation from that generally accepted today.

A quarter-size ohv JAP engine made in the works, which is now in the possession of Edward Prestwich. (Douglas Prestwich)

Appendix

The engine code system

Until the period immediately after the First World War, JAP engines had been recorded on a numerical basis, such that in the absence of any supporting evidence it is generally assumed that the number 52,000 was reached by the end of 1914. This figure, or any close approximation of it, is used by the Sunbeam MCC as the cut-off point for pre-1915 machines considered to be eligible for inclusion in their Pioneer Register and, therefore, able to compete in their annual Pioneer Run to Brighton. The Club's Pioneer Registrar, Geoff Morris, has much evidence to support this dating landmark as a result of his own considerable amount of research.

From 1920 onwards the problems of identifying and dating engines are much simplified, due to the fact that the company introduced a coded engine number sequence. By stamping symbols and numbers on top of the timing chest cover or on the top of the crankcase adjacent to it, it became possible not only to determine the year of manufacture but also to identify the type of engine, its basic specification and in some cases, whether it had been modified or produced with a specific use in mind. The way in which the engine number code can be interpreted is as follows:

1. The first letter before the oblique mark identifies the cubic capacity of the cylinder, or of each cylinder if the engine is a twin.
2. The remainder of the letters before the oblique mark identify the engine type.
3. The first letter after the oblique mark identifies the year of manufacture.
4. The serial number of the engine follows immediately after the letter identifying the year of manufacture.
5. Additional letters after another oblique stamped immediately after the engine serial number identify any deviations from standard specification. An asterisk after the serial number indicates the engine incorporates parts which deviate from the standard specification.

To provide more detail on the above, the following is a list of letters and numbers, with an explanation of their meaning:

First letter *(cylinder capacity)*
A = 300cc side valve, 70 x 78mm bore and stroke
B = 250cc side valve, 64.5 x 76mm bore and stroke
E = 375cc side valve, 74 x 85mm bore and stroke
F = 300cc side valve, 70 x 76mm bore and stroke
G = 350cc side valve, 70 x 88mm bore and stroke

I = 350cc side valve, 70 x 90mm bore and stroke
J = 500cc side valve, 80 x 99mm bore and stroke
K = 500cc side valve, 85.7 x 85mm bore and stroke
L = 550cc side valve, 85.7 x 95mm bore and stroke
M= 375cc side valve, 70 x 97mm bore and stroke
N = 200cc side valve, 55 x 83mm bore and stroke
P = 250cc side valve, 62.5 x 80mm bore and stroke
S = 350cc side valve, 74 x 80mm bore and stroke
U = 600cc side valve, 85.7 x 104mm bore and stroke
V = 175cc side valve, 60 x 62mm bore and stroke
Z = 175cc side valve, 55 x 73mm bore and stroke

Remaining letters before oblique
T = Twin cylinder
O = Overhead valves (cancels reference to side valve in preceding letter)
W= Water cooled
Z = Dry sump lubrication
S = Short stroke sports engine (or special)
C = Sports engine
R = Racing engine
Y = Twin exhaust port cylinder head
    Often, these letters are used in combinations of twos or threes.

Letters after first oblique *(year of manufacture)*
P = 1920
N = 1921
E = 1922
U = 1923
M= 1924
A = 1925
T = 1926
I = 1927
C = 1928
S = 1929
W= 1930
H = 1931
Y = 1932
Z = 1933
D = 1934
R = 1935
V = 1936
F = 1937
O = 1938
G = 1939

These letters were later reused in the same sequence to cover the years 1940 to 1959 inclusive, taking into account the war years during which machines for civilian use were no longer manufactured. It is worth noting that the JAP production year ran from 1st September of the year previous to that identified by the dating letter, and ended on 31st August of the year indicated.

Letters after the engine serial number and second oblique
A = High lift cam
B = Modified gearcover and exhaust valve lifter
C = Crankcase with inclined magneto platform
D = Cast iron, flat-top piston
E = Cast iron, dished-top piston
F = Aluminium alloy piston with domed top
G = Ball bearing gear spindle
H = Roller bearing pulley spindle
J = Roller-type cam levers and exhaust valve lifter
K = Special chainline requirement for pulley spindle
L = Outside flywheel with screw-on sprocket, for two-strokes
M = Crankcase without oil box
N = Magneto sprocket for type NA magneto of ML manufacture (two-strokes)
O = Cylinder No. 2 type
P = Cylinder No. 4 type
R = Cylinder No. 3 type
S = Double row roller big-end bearing (250cc and 350cc ohv racing engines)
T = New Type crankcase and rotary valve breather (500cc and 600cc side valve)
U = Modifications for new tappet centres (350cc side valve roadster)
V = Reduced centre connecting rods (low compression engine)
Y = 1924 pattern crankcase converted to rotary valve breather
* = Refer to engine record card

The above coding relates only to engines made during the period 1921-1925. After this period, the letter 'S' denotes the engine was made to the customer's specification. The * denotes an engine that had been specially prepared for record attempts, or specially tuned to meet a rider's requirements. Inevitably, there are exceptions to this coding and also the use of certain letters for which an explantation is no longer available. In consequence, this guide is by no means infallible.

Bibliography and sources

Books

Title	Author	Publisher
The Beginnings of the Cinema in England	John Barnes	David and Charles
Living Pictures	Henry V. Hopwood	The Optician and Photographic Trade Review
Gage Design and Gage Marking	E. Oberg and Franklin D. Jones	Machinery Publishing Co.
Automobile Design: Great Designers and their Work	Roland Barker and Anthony Harding	David and Charles
The Father of British Airships	Anthony Harding	William Kimber
The Vintage Years at Brooklands	Dr. Joseph Bayley	Goose and Son
Bikes at Brooklands	Peter Hartley	Goose and Son
Brooklands Bikes in the Twenties	Peter Hartley	Argus Books Ltd
Matchless: Once the Largest British Motorcycle Manufacturer	Peter Hartley	Osprey Publishing Ltd
The Story of Royal Enfield Motorcycles	Peter Hartley	Patrick Stephens Ltd
Brooklands: Behind the Scenes	Charles Mortimer	G.T. Foulis and Co. Ltd
Brough Superior: The Rolls-Royce of Motorcycles	Ronald Clark	Goose and Son/G.T. Foulis and Co. Ltd
The Vintage Years of the Morgan Three-Wheeler	William Boddy	The Grenville Publishing Co. Ltd
Morgan Sweeps the Board	Dr J.D. Alderson and D.M. Rushton	G.T. Foulis and Co. Ltd
The Light Car: A Technical History	C.F. Caunter	The Science Museum (HMSO)
Motor Cycles: History and Development. Part 1	C.F. Caunter	The Science Museum (HMSO)

Motor Cycles: Handbook of the Collection. Part 2	C.F. Caunter	The Science Museum (HMSO)
The Story of the Racing JAP	Cyril May	Cyril May
The JAP Story 1895-1951	D.J. Buchanan	J.A. Prestwich and Co. Ltd
Motorcycle Cavalcade	'Ixion'	Iliffe and Sons Ltd
Veteran and Vintage Motorcycles	James Sheldon	Batsford
The Vincent HRD Story	Roy Harper	Vincent Publishing Co.
Speed and How to Obtain It	J.E.G. Harwood	Iliffe and Sons Ltd
Motorcycles and How to Manage Them	Various Editions	Iliffe and Sons Ltd

Periodicals, Part-Works, Club Magazines and News Letters

Periodical	*Article*	*Author*
The Motor Cycle	Various Issues	
Motor Cycling	Various Issues	
Motorcycle Sport	Various Issues	
Speedway Express	The Story of the JAP	Uncompleted series of articles by Cyril May
South African Motor Cycle News	The Unique Mr. HRD.	Barry Sewell
Two Wheels (Australia)	The All-Conquering JAP	Peter Jones
The Brooklands Society Gazette	Double 'Double 12'	Anon. Vol 8, No. 1
On Two Wheels	Success was Pencilled In	Frank Glendinning Vol 3, Part 44
On Two Wheels	The Gamble that Failed	Frank Glendinning Vol 5, Part 66
The Official Journal of the Vintage Motor Cycle Club	Various Issues	
Wood Green and District Motorcycle Club	The JAP Story	Fred Butcher
Wood Green and District Motorcycle Club	JAP of England	Fred Butcher

Institutions, Museums etc.

The British Film Institute
The John Barnes Museum of Cinematography
The Royal Aeronautical Society
The Science Museum, South Kensington
The Shuttleworth Collection
Bruce Castle Museum, Tottenham

BIBLIOGRAPHY & SOURCES

Personal Contributions

Douglas Prestwich
Edward Prestwich
Dr. Joseph Bayley
Ron Valentine
Nelson Harring
Cyril Posthumus
Eric Corneliusen
Geoff Morris, Sunbeam MCC Pioneer Registrar
Jack Bindley
Ken Hodgson
Albert Wallis
Fred Butcher
Wal Phillips
Mrs E. Oldfield (nee Howard)
Former JAP employees

Index

INDEX

INDEX